COMPANY C

BOOKS BY JOHN SACK

The Butcher

From Here to Shimbashi

Report from Practically Nowhere

M

Lieutenant Calley

The Man-Eating Machine

Fingerprint

An Eye for an Eye

Company C

COMPANY C

THE REAL WAR IN IRAQ

John Sack

William Morrow and Company, Inc. / New York

Some of this book first appeared, in much different form, in Esquire. *The author is deeply grateful to* Esquire's *editors Terry McDonell, David Hirshey, and Will Blythe.*

Library of Congress Cataloging-in-Publication Data
Sack, John.
Company C / John Sack. — 1st ed.
p. cm.
ISBN 0-688-11281-1
1. United States. Army. 34th Armor. 2nd Battalion.
Company C—History—
Persian Gulf War, 1991. 2. Persian Gulf War, 1991—
Regimental histories—United States. 3. United States.
Army—History—Persian Gulf War, 1991. I. Title.
DS79.724.U6S25 1995

956.7044'2—dc20   94-33406
                                                                    CIP

Printed in the United States of America
First Edition

1 2 3 4 5 6 7 8 9 10
BOOK DESIGN BY LINEY LI

This is a true story. The people are real. The events really happened. The conversations are as I tape-recorded them or, sometimes, as people remembered them. The thoughts are as people reported them.

CONTENTS

"When history's written,

the arrows [on the maps] will be crisp and clean.

But down here, where the skid marks hit

the underwear, we know there were some rough times."

—Lieutenant Colonel Gregory Fontenot

to Company C, Kuwait, March 4, 1991

COMPANY C

1

The U.S.A.

★

One more beer! It was Friday, Thank God Day, the
night of This Bud's for Me, and soon the hootin'
hollerin' boys at this beer hall, pool hall, girlie-girl hall in Kansas
would whirl off to Saudi Arabia, to life or sudden death in Iraq,
well, bartender, fill 'em up! On the froth in their glasses, the red,
orange, yellow lights from the mirror-moon in the ceiling glittered
like fairy dust, ice-cream sprinkles, miniature mortar rounds, the
loudest sound was of *Little Sheba,* by .38 Special, and the off-duty
soldiers yelled, *"Whoo!"* as one of the girlies, blond, twenty-
something, wearing a red little mini-string, stripping it off, dis-
closing a white spaghetti strap, no, vermicelli strap, did
somersaults, cartwheels, shoulder stands, her legs in the air ped-
pedaling, her legs in a Y, open, closed, sending semaphore: *here's
where it is!* She leapt up, pulled a boy's nose to her breastbone, let
the boy sniff at her sweat, her secretions, her dime-store perfume,
then did a 20-hertz shimmy, her breasts slapping to and fro, slapping the boy's smooth cheeks as though bringing him to. The
music kept time, and the .38 Specials sang,

Girls on the dance floor!
Wrestlin' in Jell-O!

until the boy laid a one-dollar bill on his leg and the girl, climbing
on and *whoopie!* and rodeo-riding, sucked up the "ONE"'s and
the portrait of Washington, and the boy, now unmuzzled, yelled,
"Whoo!" turned on by that vacuum vagina.

3

The drummer went *boom!* went *boom!* and the girl extricated the bill. She then threw herself at a table of Bud-downing soldiers from C, from Company C, ten minutes away at Fort Riley, Kansas, and as the .38s sang,

> *And the crowd was reelin'!*
> *Was chompin' and chantin'!*

she got two matches from C and did her fiery finale: she put the two matches into her nipples and set them afire. Her arms above her, she looked like a Statue of Liberty, but before the two fires could reach her, she did some muscular moves and lo! her breasts went in circles, the matches did too, the fires were a couple of orange *o*'s, were open mouths saying *whoo,* and the great balls of fire went out. The girl pulled the matches out and, for her *final* finale, fell to her knees by a soldier in C, and as the .38s sang of Little Sheba,

> *Our fabled femme fatale!*
> *Spoilin' for another fight!*

she looked up at the boy and asked him, "Will you marry me?"

The boy was stunned. In his wildest dreams he hadn't foreseen this. His name, rank, to hell with his serial number was Specialist Young, he too was twenty-something, was cowboy-booted, denim-attired, slim-legged: so slim that his Levi's seemed painted on, Pittsburgh Paint Levi's. He hadn't been to this joint before, and his first sight of Mouse (the girl had a mouse tattoo and her stage name was Mouse) was what? ten minutes ago? Like some child at Barnum & Bailey's, he'd stared at her backbend, a pure parabola, her hands and feet on the floor, her hair on a boy's trembling knees, her breasts on the boy's pants pockets, her lips on a one-dollar bill in the boy's moist crotch. *My God! What visual impact!* Young had thought, but in his Texas drawl, his Rio turned dry, his voice like a basset flat on the floor, weary of all ups and downs, he'd said to his buddies in C, "That's interestin'." His flat-as-the-floorboards voice was the utter despair of his Uncle Gigi in Texas, who'd once tried to teach him Chinese but couldn't even get him to $_c a^0$ or $^c a_0$, the hills and dales of Chinese were out of his one-note range, the singsong as inaccessible as the D above C in *Lucia di Lammermoor.* "No, put some *life* in," his uncle had said.

"I don't know how."

"Just *live*," his uncle had said, but Young was still *whoo*-less tonight as Mouse, her breasts like a cat on his knees, her sequins of sweat reflecting the red, orange, yellow lights, more or less asked him to love, honor, screw her till death should take him. "Will you marry me?"

"Well, I'll have to think about it," Young said in his steam-pressed syllables.

Then *boom!* came the music of Steel Heart, and Mouse scooted off as Young sat dazed and C watched the Blond Bombshell from Hell. At midnight the boys rolled out to a Lincoln, and Young, in the cold back seat, said, "Wait," hoping that Mouse would follow him out. She did—but as she walked, well, wove, down the street, in jeans and a black leather jacket, she had one roaring civilian on either arm, she didn't even wink at her inamorato, and Young thought, *Well, I was bullshitted, bogused.* "Well, fuck her," he told the rest of C, and the Lincoln drove back to Fort Riley.

Ah youth! as Conrad once said. It still had its own imperatives. Ten minutes later, the car pulled up at C's barracks, the boys then went through a door whose lettering, COMPANY C, shone like a flare in the starlight, and Young was fixated on Mouse, on Mouse. The boys went up to their rooms—their *rooms*, the halls full of parallel beds were the long-gone things of Crimea, Korea and Nam, and C lived in one-man and two-man rooms amid an electric mess of CDs, tape players, turntables, telephones, telephone-answering machines, stereophonic speakers, radios and TV sets. On these very sets, C had heard yesterday that with its whole division, the Big Red One, it would go to Saudi and, when the President ordered, into Iraq—the pits, ditches, fire-filled trenches, the waves of spiked concertina wire, the guns, cannons, rocket launchers, the man-killing mines, the six-foot, man-high, sand-pile walls, and the cauldrons of boiling oil of Castle Iraq. On hearing this, Young (like much of C) had longed for a home to come to after the slaughter stopped: a welcome mat, a dog or a cat, the smell of hot buttered potatoes, and a good woman such as he'd met tonight at the Klub Kamille. He got undressed, and he got into his drab brown-blanketed bed. He wasn't a rocker-and-roller (his best-loved tape was Bach's *Violin Concerto in A Minor*) but tonight he was just obsessed with the .38 Specials. In his head went a never-ending drum and

> *Doncha know Little Sheba?*
> *She's the favorite one!*

and he fell asleep thinking of Mouse, Mouse, Mouse, of her somersaults, cartwheels and shoulder stands in their pretty bedroom, when he came marching home from Iraq.

A few days later, C was awakened at half past six, and it went to a warehouse for combat clothes. A woman civilian said, "What size?" and C mostly told her, "Thirty," and "Thirty-two," and got some camouflaged pants, camouflaged shirts, and camouflaged hats that it then wore with minimal chic. "We don't turn up the sides like the Aussies," the firm first sergeant (the senior sergeant in C) announced. "We don't turn up the front like Gabby Hayes. We wear them like *this,*" like *plop,* like the hair of an English sheepdog, and C didn't quibble with him, for C, sixty volunteers, sixty proud soldiers, white, black, brown, yellow and red, felt, *That's what we soldiers do. If they tell us to look like Beetle Bailey, we'll look like Beetle Bailey.* On the pants, shirts and hats, the camouflage looked like a white-pebbled desert, but, for the Saudi nights, C got some pants and parkas in darker camouflage, too. For the days when *tata!* it would storm the Iraqi walls, C got bullet-proof vests, fireproof suits, and gasproof suits, and C didn't complain that in six thick layers it would look like a crowd of homeless people. C felt, *That's what we soldiers do.*

Toward noon, C put its clothes in its olive-green bags, but it didn't whirl off to Saudi, not yet. It went to its barracks, and day after day it put in items that weren't GI, weren't Government Issued. One boy put in an American flag, and one who'd heard there was no pork in Saudi put in a larder of Beanie-Wienies. Since all of C had Walkmans, all of C put tapes in, and one boy sorted through all his tapes, selected ones like *Nowhere to Run To* by Martha and the Vandellas, and dubbed them onto a tape that he then inscribed GO TO WAR. He did this at home, and his wife (on Friday, he'd up and married her)—his bride asked him, "What does that mean, GO TO WAR?"

"It's what I'll play when we go to war."

"Do you really think you're going to war?"

"Yeah, we're going to—*aww,*" the boy said, for his bride had burst into tears.

No one in C put alcohol in his olive-green bag, for the Saudis were opposed to it. No one put porno photographs in, for the Saudis were against that, too, and C's tall captain had said, "No pornography. A girl in a string bikini's pornography. A girl or a *wife* in a pair of shorts is pornography," the captain standing with C, not smiling, not smirking, the set of his lips indicating that the string and the shorts were pornography according to *Webster's* and not just according to some silly mullah in Mecca. "This," the captain continued, displaying a girl in a bra in a J. C. Penney catalog, "is pornography, don't take it to Saudi," and C didn't put in a *Playboy, Penthouse* or J. C. Penney catalog. In deference to the Saudis, who believed in a paradise that's white, it didn't put in white underwear, but the captain said it could put in Bibles, and C conscientiously did.

One boy's Bible was church-pulpit size. The letters were like in "RUN, JIM, RUN," for the boy hoped to study them by his flashlight light in the Saudi desert. A sergeant—Staff Sergeant James—he'd been in the army twelve years, but he still prayed that someday the sky would part and God would say, "Sergeant! You shall become a Pentecostal preacher!" His father, God rest him, had been such a man in Virginia, the spirit of God issuing from him on Sundays like screaming cannon rounds. "Praise God! Praise Him!" his father would shoot as James, age three, wearing a white shirt, tie, and red blazer, sitting on the deacon's bench, seconded each of these zingers, whispering, "Praise God. Praise Him." The congregation had told him, "You'll be a preacher too," but at nineteen he'd been tempted by pool, beer, cigarettes, and he had chosen —*provisionally*—the red not the black, the soldier's life. Satan soon turning tail, James became hallelujah! saved, and, as a sergeant in C, he now issued orders in a soft, saintly voice devoid of all *damn*s and *darn*s and *dern*s while patiently awaiting the Call.

Alas. The call hadn't come from God but the President, who'd gone onto CNN and called on C and the Big Red One to go to Saudi and, most likely, into Iraq. On hearing this, James had said, "It's all God's will," but then came official word that C would whoosh off to Saudi, yes, and with some other companies would, when the President ordered, lead the American army—*lead the American army into Iraq!* It would fall on C, little C, to go to the head of Companies X, Y, Z, of one hundred thousand soldiers, and breach the fortifications of Castle Iraq, the whole medieval mess that James was hearing about on CNN. The word from the army was "Up and at 'em, Company C," and James at first, *at first*, was scared, as who in C wasn't? until he remembered some of his late father's flaming words.

He'd heard them on Sunday morning once in Virginia. "It happen' in Babylon!" his father had yelled at the breakfast table, his father serving some scrambled eggs to him, his sisters and brothers, the eggs getting cold, green-yellow, hard as art-class erasers as his father rehearsed for his Sunday sermon. "And the Hebrew boys, they was Shadrach! Meshach! Abednego! *Randolph!*" his father had suddenly fired at James's kid brother. "You don't eat till I get through!"

"Yes sir," Randolph had said.

"And Nebuchadnezza'! He *throw* those boys in the fiery *furnace!*" said James's father, possessed. "A furnace is *already* hot as it is! But we talkin' 'bout a furnace is ten times hotter than it suppose' to be! *Randolph,*" the neighbors out on their porches now, the rounds whooshing over, the neighbors pinned down. "In the *furnace* was Shadrach! Meshach! Abednego! And *when,*" James's father fusilladed, "the man which was like the guard looked in, *lo!* and *behold!* instead of he see three crisp bodies, he see the Hebrew boys walkin' aroun', for God was with them *regardless!* All right, Randolph! You can *eat!*"

"*Yes sir!*" James's brother had said, and now Sergeant James in Kansas remembered the story's moral, *It don't matter where I am,* he could be in the Valley of Death and God would be right beside him. And that being so, the terror drained out of James's brain like a quart of old motor oil.

That night James and his wife, daughter, son attended the Church of Deliverance near Fort Riley. No longer in sand-colored camouflage, he now wore a gray double-breasted suit, a purple-rosetted handkerchief and tie. In the church were a dozen other soldiers who, like James, would rather go to Iraq without Berettas than Bibles and who'd often ask at Fort Riley, "Can I wear my Cross?" "Yes, under your shirt." "Can I wear my Christopher medal?" "Yes, under your shirt." "Well, what if it just pops out?" "Well, put it back in." The church's preacher, a wild-haired woman, didn't stand like a statue of Mary but danced down the aisle crying, "Are y'all *listenin'*?" "Yeah!" In their pews the women cried, "Praise the Lord!" they leapt like on pogo sticks, their pearls flapping on their chests, they fell in the aisle still shouting, praising the Lord epileptically while the men played the trumpet, trombone and sax. The preacher added a verse to *Kumbaya,*

The boys in Arabia, kumbaya!
The boys in Arabia, kumbaya!

and James sat and lip-synched, his left hand keeping the beat like a hand with a wooden pestle or wiping a tear with a Kleenex. As always, James was subdued. He felt the spirit of God hovering over him, but he didn't surrender to it ("I will never surrender," his Code of Conduct said) and he wasn't, *kumbaya,* possessed. He knew he had answered his country's call, but he wondered when, dear God, he'd get the Call from Thee.

The first soldier into Iraq would be Second Lieutenant Russell. One day C's captain chose him, but Russell didn't know it: he'd just had an eight-pound, ten-ounce son, and he was in Texas with him. "You don't understand me, Tom," said Russell, peering into Tom's white crib, "but Daddy's going away. If my country calls, then I have to."

Every cell in Russell believed this. He too had an army father, had been born on a base in France, had grown up on bases in Germany, Georgia and Texas, in worlds whose dimensions were red, white and blue. His neighbors had put their hands on their hearts for *The Star-Spangled Banner,* and at five every day as the cannon went *boom,* they'd whispered to Russell, age three, "Hey, fella, the flag," and Russell had jumped from his tricycle, hand on his heart, as *tatata,* the flag came down. On these bases he'd learned the eternal verities, which, after all, by definition, were true. God is good. A man cares for his son. A man cannot love unless he loves honor more. If duty calls, a man answers, and Russell was going to Saudi to the interior music of *Yankee Doodle,* of *Glory, Glory,* of *Over There.* He believed that America's wars, America's boys, had given him his America and he must preserve it for all the boys after him.

"I have to go, Tom," Russell said now. "But when I come back I'll be here for you." The tears welled in Russell's eyes, they rolled down his soft, smooth, baby-skin cheeks, they dripped off, *pit, pat,* and Tom looked at Russell baffled. "I love you, Tom," Russell said, but Tom looked puzzled and Russell said, "I," said, "Love," said, "You. Well, someday you'll know what I mean." Tom's ears were like Mickey Mouse's, they probably picked up Comsat, come in, London, I copy you, but Tom hadn't understood and Russell thought, *What if I die? And don't come back? And Tom doesn't know that I loved him?* and Russell thought, *I know what I'll do,* Russell would write a diary that Tom, his beloved orphan, could read in the year 2000-and-what. Then, Russell told him, "I love you," gave him a swallow-tailed pennant of Company C, and flew to an airport in Kansas.

Another lieutenant drove him to C. "There's something you've got to promise me," Russell told him.

"Yeah."

"I'm going to write a diary for Tom. I'll wrap it in Nomex," in fireproof fabric. "I'll put that in a .50-caliber ammo can, and I'll put *that* in a 20-millimeter ammo can."

"Yeah." The other lieutenant, a black one, was driving and watching the snow-covered road.

"I'll then tie *that,*" Russell said, "to my bustle rack," to the cage at the back of Russell's tank. C was a tank-riding company, and Russell commanded one of C's tanks—indeed, as a second lieutenant, commanded four. "Promise me if I get killed, you'll get the diary to Tom."

"Yeah," the other lieutenant said. He hadn't listened closely, and he wasn't prepared when a few hours later he, Russell, and another lieutenant sat on a Sunkist-colored couch and the captain of C said, "Here's what we'll do in Iraq. We'll be the breaching unit, and Russell," the captain continued, the captain his usual solemn-as-a-Roman-senator self—"and Russell, you'll be the plow platoon." The captain meant that a six-foot plow would be welded to Russell's tank to *boom!* to plow up the man-killing, tank-killing

mines as Russell, the happy daddy, led the American army into
Castle Iraq, and the black lieutenant gasped. He blurted to Russell,
"Uh, where'd you say the diary would be?"

Russell sat stunned. He felt like a star when the MC says,
"And the winner is *YOU!*" He was proud of the captain's confidence, but he couldn't account for it. He was the junior lieutenant
here—he'd been thirty days in C, the other lieutenants three *hundred* days, well, why had the captain rejected them? The black
lieutenant had wanted to be in combat since he was a boy in Ohio,
age nine. His mother, he'd once told Russell, had given him a
quarter one day, and he'd bought the May, 1975, issue of *GI Combat*. In that comic book was the story of Jeb, a tank commander
in Europe in World War II. And WHRANG! The boy in Ohio had
gaped as a German pilot dived and, the tank colored green, the
explosion yellow, as Jeb's tank exploded and Jeb and his crew
climbed out. On the ground was the cannon, but Jeb and his crew
hand-hoisted it as RAT-TAT! the German dived again. Jeb shouted,
"FIRE!" and Jeb's loader shouted, "YOU'RE LOADED!" but Jeb's gunner shouted, "I NEED ELEVATION!" as bullets bounced off the cannon, VIP! VIP! and BEEOOW! Then BLAMM! the cannon went
BLAMM! the round hit the German, WHRAAMM! and in orange-
edged smoke the German exploded. On seeing this, the boy in
Ohio had chosen to be the tank commander that lo! he'd become
at C, and today he looked combat-ready as Russell thought, *Why
did the captain pass over him?* The third lieutenant, from Washington, had been to West Point, so why had the captain scorned *him?*
And then Russell saw: the honor of being first in Iraq had gone to
the most expendable soldier, the one who could die with the least
inconvenience to C.

"Uh, where'd you say the diary would be?"

"On the bustle rack. In an ammo can. In Nomex," said Russell, thinking of Tom, dear Tom, his desolate son, the boy who
would read his last, loving, sweat-stained words. "Sir," Russell said
to C's captain, "can I put up a sign in Iraq saying compliments of
Company C?"

"I'll look into that," the solemn-as-Caesar captain said.

The conference ended. The three lieutenants went to C's cinder-block corridor. The one from West Point thought, *If I were Russell, I'd be afraid,* and, not knowing what to say, said nothing, but the black lieutenant tried humor. "The diary'll be on the bustle rack?"

"Yes," Russell said.

"As long as it ain't in the turret! I don't want your guts on me!"

Russell laughed. He was now, for whatever reason, someone special in C, a boy who'd one-upped the other timid lieutenants. He jabbed the black one, who called his soldiers the Dogs of War, after the song by Pink Floyd, and said, "The Puppies of War!"

From then on, the two boys laughed at Russell's predicament. One day they went to a class on Russell's nemesis, the Iraqi mines—the Iraqi *moins,* for the instructor was an Australian who in his shrimp-on-the-barbie accent said, "Oi will pass this moin aroun'." As the mine (it had been disarmed) went around like a church's collection plate and as, in its innards, a loose nut or bolt or washer went *clink!* like a dime dropping in, the Aussie told of the mines that, like truffles, would lie in Iraq in Russell's way: of dumb mines, smart mines, of seismic, magnetic, pneumatic mines, of mines that a mine detector couldn't find: of wood, plastic, paper mines, no, there were no paper mines, of mud-colored, muck-colored, sand-colored mines, of mines that, like scorpions, could crawl into Russell's tank, well, almost, of mines that if Russell rolled over them, would send a plague of hot molten metal into Russell's poor tank. "Ten years ago," the Aussie said, "the Iraqis had fourteen million moins. They used four million against Iran." He then tapped his forehead and said, "Me being a mathematical genius tells me there's ten million left."

Russell laughed blackly. He turned to the black lieutenant, put his thumb and his index finger into an O, and put his other index finger through the O, the configuration of a man's penis in a woman's vagina. The gesture meant *I'm fucked.*

"Better you than me!" the black lieutenant laughed.

"The Puppies of War!" said Russell.

"The *alive* Puppies of War!"

Russell raised his two hands. He pretended they were a megaphone and, at the black lieutenant's ear, whispered, "The Puppies of War!"

"Hey, motherfucker," the black lieutenant laughed. "You'll be a smokin' hulk inside an Iraqi," he called it *I-rack-ee*, "minefield and I'll be in Baghdad!"

Of all of C's chores before going to Saudi, the most important was to rehearse, and one day C rolled from its barracks to rehearse, rehearse. It was cold out, the clouds hid the sun, the wind was a wolf going *ooooo!* but C wouldn't suffer today, for its tanks were at sea somewhere east of Suez and C wouldn't rehearse on a bison's old stomping grounds but in a warm classroom, indoors. C got to the classroom after lunch. It stood at the room's south wall, and at one o'clock it walked three feet to the north, to a row of 3-by-5 cards that lay on the brown linoleum floor. On the cards were a lot of green ⊓⌐⊔⌐⊓s, representing the six-foot wall—the *berm*—that would be C's first obstacle in Iraq. C's sober-sided captain stood with his toes on the ⊓⌐⊔⌐⊓s, saying, "We hit the berm, and the CEV," the combat engineer vehicle, "goes up and shoots it."

"Well . . ." In the room was a voice like in "Well, I don't know." It came from the captain's boss, a tough little scar-faced lieutenant colonel, commander of Companies A, B, C, D, who was squatting at one cold window, watching. For one long moment, the colonel inhaled a Carlton, reflecting, then said, "Well, I guess Abdul knows we're here. I just don't like making kabooms."

"Yes, sir." The captain spoke as though every word was a life-or-death matter, for, like everyone else in C, he'd never been in a war before and he wasn't nonchalant about it. "Next," he said, "we fire a red star cluster."

"*Was meint das?*" the colonel said. In his twenties he'd served in Germany, and he'd asked in German what the red flares meant.

"They mean we've reached the berm," the captain said, then he turned to Lieutenant Russell and said, "The plow platoon will be Russell."

"Yes, sir!" Russell stepped forward over the ⌐‿⌐‿⌐s, meaning that he and his tanks would go through the hole in the six-foot wall. "We roll through the berm," he began, "and we roll through the wire," and he stepped over a row of 3-by-5 cards with a lot of black ✳✳✳✳✳s, representing the sharp barbed wire in Iraq. He spoke at Amtrak speed, for he was a cat confronting a king: the scar-faced lieutenant colonel, and a pause might imply indecisiveness.

"Yes, plow through all the wires you can," the colonel said.

"Yes, sir," said Russell, the Twentieth Century Limited. "We roll right over the ditch," and Russell stepped over a row of green ⋁⋁⋁⋁s, representing the moatlike thing in Iraq. In his hurry he kicked it, but it didn't budge, for the 3-by-5 cards were held to the floor by Scotch tape. "We get to the moderate minefield," said Russell, and he stepped over a row, a row, and another row of green : : : : :s, representing the tank-killing mines in Iraq, "and I'll know we're through when we get to the concertina wire. We roll right through *that*," and Russell stepped over a row of green ಠಠಠಠಠs, representing the spiral wires in Iraq, "and we get to the heavy minefield. We start plowing again—"

"What if your tank gets hit?" the colonel interrupted. In the window behind him, a crow flapped across the tin-colored sky.

"I would unman," Russell said. He meant that he and his gunner, loader and driver would get the hell out.

"Mm." The colonel turned to the rest of C, which still was in back of Russell. Young, the boy who dreamt of Mouse, and James, who awaited the Call, weren't there, for Young was manning the telephone saying, "May I help you, sir or ma'am?" and

James, who'd done this yesterday, was now off duty, off post, and painting his daughter's playroom white, but to everyone present the colonel said, "Keep firing. We don't want Abdul to stand up and put some rounds up Russell's poop-chute." C nodded professionally, and the colonel said, "What next?"

Russell resumed his and-then-you're-in-Baltimore speed. "After clearing the second minefield," and he stepped over the : : : : :s, the : : : : :s, and the : : : : :s, "we come to more barbed wire," and he stepped over the ＊＊＊＊＊s, "and to more concertina wire," and he stepped over the ರರರರರ s, the last row of 3-by-5 cards. "At that time we'll stop," Russell said, for Russell was on the bare linoleum now—was where, in Iraq, the Iraqi trenches would be.

"No! The last thing I want to do," the colonel said suddenly, "is to lose infantry in a fight with a bunch of semiliterate half-assed savages. *You,*" he continued to Russell, his feet a few feet apart, his boots on the glossy linoleum—"you straddle the fuckin' trench and *go!*" his boots going *clomp!* and *clomp!* "I don't want to fight fair!"

"No problem, sir," Russell said.

"Make sure nothing there will hurt us!"

"Yes, sir."

"Make them convulse until death!"

"Yes, sir."

At last C relaxed. It went back to its barracks, and the colonel went to his old stone home at Fort Riley and, with his wife, had a couple of rum-and-Diet-Cokes. As tough as he looked, the scar from the colonel's ear to his mouth wasn't from Heidelberg, as he would sometimes joke in Kansas, saying, "We used epées," but from Kansas itself, the colonel, age seventeen, crashing a Mustang, tottering out, and knocking on someone's door, *tap-tap,* a woman in rollers opening it, seeing him, and screaming, *"Aiii!"* A former history teacher, the colonel knew the Iraqis weren't semiliterate savages, were, in fact, the inhabitants of the Cradle of Civilization, but he willingly called them the "Savages," "Abduls," and "Fuckers" to help sustain the fighting spirit of C. He knew the Iraqis had three times as many tanks as America did, but he'd shown confidence at the paper rehearsal today. To have acknowledged that C might get to the ⎍⎍⎍s but not to the *****s, the ⋁⋁⋁⋁s, the : : : : :s, the ०००००s, or the end-of-the-rainbow trenches would have been, well, defeatist.

Like all of C, the colonel, who'd enlisted in 1971, had never been in a war before. The closest he'd come was in Germany, his tank catching fire, his rounds heating up, he and his crew unmanning fast. That near-disaster in 1977 now flooded his thoughts as he went to bed at Fort Riley. He fell asleep, but he dreamt he was suddenly in Iraq, was being hit by Iraqi mortars, cannons, rockets, by Iraqi iron, wood, plastic mines—by an Iraqi Fourth of July around him. He dreamt that, yes, his tank was on fire, *many* of his tanks were on fire, they were glowing, exploding, the red-hot turrets rising like Roman candles, dreamt he was shouting orders to Companies A, B, C and D, "Alfa, this is Dreadnought!" "Bravo, this is Dreadnought!" "Charlie—" His dream was a nightmare, for no one was answering, no one was living, his A, B, C, D were charcoal now, and the colonel woke up with sweat pasting him to his sheets, his wife beside him and C in its barracks, sound asleep.

The next night was Friday, the Goddess of Love Day, and C did its first priority: *girls,* and in sneakers, jeans, and T-shirts with pictures, say, of Bart Simpson, its bachelors drove to a disco outside of Fort Riley. This being the '90s, the boys didn't ask, "May I have this dance?" but stood with a Bud till a girl, approaching, punched a boy's stomach saying, *"Heyyy!"* or threw a nelson around his neck saying, *"Heyyy!"* the subtext being "Hey, brother, I'm your sister, don't try to ball me." One boy in C, who was white, was sipping his Bud when a cute black girl, a black lace on one of her sneakers, an orange lace on the other, the laces dragging behind like the train of a bridal gown, *here I come,* walked up and more or less goosed him. *"Heyyy!"* the girl hailed him. "It's you and your big fat Amazon ass!" The boy answered, *"Heyyy!"* and the two repaired to the dance floor to lie on their backs and to wiggle their arms and legs overhead like a pair of upended beetles to Sam Cooke's *Shout.*

The introductions concluded, some of C actually scored. Or was it the girls who scored? for at midnight a girl in a Hi-I'm-a-wild-thing tie-dyed shirt went to Sergeant Spence, a close-mouthed boy from Texas, and said, "You ready?" Spence said, "Yeah," and the girl drove him to her house, took him in, and at her bed tossed out the teddy bears, teddy lions, teddy hippopotamuses, and Rag-gedy Anns. She then seized a jar of gel that looked like Dippity-Do, slapped some of it behind her (her pants and panties were off) and cried, "Oh, Mike!" though Mike wasn't Spence's name, "Oh, fuck me up the ass!" and Spence said, "Yeah." The only aggressor in C tonight was Specialist Walters, from Arkansas, a soft-cheeked boy who approached a girl in I-got-frills and yes-I-can-shimmy jeans and who, saying nothing, picked her up and carried her out. The two had been lovers once. But that week at Fort Riley, Walters had tested his gas mask *(hoo!* he'd sat in a gas-saturated tent, and *hoo!* he'd breathed like Darth Vader) and, com-ing back to his room, he'd heard the girl on his answering machine, for a girl in the '90s seldom wrote a Dear John. "It's not working out," she'd said, "and we need to end things between us," but Walters just went to the disco on Friday and, like Lochinvar, car-ried the giggling girl to her apartment and bed. "Hey, Walters!" the rest of C said when he bounded into the barracks on Saturday afternoon. "What's with this Romeo stuff?"

"Aw," Walters said. "She's crippled," the girl used a cane, indeed. "And when she's looped, she—"

"No, no, no," C needled him.

For the bachelors in C, the girls, pretty girls, were of sudden immense importance now, a lot of C even proposing. One such boy was Sergeant Medine, from Louisiana, half Irish, half Sioux, who didn't propose to a girl at the disco in Kansas, Bushwacker Bar, but to a pen pal in England, the border of Scotland. The two hadn't met, but as soon as Medine had gotten his orders to Saudi he'd longed for a wife in the Wordsworth lands, *Behold her, yon solitary lass,* and he'd popped the "Will you?" by telephone and Carol had answered, "Yes." Specialist Young, the boy who'd dreamt of Mouse, of Mouse, one night went to the Klub Kamille and, his voice still flat as his shadow, came back to C asking friends, "Will you be my best man?"

"What what? You want to marry the *dancer*?"

"Yeah—"

"You idiot! Did you *sleep* with her?"

"No—" In fact, Young had only played pool with her and, to woo her, had purposely lost.

"She just wants your *money*," said C. "She just wants your BAQ," your Basic Allowance for Quarters, $324 each month. "She just wants your SGLI," your $50,000 for dying in Iraq.

"No, she's not—"

"She's hopin' you'll die! She'll send you a package of poisoned cookies in Iraq!"

"Well—"

"She'll write the Iraqis, 'My husband's in Company C. He has brown hair, brown eyes, and—' "

"I'll have to think about it," Young said.

By now, a number of bachelors in C (some specialists, sergeants, the black lieutenant) were even getting married. One such was Specialist Penn, a boy with a rough-looking face, from California, who'd dated a girl he'd met in a disco who told him one day, "I'm pregnant." Penn was white and the girl was black, so Penn asked his virtuous sergeant, "Should I marry her?"

"Do you love her?"

Penn didn't answer.

"Well, marriage," the sergeant said, the sergeant was James, the when-will-I-get-the-Call? boy, who was black himself, "is not a vow you can make and break. We talkin' 'bout a vow you make before *God*. You can't say, 'Well, now I'll break up.' "

"I think I'll marry her," said Penn, and he married the quiet, corn-braided, big-bellied girl and had the reception in C's crowded barracks, C in its jeans with its Sprites.

One day, Specialist Gebert, a never-ending-smiling boy from Texas, married a girl he'd known since second grade. At two on their wedding day, Gebert in camouflage and his bride-to-be in jeans and a *Coca-Cola* shirt sat in a room like a mausoleum that, in fact, was a $20,000 computer game. Up front on a TV screen was an image of Egypt, the sand was new-mustard-colored and the pyramids old-mustard-colored, and the "camera" panned right and left as Gebert, his hands on a wheel called the Cadillac, turned it first right, then left, then— Suddenly, from in back of a pyramid came two Iraqi tanks, and the bride stopped embroidering as a sergeant shouted to Gebert, "Two tanks! The right tank first!"

"Identified!" Gebert cried. He turned the Cadillac right, and his thumbs hit the two red buttons on it. A laser hit an Iraqi tank, and a "2200" for 2200 meters appeared on the TV screen. The sergeant cried, "Fire!" and Gebert cried, "On the way!" and his fingers pulled the red triggers, and his head snapped back as his headrest recoiled. His bride put her fingers to her lips, apprehensive, and her diamond glittered in the mustard-colored light. The audio went *boom!* and the video showed an orange-edged flash like the one on Jeb's stricken tank in *GI Combat* in May, 1975. "Target!" the sergeant cried, "Bull's-eye!" the sergeant meant, and Gebert turned the Cadillac left. "On the way!" Gebert cried, *boom!* went the audio, *flash!* went the video, and the Iraqi tanks were two smokin' hulks. The bride murmured, "Two out of two," she picked up her aida cloth, and she continued her count-across stitches, XXX, a bear on a Christmas stocking.

By six, Gebert had killed about forty tanks (he'd also missed, the Iraqis had fired, the screen had gone black, and the bride had said, frowning, "I *guess* they're alive") and for the wedding he'd changed to his brass-buttoned uniform, the bride to a navy-blue suit. At six she walked down the aisle of St. Mary's Chapel. With her was her father, a man who'd obeyed the words of Jesus, "Ye have heard that thou shalt not kill," and who during the Vietnam War had served at a school for the mentally retarded rather than in Vietnam. He still belonged to the War Resisters League.

"Who gives this woman away?"

"My wife and I do."

"Do you, Russell Gebert, take . . ."

They were married. They honeymooned at Motel 6. Then Gebert, who, like the rest of C, would rather make love not war, but who'd also promised, "I do," to an army recruiting officer, returned to the barracks and put his wife's picture into the olive-green bag that he'd carry to Saudi any day.

But not just yet. C had one thousand things to do—no, 1001, for Operations had calculated that most of C, about forty-five boys, would be hit as they stormed into Castle Iraq and had scheduled a course in first aid for C. The course, a refresher, really, was held in the barracks in the room for the TV set and the sand, pool, ping-pong and Foosball tables—the TV set that C had seen the Pentagon movie *The Breach* on, the sand table that C had put Iraqi trenches on and, *whoosh!* with a gesture, erased, the pool, ping-pong and Foosball tables that C had had little time for, and one more thing: a piano that C never played. Today, C turned the TV off ("Yes," said Dracula, "the other guests will be *dying* to meet you. Yes, *dying*") and sat on the floor as a fast-talking, syllable-dropping medic told it what it should do when someone is hit by Iraqi fire. "The first thing," the medic said, "is to make sure he's conch," meaning conscious. "Ask him, 'What day's to-day?' He says Thursday, but you know it's Monday. Ask him, 'What plant are you on?' " meaning planet. "If he doesn't know, well, somethin's wrong. Check him for Paris," paralysis. "If you kick him in the foot, *wham,*" and the medic kicked the linoleum, "and he doesn't move, well, somethin's wrong. If he's unconch (and he may be unconch for a second, a minute, or maybe forever) don't go and pull a John Wayne. You know? And slap him around?"

On the floor the soldiers of C were alert and amused, like the flyboys of World War II, "We'll have flak over Düsseldorf," "Okie doke." By now C had had many classes on combat first aid, and it sat sipping its Pepsis thinking, *Get on with it.*

"He may have a head wound," the medic continued. "I don't mean somethin' sufficial," meaning superficial. "You cut yourself shavin', you put some toilet paper on: that's somethin' sufficial. He may have cerebrospinal fluids comin' out. The stuff that your brain is floatin' in. It smells sweet, it looks like white honey, like corn syrup that your mother made. He may have some brain matter seepin' out. Don't try to put the brain matter back in, and don't give the guy any painkillers, cause when he gets to the rear, they'll jab him and ask him, 'Are you feelin' this?' 'No,' and they'll think he's doin' the sick-call shuffle."

C chuckled. C gave the medic credit, he was trying to make the class interesting.

"If he's layin' there on the ground," the medic continued, "and if his intessins," intestines, "are all strung out on the ground, don't try to repack 'em. Don't try to take 'em, *klup, klup, klup,*" and the medic pretended to scoop something off the linoleum, "like a garden hose, and put 'em back in. You take the cleanest thing you've got and you lay it here," he patted his tummy. "If his eyeball is hangin' out— Has anyone here ever seen anyone with his eyeball hangin' out?"

C laughed and said, "No."

"Anyone here seen *Rocky IV*? And his big swollen eye?"

C laughed and said, "Yes."

"Well, Rocky," the medic digressed—"Rocky was stupid. To hit that guy Drago? The guy with the crew cut? You don't go and *hit* anybody that big. Well," said the medic, reconsidering, "I'd go in the ring with Tyson, I think. I think anyone in this *room* would go in the ring if they're payin' us eight million dolls." The medic pretended to climb in a ring and suddenly slip. "Ooh, I just pulled a muscle!" he moaned. "I quit!"

C laughed. A platform was all the medic needed.

"Um," the medic continued. "I'm lost, I'm on Mars. Oh, sometimes the eyeball is hangin' down by the optical nerve. Do not attempt to replace it. What you do—"

"Can the guy still see?" said someone in C.

"I don't know."

"He won't be lookin' aroun'," said someone in C. "He'll probably be in shock."

"He'll be lookin' aroun' the corners," said someone in C, who then craned his head around like the Extra-Terrestrial.

"What you do," the medic continued, "is be really careful with it. Pick the guy's eye up. Then take a Styrofoam cup. Put the guy's eye in."

"Who's gonna find a cup layin' aroun'?"

"Take some copper," some cardboard, "and roll it up."

"Well, who's gonna find any cardboard?"

"Use an MRE," said someone in C, who referred to the cardboard boxes for MREs, Meals Ready-to-Eat. Far from being repelled by these vivid instructions, the boy felt, *Well, that's what we soldiers do. We put eyeballs in cardboard boxes.*

"You want to pad it," the medic continued. "You don't want to put pressure on, cause they'll operate and say, 'Can you see?' and he'll say, 'Well, everythin's blurry.' If his aisle," his eyelid, "is layin' on the ground, wrap it up. Don't tell him, 'Hey, here's your aisle,' but give it to someone who's bringin' him in. Give him his glasses, too, so he doesn't wake up in the hospital and say, 'I can't see!' 'Well, bonehead! Your glasses aren't here!' Any questions?" No one in C had questions, and the medic concluded, "You see the guy sitting next to you?" The medic intended to say to C, "Don't forget what I've said. Or the guy sitting next to you may not be coming back," but he'd talked for an hour now: he was pooped and he simply said, "He may not be comin' back."

"*I'm* comin' back," said someone or other, and C skipped out of its pool, ping-pong and Foosball room and out of its busy barracks.

A lot of C went to a Christmas party. It went in its cars, for a genial sergeant in C had invited it to his home outside of Fort Riley. Long gone were the sergeants who cried, "If you needed a wife, we'd have issued one," for much of C was married, especially now, and at four every afternoon the genial sergeant drove to his dollhouse home, to his Christmas tree and his red MERRY CHRIST-MAS festoons, and to a wife and kids who often sat staring at CNN. "That's Santa Claus!" his three-year-old at the TV would shout. And two minutes later, "That's Saddam Hussein!"

"Who is he, Joshua?"

"The bad man!"

"What did he do?"

"He took stuff away!"

"And Daddy—?"

"Has to go get it back!"

At five o'clock, C in its civvies came to this home sweet home. The sergeant's wife said, "I'm Penny," and offered her cookies to C: her graham-and-coconut cookies, her peanut-butter cookies with Hershey kisses, her chocolate-covered pretzels, her coconut cookies with M&M's (red ones and green ones for Christmas) and her melted marshmallows with Rice Krispies, a snap! crackle! recipe that Penny revealed she'd seen on a Kellogg's box. "Thank you," said C, and with cookies and red paper napkins it went to her son saying, "What do you want to be?" "A fireman!" and to her pretty blond daughter, "You drive the boys crazy, don't you?" One green-sweatered boy in C even kissed the daughter's hand.

"Ooh!" the girl said. "What's that?"

"No one has ever kissed your hand?"

"No."

"How old are you?"

"Two."

"Well, what kind of boys do you date?"

The girl giggled. She climbed on the soldier's lap, and her father the genial sergeant said, "She's in love with you."

"Well, I'm in love with her too."

"You are?" said the girl, looking pleased. "When I grow up, I want to be a policeman."

"How come?"

"Because: I want to fix people's teeth."

"Oh, you want to be a *dentist*."

"A dentistman?"

"No, you want to be a dentist *woman*."

"Why?"

"Well, blue is for boys and pink is for girls and *you*—"

At their side was Penny, beaming. The sergeant's wife had the red round face of a girl on a cake-mix box. She surely didn't mean to turn this nice conversation to the topic of mayhem and murder, for she simply asked the hand-kissing boy, "Do you go out with girls around here?"

"Not for more than fifteen minutes, no," the boy laughed.

"Do *you*?" Penny asked another bachelor in C.

"Well," the boy laughed, "I try."

"But the girls know better?" said Penny. The boy laughed again, and in her motherly way she asked him, "Do you have sex?"

"Well, that's what they call it."

"Do you use protection?"

"No," said another bachelor in C. "You don't want a rain-coat on."

"You don't think of AIDS?"

"No, we're gonna live till it's our time to go."

"You don't think of dying? I don't mean in Saudi Arabia."

"Hey, I don't want to die *anywhere*," a boy in C laughed.

"Well, I want to die with a sabot round," a cannon round,

"through my turret," said Penny's husband, the Christmas host.

"As long as I'm not in that turret with you," a boy in C laughed.

"I know what he's sayin'," another boy laughed. "A sabot, you die very fast. Unless with my luck it takes off my legs and I bleed for a while."

"I'd rather die than lose a leg. Get it—"

"I wouldn't."

"—get it over with. I wouldn't care."

"Well," a boy laughed, and the conversation came back to Kansas as fast as it had vaulted to Iraq—"well, I'm goin' out with a DUI on the way to a club in Topeka."

Everyone laughed—Penny too, for she was married to C for better, for worse, and she knew what people in C did: they lived, they laughed, they lost legs, they died, they ate Rice Krispies at Christmas. "Is anyone for Trivial Pursuit?" said Penny, and C said enthusiastically, "Yes!"

It was now the eleventh hour, and Young, the boy who dreamt of Mouse, had yes! had decided to marry her. For days, he'd seen other companies go *poof!* go in their combat clothes, the black rifles on their shoulders, bayonets at their hips, as though they planned to parachute-drop on Missouri, to rows of bright yellow buses with this sign: JUST PASSING THROUGH, the soldiers had gotten aboard, then (*poof!*) the buses had left, and nothing was ever seen or heard of Company A or Company B. Not one little cigarette butt! It was like—*death,* it was even worse, it was as if A or B had gone on a tangent off of time's circle and so had never existed, *never,* and Young had remembered that C would fade away too. In the depths of his heart, he wanted part of himself to stay in Kansas intact till the rest of him reemerged from the fourth dimension, and he'd said yes to the girl who a couple of Fridays ago had fallen to her knees and, the sweat on her breasts almost blinding him, had asked him, "Will you marry me?"

And now, Young and his bride were in a Dodge en route to a Methodist minister. On normal days Young was a boy who couldn't get to *do-re-mi,* but on this momentous one he couldn't even get to *do,* for he was afraid that the girl might renege and say, "Stop the car!" and say, "Lemme out!" and say, "See you later, potater!" and he was stifling the cry inside him, *"Marry me! Or I'll die!"* He'd been in the army eight years, he was normally cool, but in this past hour he'd driven out of Fort Riley, had gotten lost, had called up Mouse reporting, "I'm lost," had sensed a certain emptiness, had thought, *Jesus Christ, am I fucking up,* had called her again, "My wallet, I forgot it," had driven back to Fort Riley, had gotten his wallet but met a sergeant who'd said, "ID card?" "Dog tags?" "Code of Conduct?" to ascertain if Young was ready for Saudi. "Here," "Here," "Here," Young had said, taking the ID, et cetera, out. "Hey, I'm running *late,*" the *late* not a decibel louder nor a semitone higher than Young's other words, simply longer: *laaaate,* the sergeant telling him, "Go," and Young now driving the Dodge, sitting as stiff as a mannequin in a car-crash commercial, glancing at Mouse and thinking, *Oh God! She might say, "Stop the car!"*

He turned onto Washington Street. On the seat beside him, Mouse carried on the conversation by Young's default. "I called you up," she said with zest. "The guy who answered said, 'Who may I tell him's calling?' and I said, 'Tell him it's Mrs. Young!' The guy said, '*Mrs.* Young?' and I said, 'Yeah! We're getting married! Doncha know?'" She laughed, her whole body shook, then a new mood possessed her, and she looked at her $1000 ring and the streetlights shining inside it and whispered, "Gee, I'll be Mrs. Young," and, like a girl who meant it, "Even when I'm old I'll still be Young." On her first date with him, his ball going slow, slower, slow-a-slug toward a side pocket, *stop,* his ball standing still like a soldier scared of a parachute jump and Mouse crying, "I'm gonna win!" she'd told him that no other soldier had ever inspired her to end her act asking, "Will you marry me?" With evident feeling, she'd said that Young had watched her so stoically, so totally empty of "Whoo"'s, so—well, so Gary Cooper that Young had truly intrigued her. "I'm like that," said Mouse, who wore jeans and a modest pink sweater, her face full of happiness, as Young pulled up at the home of the Reverend Walls.

They got out and knocked at the Reverend's weathered door. The man who opened it looked at Mouse and said, "Mm-*mm!* I goin' boil me some sweet potatoes so I can make sweet potato pie!" The man, who was old, fat, black, and exceptionally jolly and was the Reverend, apparently, then said something that Young wasn't ready for. He didn't say, "Do you take this woman," but "Do you know that husban's shou' cook?"

"I can boil water," said Mouse, who was doing the talking today, "and I can cook meat loaf." She laughed and the Reverend chuckled, and Young sat down uncertainly on the Reverend's over-stuffed couch. It was six o'clock, suppertime, but Young hadn't come for a wedding reception, just the "I do," "I do." Mouse sat down beside him, the Reverend stood at a make-believe pulpit: an overstuffed chair, then he started and Young wasn't ready again.

"So who's the boss?" the Reverend said.

"We both are," Mouse laughed.

"You both the boss," the Reverend said, approving. "You," he said to Mouse, "shouldn' buy a mink coat unless he know about it."

"I don't want a mink coat," said Mouse.

"And *you*," to Young, "shouldn' buy a Cadillac unless *she* know about it. You put all you' money *together*. You," to Mouse, as Young thought, *Oh no! He's preaching to us!*—"you don' have to feed him steak every day."

"Do you like veal, honey?" said Mouse.

"You give him steak today, tomorrow you give him some beans. But make sure there's A.1. sauce."

"*Mm.* I love A.1. sauce," said Mouse. "We both are for A.1. all the way."

"Heh heh. You'll have no problem then."

"No problem," said Mouse. She looked pleased with the Reverend. She didn't look as though she'd say, "Stop!" "I'm bored!" or "I'm outta here!" but Young watched the Reverend's door to assure himself, *Yes. It's chained.* In his throat was a cry of *"Hurry! I'm going to Saudi!"* and, to suppress it, he cut off the power to it: his breath, and he breathed minimally, *iiiin, ouuut,* as the Reverend, his hand on his pulpit, his pulpit upholstered with foam, the foam full of egg-crate indentations, resumed.

"You don' have to have a $150 dress," the Reverend said to Mouse. "And *you*," to Young—"you don' have to have a $400 suit. One that cost 200 look jus' as good nine times outo' ten. You know what you dislike. And *you* know what *you* dislike. And when you find what each other dislike, don' *do* it! If you know you' husban' don' like steak, and you buy him a steak, what he gonna do? Get angry! If you know you' wife don' like stuffed po'k chop, and you buy her po'k chop—"

Mouse laughed. She smiled at Young, discovering that he was nearly apneic, for he was breathing as someone might on his dying day.

"—she gonna get angry!" the Reverend said.

"It's okay to breathe," said Mouse to Young. The Reverend chuckled, but Mouse put an ear to Young's motionless chest. "Are you alive?" she said, and Young took a teeny-weeny breath, meaning yes.

"Don' pass out, please," the Reverend said, "cause I can' stand the sight. A lotto' times," he continued, "a lotto' things happen to a marriage the *husban's* the cause of. You," to Young—"you get off work at five o'clock, you shou' be home by five-thirty. Not sto' by the tavern and get you four or five brews and come home and can' hardly walk. And come in the door, start in undressin', go to the bathroom, and let you' wife pick up the clothes—no, you put you' clothes in the clothes hamper, *tha's* what you do!" Young didn't respond, he was virtually *in extremis* now, but Mouse laughed appreciatively and the Reverend switched to an Amos-and-Andy voice to mimic some macho man. " 'I don' pick up no clo's cause I don' wash 'em,' " the Reverend said, then returned to his normal voice. "Why *not?* If you never do it, *she* goin' have to do it. Any questions?"

Mouse laughed. She shook her head no, and Young stifled a *"Yes! One question! When will you marry us?"*

"Now, when I finish," the Reverend said, addressing himself to Mouse, "you' last name will be his last name unless you a movie star. I know how old you are," the Reverend suddenly told her.

"You do?"

"Mm-hm. I bet you a Coke, I can tell you how old you are."

"You can guess it?"

"No, I can tell you *'xactly* how old you are. Or I buy you a Coke."

"All right," said Mouse, and Young went to all-systems-shut-down, a mode that a coroner couldn't distinguish from that of a corpse on the Reverend's couch. "How old am I?"

"You as old as you' tongue but not you' teeth."

Mouse looked puzzled and Young was now out of it.

"You as old as you' tongue but not you' teeth!" the Reverend cackled. "Cause everyone in the world today, tha's how old they are! As old as they tongue but not they teeth! Cause when they came here they had a tongue, but they *teeth* came later!"

"I love it!" Mouse laughed.

"Everyone tell me," the Reverend continued, " 'Well, maybe you got that wrong,' but I say, *'How?* Cause if you' teeth came before you' tongue you better go back!' " Mouse laughed loud and long and the Reverend cackled, "Any questions?"

"No sir!" said Mouse.

"Well!" the Reverend said. He reached in his pocket and took out a piece of white plastic the size of a tongue depressor. Till now, he'd worn his black collar open, but he now buttoned it and put the white plastic in, an instant clerical collar. "Well, I goin' hook the horse to the plow and the plow to the horse," the Reverend said. "Any questions?" He paused, then he stared at Young and practically yelled, "Any questions?"

"Mike!" said Mouse, and she banged on Young's chest like a nurse doing cardiopulmonary resuscitation. "Breathe! Loosen up! You look like a mummy sitting there!"

Somewhere inside him, Young knew he had to answer her, and his voice issued from the Beyond. "I'd hate," said Young, "to be declared *deaaaad,*" then he fell silent again.

"Excuse me?" said Mouse.

"If you nervous, don' pass out," the Reverend said. "Stand beside me," he said, and Mouse hopped off the couch as Young slowly rose like a maharishi accomplishing levitation. He had white sneakers on, he had clean jeans and a turtleneck, in his hair was a pint of Aussie but in his mind he was light-years away from the Reverend's parlor in Kansas. "Now don'," the Reverend said to Mouse, reprising his Polonius bit—"don' go in the kitchen and break all the dishes, cause a fork doesn' make a tinglin' soun' on a paper plate. And *you,*" to Young, "don' tear off the roof, cause the house with no roof it'll *rain* in it. Dear Lord," the Reverend said. "Thank you for blessin' this man and woman. Let them be able to climb the Mountain of Disappointment and go through the Valley of Despair. Are you ready," he said to Young suddenly, "to repeat after me?"

"Yes," Young murmured. He was like under hypnosis, ready to see, hear, smell and certainly say whatever the Reverend told him to.

"I—" the Reverend said.

"I—" Young murmured.

"Your name—"

A pause. Then "Michael Keith Young—"

"Take thee—"

"Take thee—"

"Her name—"

A pause. A very protracted pause. Young wondered: Who was

this *her?* Why was he, Michael Keith Young, a man who should know it? Why was he in this solar system? Why did space itself exist? At last, the girl standing next to him laughed and said, "Karen."

"Karen—" Young murmured.

"To be my wedded wife—"

"To be my wedded wife—" Young murmured, and Mouse *née* Karen put her two index fingers at the sides of his mouth, lifting them into a smile that, as her fingers dropped, remained like a *risus mortis* on Young's otherworldly face. The smile was quite scary as Young, then Mouse, repeated the Reverend's words.

The two exchanged rings. "With this ring, I thee wed," the Reverend said, then Young then Mouse repeated this, then the Reverend quoted from Longfellow, calling him Shakespeare,

> *Life is real, life is earnest,*
> *And the grave is not its goal,*
> *"Dust thou art, to dust returneth,"*
> *Was not spoke' of the soul,*

then the Reverend said, "Any questions?" No one had any, and the Reverend, a 60-watt bulb above him, a fan revolving around it, a 60-rpm halo circling above him, said very suddenly, even anticlimactically, "You are now husban' and wife. You," he continued to Young, who looked like the face on a Jolly Roger—"you can smile now."

"You can breathe now," said Mrs. Young.

"You can breathe," the Reverend concurred. But Young was now anoxemic, he needed intensive care, and Mouse (after thanking the Reverend) shepherded him to their car and to their narrow apartment on Jefferson Street. In the bedroom she pulled off her boots, but she didn't employ them to pound him to death for his $50,000 insurance as C had often predicted. *Au contraire,* she pulled off her jeans, her sweater, her underwear, and as Young lay supine on the bed, half dead, she climbed on and straddled him and *up, down, up,* like a man pumping up a flat football, she pumped a semblance of life back into him.

By morning, Young wasn't half dead but as usual half alive, and to Mouse's mischievous question "Do you still love me?" he only could say, "Well, I *maaaaried* you," although in his eyes a distant twinkle said, "I adore you." For breakfast, Mouse scrambled some eggs, and at night they went to the Klub Kamille, where Mouse had a hasty peppermint schnapps, then *boom!* then danced to the music of *Little Sheba,*

> *And the joint was jammin'!*
> *They were rappin' and clappin'!*

and Young, twenty feet away, the red, orange, yellow confetti on top of the table, played pool with a boy from C. The boy was ahead, but as Young lined up his cue, cue ball, and four ball and as the hard beat of *Sheba* stopped, Mouse, having bowed, having put something on, came up behind him, reached under him, did a fig-leaf thing with her fingers, and, as her way to wish him "Good luck," slowly massaged him as *click! clack!* and his four ball dropped like a putt in the far corner pocket, *plop!* "You see?" Mouse laughed. "You can't make it without me. Blow," she continued, and she bent forward to Young, her blouse drooping down, the light at the table lighting her hot wet breasts, and Young, grinning, chalking his cue, administering lip-conditioned air.

It was Friday again. By now C had gotten its shots, its coconut haircuts, and its orders to fly to Saudi on Monday, and most of C's bachelors were at the bars saying, *"Heyyy!"* "Let's dance," "Let's leave," while the husbands and fathers in C stayed home saying, "Daddy goes bye-bye."

"Why do you have to go?"

"Well, I'm in the army."

"Why?"

"Well, that's what I've chosen to do. When *you* grow up, what'll *you* do?"

Sergeant James, who awaited the Call, and his wife and two children were at the Church of Deliverance tonight. James sat placidly as, at a POWER THROUGH PRAYER banner, the wild-haired preacher said, "You need Christ! He'll get you through this!" and as most of the congregation shouted, "Amen!" But later on, James stood up, he held up a bottle of olive oil—of anointing oil, and as tears came to his eyes, as his gold-rimmed glasses magnified them, and as ushers offered him Kleenex, the preacher blessed it in Jesus's name. Lieutenant Russell, the boy who'd be number one in Iraq, wasn't with Tom, his baby boy, for Russell in fact wasn't married to Tom's pretty mother. He loved her, he'd wanted to marry her, but she'd suddenly married an air force man, and she, he and Tom were in Texas and Russell was alone in Kansas, packing, putting in a diary for Tom. Specialist Penn, the boy who'd married the quiet, corn-braided, seven-months-showing girl, was at her home crying and thinking, *When will I see him?* his still-fetal son, and Specialist Gebert, who'd married the war resister's daughter, was *shh!* in his bed in the barracks with her, and at the Klub Kamille, Specialist Young, who'd married the feature attraction, was at the bar draining a plastic pitcher of Bud as big as an Attic amphora, listening to *Sheba,* contentedly looking at Mouse, and, with another boy from C, doing prognoses on what would become of C in Iraq.

Now, C had exactly sixty-four soldiers. Their names went from A to Y for Young. Young knew that some would live, some die, and he felt that each soldier's destiny lay in each soldier's know-how, the good ones living, the bad ones dying: a pretty little theory, and as Young and his pal clean-jerked the pitchers of Bud, heave ho! the ultimate bent-elbow exercise, he tried to foretell the future for every soldier in C. He started in tank number one.

"Survivor," said Young.

"I agree," said Young's buddy.

"Another survivor," said Young.

"I agree. An ass-kickin', I'm-goin'-to-live motherfucker."

"Survivor," said Young.

"A throat-cuttin', knife-wieldin', ass-kickin', better-not-stomp-on-my-peter motherfucker."

"But *this* one," said Young, coming to soldier number four. "He's livin' in the twilight zone."

"In the dream world, yeah."

"He's walkin' around," said Young, commencing a one-note song, "going *do-da-do, da-do-da-do.* We get hit with chemicals, he'll be sittin' outdoors and gettin' a fuckin' suntan, he's dead."

"I agree."

And himself, the Good Soldier Young? "Survivor," he said without hesitation, he was a specialist, after all, he had an achievement medal and two good conduct ones, such a competent soldier couldn't die. His bottom line for C for day number one in Iraq was ten dead, forty wounded, that was his buddy's estimate, too, but it was pessimistic, for at Operations the estimate was nine dead, thirty-six wounded. "Well, cheers," said Young, and the boy who'd come home, hurrah, hurrah, had his last bubble of Bud, his one-for-the-road to Jefferson Street and to Mouse's warm bed, her waterfall laugh, her soft supple shoulders, her—and at half past two in the morning on Monday, putting on camouflage clothes, saying to Mouse, "I'll see you," he took the first steps of a 10,000-mile trip: to his bedroom door, then apartment door, then snow-covered-street door, then by car to Fort Riley.

2

Arabia

★

A half hour later, the first sergeant said, "Fall in," and Young and all C lined up. The moon was full, and the snow at C's feet fluoresced like the plates of glass that a doctor attaches x-rays to. It was five below zero and C was in its thick parkas, but C was also in helmets, not hoods, and its ears were now pepper red. C had its mean black rifles or, for some, its Berettas, on its chests like a general's medals were its red-lensed or blue-lensed flashlights and its first-aid and first-aid-for-gas kits, at its hips were its ammo, bayonets, canteens, gas-mask bags, and, *be prepared,* two more first-aid-for-gas kits, in some of its black-gloved hands were flags, it looked like the Bagman Army. By now C had done its one thousand chores. It had filled in the papers saying,

I give, devise and bequeath, absolutely and forever, all of my estate and property, to . . .

it had signed, triple-witnessed, and notarized this, it had signed up for life insurance (sometimes $600,000 worth) from a man who had perched like a raven inside its barracks, and it had told its women sometimes, "Get real, I could die," the women saying, "Oh, *you're* coming back," and C saying, "Yes, but I also could die." And now, three o'clock in the morning, it was ready! was set! and started to Saudi Arabia.

C didn't march. C seldom marched anywhere, for it wasn't a crowd of 'cruits, of recruits, doing its basic training down at Fort

Diddle Doo. At times a nostalgic sergeant had told it, *"Attention!"* and *"Forward march!"* and

> *Mama, mama, can't you see,*
> *What the army's done to me!*
> *Took away my bluuuue jeans,*
> *Now I'm wearin' army greens!*

and then like a bellowing elephant the sergeant had said, *"Sound off!"* but C had seldom sounded off, had seldom shouted, "One!" "Two!" it had laughed and the sergeant, defeated, had said, "Aw, stop fuckin' aroun'," and C was now strolling to war in this gaggle-of-geese arrangement, going east. No one said, "Left, right, left," for C was going voluntarily, going so as to come home again asap, and the only loud voice was the black lieutenant's,

> *We're off to see the ragheads,*
> *The wonderful ragheads of Iraq,*

as C was strolling along.

In this unceremonious way, C went to the yellow buses with the JUST PASSING THROUGHS. It got on and ten minutes later got off at an airport where, in a hangar full of HURRY HOMES, it got some coconut doughnuts, then it got on the buses and one hour later got off at an airport where, in another hangar, it got some more coconut doughnuts. The girl who handed these out was very good-looking, her hair was bobbed like the nurse's in *China Beach,* and C looked at her with yearning. One boy showed her his photos: his wife and baby, and one boy showed her a magic trick: he took a dab of Cremora, then *whoo!* then blew it onto the red-hot heater, and as the girl cried, *"Oh!"* the Cremora exploded. Lieutenant Russell, who didn't have a girl-to-come-home-to in Kansas, gazed at her wistfully till she, looking back at him, laughed and said, "You were looking at me."

"No, you were looking at me," Russell said.

"So where are you from?"

"Texas." His son and his heart were in Texas.

"I've never been there."

"Well, you and I'll have to go there someday."

The girl just laughed, but Russell pulled out his calling card: an ace of spades, for the soldiers who'd been in C in the '60s had supposedly put the ace of spades on the VC they'd killed in Vietnam. The card had Russell's name, too, and C COMPANY, 2D BATTALION, 34TH ARMOR, and Russell handed it to the bobbed-haired girl, the last girl he'd see for months? for years? for eternity? saying, "Please write me in Saudi," "Sure." Russell and C then walked to the wide-bodied plane, they sat on the ten-across seats and the plane took off, the wheat fields below it: the fields with furrows were full of white snow, the ones without furrows were brown, and the white-and-brown quilt of Kansas shrank as C gazed at it.

The plane turned east to Arabia. In minutes, most of C was writing its wives, brides, girls, but Russell couldn't write to Tom saying, "Dear son," for Russell suspected that Tom's new father would throw the meddlesome letter out. Instead, Russell pulled out the diary that Tom, dear Tom, could read in the year 2000-something, and, the Missouri beneath him, the islands of ice like spattered white paint, he opened the green plastic cover and on the blue-ruled pages wrote,

The plane took off at 1608. . . .

In time, Russell passed over the Great Lakes, the water was rose in the setting sun, the sun set and Russell wrote,

We land in Bangor at 1830. . . .

The last lights that Russell saw were in Newfoundland. He fell asleep, the sun rose in Belgium and Russell wrote,

Well, son, we made it to Brussels. . . .

He flew over Germany, Italy, the Mediterranean Sea, the sun set and Russell wrote,

> *We're about fifteen minutes out of Saudi Arabia. I've watched my second sunset, this one was special, though. There was a single star against a blue and orange background, like a Nativity scene. Well, Tom, the star seemed to say that there was still hope. . . .*

C landed in Saudi on New Year's Day, and with its rifles, pistols and bayonets it walked down the steel staircase. The weather was cool, not cold, but in the moonlight the sand looked like snow, like a snow-covered prairie in Kansas. No houses, not even huts, interrupted it, but someone turned on a Walkman and C comprehended that Toto, it wasn't in Kansas, for the music on every station was *"Nyaaaa!"* was music to belly-dance to, to sway a limp spine to, to charm a numb cobra with. A lot of C sang along with it, *"Nyaaaa!"* slapping the sides of its hands on its Adam's apples, and one boy even danced along, moving his arms like in ⚓ and ⚒ , the Egyptian hieroglyphics he'd seen in *National Geographic*. "The guy," the boy said, meaning the vocalist, "sounds like he's in pain."

"He must have seen one of the women here," said someone else.

"Her veil must have dropped," the boy who was dancing agreed.

The moon behind it, C started walking north, and in ten, twenty, minutes it stopped at a rack full of Al-Ghadir Bottled Water. At this oasis were two dozen men in dirty white robes, and one boy called to the black lieutenant, "Sir! It's the ragheads!"

"Yeah, I see those motherfuckers."

Now, C wasn't normally racist, but C didn't like any Arabs. If ever in human history an Arab had told an American, "Hello, how are you," C hadn't heard about it on CNN. No, the Arabs just called us Satans, they blew up our passenger planes, they were pirates: they got on our ships, then *splash!* they pushed the people in wheelchairs off, they killed the U.S. Marines, the athletes at the Olympics, the brother of President Kennedy, they said *death!* to a British novelist, oh God, what else? they bombed the Jews, they gassed the Kurds, they went to the Arab hospitals killing the Arab babies, and if C told an Arab, "We'll help you," the Arab responded, "Sure. But don't let the Cross pop out." Basically, C had left hearth and home to kill an Arab for Uncle Sam, but since it believed in "Thou shalt not kill," it had had cognitive dissonance and it had resolved it like this:

1. *We must kill Arabs.*
2. *We don't want to kill any human beings. So*
3. *Arabs aren't human beings.*

One night, for instance, at home in Kansas, the black lieutenant had said, "Well, Hitler didn't kill the right people. He should have killed the Arabs."

"That's mean," the lieutenant's wife had said.

"You don't understand," the lieutenant had told her. "The Arabs my *enemies,* and if I like 'em and love 'em it's harder to kill 'em, but if I hate 'em it's easier." A few days later at the Beretta range, C going *bang bang bang,* the Iraqi silhouettes toppling, the lieutenant had called the Arabs towel-headed motherfuckers, a PFC had called them sand-dune-climbing motherfuckers, the lieutenant had said, "Hey, let's write this down," and the two had announced to C that the Arabs were towel-headed, sand-dune-climbing, camel-spitting, goat-cheese-eating, third-world-living, *ma-hakana-hakana*-speaking motherfuckers.

"Yeah," the lieutenant, whose name was McRae and who of-

ten said *fuck, fucker, fuckin'* and *motherfucker* as though these words
meant space, next word, said in Saudi now. "I see them, they look
pretty nasty."

"They probably stink," someone said.

"Hey you!" someone said to an Arab. The boy said it *sotto voce*
so C could hear but the Arab couldn't, and he pointed straight at
the Arab, a gesture (as C knew from Kansas) that an Arab uses to
summon his dog. "Hey, you're okay!" the boy said *sotto voce,* and
he gave the Arab the O-shaped sign that an Arab uses for "Hey,
you're an asshole." The rest of C, laughing, did a strange little jig:
it stood on one foot and pointed its other sole at the Arabs, a great
insult in the Arab world. Ten yards away, the Arabs (who probably
were Pakistanis) rolled up their prayer rugs and got on the buses
behind them, one Arab per bus, and C, after picking up two plastic
water bottles apiece, got on the buses too.

The buses drove off. The drivers were the Arabs, who'd apparently understood the "Hey you"s and "Hey, you're okay"s, and
who retaliated by driving eighty mph, the Arabs drag-racing, passing on the right, left, right, with an inch of *squeeeeak!* of clearance,
the buses bouncing, the windows rat-rattling, the Arabs turning
their lights off and, Allah help us, driving on the *left,* the stars,
the planets, all the red lights in Arabia passing like UFOs as
whoosh! as *whoosh!* as C sat stunned by Mohammed's sons, "They
think they're Mario Andretti!" In Kansas, C had heard of Arab
terrorists, C had been told, "They follow, I can't pronounce this, a
modus operandi," and C had taken a terrorist test,

Terrorists follow a modus operandi, (a) true, (b) false,

but C hadn't guessed that the MO was, the terrorists worked for
the U.S. Army, driving in Saudi Arabia.

Screeeech! A concrete wall stopped the Arabs, and at five mph
they continued into a town of a thousand tents: a Camelot, moonlit,
silent as stars, and C got off and the Arabs left. In one of the tents
were cots, and C fell asleep and at dawn discovered itself on a spit

of sand on what it assumed was the Persian Gulf. At one of the wharfs was the SS *Jolly Rubino* with C's indispensable fourteen tanks, and C unloaded them as, on its Walkmans, it found the army's radio station in Saudi, "How are you, Zsa Zsa?" "I am vonderful," and Baghdad Betty in Iraq, "Your wives are sleeping with Tom Cruise, Tom Selleck and Bart Simpson." ("I don't mind," said someone in C, "as long as Homer don't touch her.") The news was, the war hadn't started but American boys and American girls were dying by stumbling into the Persian Gulf.

At dinner C had another lesson on Arabs. C lined up, and Arabs, some with red-and-white headdresses ("They must have worked at Country Kitchen. They have the tablecloths on")— and Arabs served sizzling chickens. No one in C said *"Shukran,"* the Arabic word for "Thank you" in C's little *Soldier's Guide to Saudi Arabia,* but the black lieutenant said it in English, "Thank you," and then looked up in astonishment when the Arab said, "You're welcome." The lieutenant gasped as he might if his miniature schnauzer back in Ohio had said, "Oh, don't mention it," and he stared at the Arab's mustached face. The man (who probably was a Pakistani) was very well-mannered: he had his left hand behind him, and he smiled at the wide-eyed lieutenant like a caterer at a country club in America. *Damn!* the lieutenant thought, *if he's subhuman, then so am I,* he got his chicken, his vegetables, and he sat down on the sand meditatively.

"You eatin' that seagull?" said someone in C.

"Mm," the lieutenant said.

"You ever feed a seagull an Alka-Seltzer?"

"No."

"You do and the gull'll go off and explode."

"Oh, yeah?" the lieutenant said, but he wasn't concentrating. He was still eyeing the Arabs, thinking, *They're human like me,* his white plastic knife going *kkk!* like a fingernail file, *I couldn't kill 'em,* the chicken succumbing, *I couldn't.* At last the lieutenant decided there were Arabs and Arabs, some good, some bad: the Saudis were good, the Syrians good (well, this year they were) and the real camel-climbing, sand-dune-spitting, *ma-hakana-hakana* mothers were the Iraqis, let's kill 'em! and flipping his empty plastic plate into a garbage can, he stood up, took out an Alka-Seltzer, and *here, little birdie,* tossed it to the gullible gulls of the Gulf.

A few days later, C put its tanks on trucks to be driven by Arabs and got on buses driven by C, by sensible boys with Georgia and Oregon licenses. At ten o'clock on this rainy—rainy! in Arabia!—morning, it left the sand spit, and it went west on an eight-lane, then four-lane, then two-lane road. On the army's radio station, the words of *My Love Is Iraq,* correction, *My Love Is a Rock,* by REO Speedwagon, got more and more unintelligible, the DJ faded to Jabberwock, "We'll keep things jammin' *crackle,* across the Saudi airwaves *crackle,* headin' across the desert *crackle,* for you," and C put its tapes on its Walkmans instead. C had the windows open, and as the unadvertised rain splattered in, it stared at the desert: at one-and-two-inch-deep ponds, at islands of bone-white salt, and at occasional palms and crows and "Hey, camels!" Of all of Arabia's wonders, C was most amazed by the traffic, for the United States had one half million people there, the British, French, Egyptians, Syrians and Saudis had people too, and in the one westbound lane was a bumper-to-bumper procession of cars, buses, trucks, tanks, 5000-gallon tankers, etcetera, all mud-colored, caked with mud, the rain whipping down, the mud running down, the tarps on the trucks going *whap!* like some giant pterosaur wings. The sights seemed out of the Bible: the Apocalypse perhaps, for a lot of the westbound vehicles had hit the eastbound ones, and at the roadside they lay on their backs, their tires groping at—*what?* their bodies subsiding into the mud like dinosaurs in the La Brea tar.

At seven the world became black, but not until four did C turn off "Suicide Drive" and onto the desert, heading north, and

C didn't stop until dawn. C was now in a flat, flat, *flat* locale, no molehills, no moleholes, in any direction, though at the horizons were other oases of buses, trucks, tanks and Americans. It was still raining camels, and C, getting off, the buses withdrawing, discovered it wasn't on sand but mud, the same sort of mushy mud its fathers had sloshed in in Nam. Most of C got into tanks, and *arrr!* it maneuvered them into a circle, but the first sergeant drove a humvee, a hummer, a low, wide, cockroach-looking jeep, to the horizons looking for Bedouins, twentieth-century Bedouins in Chevrolet trucks. He found two and, not looking up the Arabic for "Scram" in his *Soldier's Guide to Saudi Arabia,* he put his palms together, then in a violent gesture threw them apart saying, *"Boom!"* and the Bedouins, catching on, got in the Chevrolets and silently stole away. They were well advised, for two nights later at three in the morning the war began: the clouds were loud with a thousand locusts: the roars of the bombers heading north, and C in its tanks woke up, stood up, and watched the white flashes up in Iraq, the part of Iraq that till recently was Kuwait.

In one tank was Sergeant James, the boy who'd listened to "You need Christ!" at the Church of Deliverance and who was a tank commander in Saudi. Alone in C, James had a big box radio, it was as big as an ammo can, he tuned to the army station, and, his feet in the tank, his head out the top, his eyes on the lightning thirty miles away, he heard the President say, "Why act now? Why not wait? The answer is clear." And *boom!* from Iraq came the tardy thunder, two minutes thirty seconds late, and the President said, "The world could wait no longer." Now, sitting on James's tank was Specialist Penn, the boy who'd married the quiet, corn-braided, pregnant girl and who now behaved like in church: solemn and silent, intent on the sound-and-light show up in Iraq. His eyes were still, like a boy's who's scared, for he was thinking that if a war is so bright and boisterous when it's 150 seconds away, what will it be when he's under it? On the radio the President said that Penn (well, every soldier, sailor and airman) was in his prayers, the President said, "God bless them," James's head bowed reflexively, and Penn said, "I'm sorry I wasn't saved when I was in Kansas."

"Well," said James without thinking about it. "You can be saved right here."

"I can?"

"Jus' cause you're not in a church don't mean that God can't save you," said James, still matter-of-factly. He bent into the tank, and from a rack behind him he took his big Bible and, using his blue-lensed flashlight, looked for Romans 10:9. He'd highlighted this when God had saved *him,* and he read it to Penn,

> *If thou shalt confess with thy mouth . . . and shalt believe in thine heart . . . thou shalt be saved.*

"And that's it," James explained. To the north an Iraqi rocket went up, it disappeared into the rain clouds and James turned the blue-lensed flashlight off. "You confess and believe it," James explained.

"Let's do it," Penn said.

James wasn't expecting this. He was just explaining things to Penn. "No, you can't do it," James said, "and then say, 'I think I'll smoke, I think I'll drink, I'll listen to all my music again.' "

"I know," said Penn. "Let's do it."

"You want to?"

"I want to. Let's do it," said Penn.

Well, glory to God! The helmet on James's head was a weight-less halo now. For years he'd been wondering when, dear God, he'd get the Call, but he now understood that God (and not just the President) had sent him to Saudi to do God's work. And *boom!* amid sounds like a distant natural disaster, he turned to Penn and said, "Do you confess that the Lord, Jesus Christ, is risen from the dead?"

"Yes, I do."

"Do you *believe* that he's risen from the dead?"

"Yes, I do."

"Repeat after me," James said with the hesitancy of a man who'd never once done this. "Lord—"

"Lord—" said Penn. His eyes were wet, and the drizzle licked at his ears, cheeks, chin like a Towelette. In his ears were the ominous *boom*s.

"I'm asking you to forgive my sins—"

"I'm asking you to forgive my sins—"

"To come into my life—"

"To come into my life—"

"To clean me up—"

"To clean me up—"

"To make me whole—"

"To make me whole—"

"And that's it," James said calmly. "Thank you, God, for another soul that's come to Christ."

And *boom!* The sounds to the north seemed part of Creation now, like the roar of a far-off waterfall. "I'm saved," Penn said, "I'm saved," and he started crying as though, hallelujah, the war were over and he hadn't died. His sudden pastor, Sergeant James, sat with his Bible thinking, *Thank you, God,* for James had a new priority now, James would be pastor pro tem to C. Some, many, most of C would die in Iraq, their summons to God would come in Iraq, no one could save them but he could exhort them to save their immortal souls. *God has that mission for me,* James thought. *That's why He called me to Saudi.*

The sun rose, the sun was a pale gray stain and C ate its scrambled eggs. C heard the *boom*s, but it still wasn't going over the top and it could rehearse, rehearse. To date, C had had one, just one, rehearsal in the outdoors: in Kansas, a cold wind blowing from Colorado and C walking toward Nebraska saying, *"Arrr!"* To simulate cannons, C had held out its arms like elephant trunks, *gimme a peanut, please,* then someone in C had said, "Tank!" and C, its arms recoiling, had shouted, *"Boom!"* But here in Saudi, the engineers put up fifty acres of berms and ditches, wires and mines: the engineers built a Mini-Iraq, and two days into the war, the rain coming camels-and-cats, the tall, thin, sober-sided captain picked up his radio microphone, *crackle!* and said, "Move out," and C rolled north into Mini-Iraq.

C really screwed up. It went the wrong way, and the captain abandoned some of his cool, saying, "No! Get this goddam thing turned around." C did but it went too slow, then *arrr!* too fast, then got to a berm as the army's artillery hypothetically was falling on top of it. C remained chipper. One boy half said, half sang, *"Stress monsters,"* one sang along with the Rolling Stones, *"I can't get,"* and everyone laughed when the captain said, "Go right," when he meant "Go left." The berm was six feet high, and the mud hit the fan as C went over it. Next, C came to a ditch: a moat, a mud-swollen gully, there could be crocodiles in it, C went across it and *whack!* a tank threw a track, a tank fell in ("We'll pull you out after the war," someone chortled) and C saw the mines ahead. They were silver discs, like a fortune in $1000 coins, scattered like at a yard sale, they were minus the TNT but the lieutenant from West Point radioed, "We have a casualty!" He then went limp, for he'd been appointed a hypothetical casualty and now was affecting a torn-open leg, a torn-open chest, and a possible broken neck. "Sit-rep!" the captain radioed, meaning "Send me a situation report," but for once in his life the slumping lieutenant didn't say, "Yes sir."

Wounded and not, C went around and *uh-oh,* right over the mud-hidden mines. The tank in the prettiest pickle was Lieutenant Russell's, for Russell's gunner down in the tank's intestines at Russell's feet was uncooperative. "Start scanning," said Russell.

"For what?"

"For Iraqis."

"But there's no Iraqis there."

"Well, pretend."

"But there's nothin' there."

"I understand that," said Russell. "But you won't see the Iraqis when we're in *Iraq*. So now you can practice."

The gunner grunted. He turned his Cadillac, and the ten-foot cannon (and the turret, himself, his loader, and Russell) turned to the left, then right, as he peered through the periscope sight. He did this for thirty seconds, then stopped.

"Keep scanning," said Russell.

"But lieutena'. There's nothin' there."

The gunner was from Samoa. In the rainbow of C his color was coffee-with-cream, and his head and body were compressed like a man's who's standing on Jupiter. He wasn't fluent in English (he'd had two years in Pago Pago) and at the mausoleum in Kansas, the $20,000 computer game, he'd listened to Russell's rapid commands, "Two tanks!" "The right tank!" "Fire!" and he'd lost some precious seconds by mentally translating this to Samoan, *"Lua tane!" "Tane taumatau!" "Fana!"* Every night, the Samoan had gone to his home outside of Fort Riley, had changed to a red sarong, had put bananas in boiling water, had sat at the telephone talking *click-clack,* like in Morse, had, after forty-five minutes, pulled out the well-boiled bananas, dunked them in coconut milk, devoured them, and—the Samoan was Christian—had sat and studied his Bible, how God had created the *lagi* and *lalolage.* One day he'd read the Sixth Commandment, *"Aua ete fasi oti.* Thou shalt not kill," the Commandment didn't say, "Except for the Arabs," and he'd concluded he mustn't shoot at Iraqis. He hadn't confessed this to Russell, though.

"But there's no Iraqis there."

"Well, there's mud, there's pebbles, there's tanks. So pretend," Russell said.

"But there's nothin' there."

The mines behind it, C now rolled to the sharp barbed wires, and it towed these balls-and-chains through Mini-Iraq. It then stopped, and the medics in red-crossed vehicles came for the "casualties" like the slumping lieutenant from West Point. The "casualty" on Russell's tank was Russell's loader, and Russell climbed out of his hatch, reached into the loader's hatch, opened the loader's shoulder pockets, pulled out two straps, and, with the Samoan, hauled out the loader by the two handy-dandy straps. *"Ohhh!"* the loader was smiling and saying like a bad actor in *Combat,* for he'd lost his arm, hypothetically. "I don' wanna die!"

"Don't worry," Russell smiled. "You're not going to die."

"Ohhh! I don' wanna die!" the loader said. The boy had an Asian accent, for he'd been born in China, had grown up in Laos, had fled with his Thailand mother (telling her, *"Hao yah mah han!"* "I want to go home!") to Thailand, and at age ten had flown to America. At sixteen he'd entered a Buddhist monastery in Washington and learned the ten Buddhist commandments: the first was *"Ham kha.* You mustn't kill," and his yellow-robed master had told him, "Not even the flies." For three years the boy was a Buddhist novice, then, to his master's disappointment, he'd joined the American army and C, in whose chaos he'd smiled and smiled like someone at one with the Absolute, flies and all. He too, in his heart, was a conscientious objector: in Kansas he'd declined to be Russell's gunner, telling him, "I get crazy," "You get claustrophobic?" "Yes, I get clo— Yes," and he'd become the loader, instead, the boy who shoved in a round, then *boom!* then shoved in another one. *"Ohhh!"* he was saying, smiling like God's own houseboy as Russell laid him on the mud-spattered tank. "It hurts! It hurts!"

"Oh, quit crying," someone said.

"My arm! My arm!"

"Oh, you still got another one."

For one half hour the Laotian (he didn't think of himself as Chinese)—the loader lay in the rain, smiling, then the busy medics carried him, the lieutenant from West Point, and ten other "casualties" off, and the rest of C drove out of Mini-Iraq. At night Russell pulled out his diary for Tom, but Russell didn't write what he felt: that he, Tom's dad, was the most expendable lieutenant in C, and that his Samoan, Laotian, our-second-language-is-English crew was expendable too. Tom, Russell felt, was pulling the pages straight off the fax, and Russell, to not upset him, wrote,

> *Practice practice practice. I know I'll be back, I just know it, God's given me this feeling that I'll be back. I love you, son, and I'll see you soon.*

He then put the diary behind him, and he went into the, what else? rain to get his wet beef, wet potatoes, wet beans.

I t rained every day. Russell rehearsed every day, and at night he wrote in the diary to Tom,

> *It rained all day. My wash fell into the sand again. They told us it didn't rain here. Were they wrong. . . .*

> *It rained again, and my wash fell into the mud. But I know that all will be good when I get back, I know that I have you, son. . . .*

> *Well! It rained again, and the temperature dropped a few degrees, so we were cold, wet and miserable. I miss you so very much, take care, my son. . . .*

> *I woke up to rain. . . .*

> *It rained. . . .*

But one day when Russell woke up, it wasn't raining and lo! the sun rose and Russell saw something unprecedented in Saudi. In front of his tank was the color green, and Russell wondered,

What's this? A mirage? As tank commander, he had his own Cadillac, and, turning it, he aimed his ten-foot cannon at the enigmatic patch. He peered into the ten-power sight, and he gasped when he saw the dirt and, like five-o'clock shadow, a lot of little green stems. "Sonofabitch!" Russell cried. "It's *grass,*" and he got off and walked to that strange vegetable from the Pleiades. He squatted beside it, took his black gloves off, ran his fingers across it. He thought, *It's really grass!* then he had a sudden insight: the grass was a symbol for Tom, his son.

His life, Russell saw, was a desert too. It was virtually empty: his girl had married an air force man and his son was probably calling the man his daddy. The two would be, what? playing pattycake? piggyback? counting toes? saying, "This little piggy went—" as Russell led the American army into Iraq and, face it, as Russell died. In minutes, the sand would erase his tank tracks, and the sands of time would erase every clue that he'd walked on this earth, *except:* on one wondrous night, he'd planted a seed that, like the magic grass, would grow, even when he himself was dust. He'd not only planted it but, in his diary, nurtured it: he'd written to Tom, age ten, age twenty, age everlasting (for Tom would have sons, daughters, too)—he'd imparted to Tom the essentials, like God,

> *I went to the Protestant and Catholic masses. It doesn't matter how you believe, son. Just believe,*

like the purpose of Man,

> *Son, power is sometimes said to be all-important. It's not, son. God, love, family, that's important,*

like women, defend them, like wars, we must end them—yes, Russell had fathered a Mini-Russell,

Tom, may this journal find us together as a father and son should be. If I'm nowhere, Tom, realize that my country called and I answered that call,

and Russell, through Tom, was immortal now, Russell had now outwitted death.

From that day on, Russell watched over the Saudi grass like an orchidologist watching a $5000 specimen. In days it got two inches taller, greener, it spread to the width of a batter's box: it now was a symbol for Tom age ten, and Russell now couldn't resist it, Russell wrote in his diary,

I am your father, Tom! And Tim,

and Tim was the air force man, the sergeant in Texas, the man who was teaching the air force recruits to polish their boots, their brass, *no, I can't see my reflection, private,*

and Tim has cheated me of you, and when our country called, I was ready, not Tim. Those who are warriors fight and win. Those who ain't warriors teach what they wish they could do. Tom, it's my job to lead men to battle and,

and it's not Tim's, not Tim's. A little reflection, and Russell might have seen that the passage might not be best for Tom, that Tom, age ten, might prefer a dad who was *there* to a dad who'd died hideously in Iraq, that Tom might prefer a Tim the hero to a Tim the REMF, the Rear-Echelon Mother Fucker. But this was war, was life or death, and Russell continued,

Son, I fought to get your mother, and she never put up a fight for me. What angers me most is Tim is using her and,

and *and* and *and*. And soon the fond little diary was a diatribe, too, a petition to Tom to honor his dad, who don't forget isn't Tim.

The grass grew like Topsy, like Tom. One day was dress rehearsal for Companies A, B, C, D, and as Russell rolled out, his driver headed for Russell's emerald isle. "Ha!" the maniacal driver cried. "Grass!"

"Don't you run over it!" Russell cried.

"Why not?" said the driver, gunning the 60-ton tank.

"Just don't!" Russell cried. The driver swerved, the grass escaped, and Russell, his head out the hatch, gazed in relief at his monument, the Russell Memorial Meadow. That day A, B, C and D had their dress rehearsal, they came back from Mini-Iraq and Russell wrote,

> *You're on my mind a lot, son. I hope you'll never face the horrors of war as I will. . . .*

Whoop! One night C, to its horror, heard the mad metal instrument that lay on the desert to try to detect the Iraqi menace, Iraqi gas. *Whoop!* For days the Iraqi missiles had fallen on Saudi, exploded, so far they hadn't emitted gas but C had done drills every day. C might be in its T-shirts hitting its one precious volleyball when a sergeant cried, "Gas!" and the ball would fall like a meteorite as C went *snap!* unsnapping its gas-mask bags. The sergeant would count off, "One!" "Two!" "Three!" and the boys who didn't look like Darth Vader by "Nine!" could assume that if this were real, they'd be spitting, drooling, vomiting ("It sound like a drunk, don't it?" the medic in Kansas had said) and two minutes later be checking out. But tonight, C was in sleeping bags in (or on top of) its tanks when at two in the morning the world began going *whoop,* and C was still putting its masks on nine seconds later.

C was near panic. It was pitch black, and C didn't know which end of the mask was up. One boy had symptoms: he gasped like a four-minute miler, thinking, *It's from the gas!* and one boy thought, *I can smell it!* C had the creeps about gas, it couldn't fight the shapeless stuff, it only could wait like at Auschwitz, thinking, *Well, will I live? Have paralysis? Die?* To do something, *anything,* the first boy to put on a mask then radioed in a Luke-I'm-your-father voice, "Gas! Gas! Gas!" One boy who heard him thought, *I'm gonna die!* but another slept till the black and black-masked lieutenant, a thing from the black lagoon, shook him and told him, "Gas! Gas! Gas!"

"Yes sir," the boy mumbled, still asleep.

"*Gas!*" the lieutenant repeated.

"Oh shit," the boy said.

C's sober captain was in his tent, not tank, when the *whoop!* awoke him. His dog (he'd found it in Saudi, he'd fed it the army's corned beef hash)—the dog began running in circles, snapping its black-and-white tail, and the captain thought, *God! It's had nerve gas!* and *slap!* he slapped on his mask as fast as a fireman's helmet. The dog, like a pigeon in World War I, then dropped to the ground prostrate, and the captain thought, *God! It's dead!*

One boy, one, wasn't apprehensive: the Mouse-married Specialist Young, for Young was certain he'd go back to Kansas alive. Recently he'd been a "casualty," he'd suffered a "broken leg," he'd been hauled from the loader's compartment (he was a loader) and he'd said confidently, "A broken *leeeeg?* I can't understand how I could've gotten *thaaaat.*" And tonight the *whoop!* was the raven of death but Young didn't think, *I'm gonna die,* he simply followed the SOP: he masked up, stood up, and closed the lid of the hatch so quickly that *ow!* it hit his gold wedding ring from Mouse.

"Oh shit," Young said. The lid was 125 pounds, the ring was heart-shaped now, and Young imagined that Mouse might frown, Mouse might conclude that Young didn't *care.* Around him the tank was a bathysphere, deep in the sea, lighted green, to his left was the screwdriver box and Young took a screwdriver out. He couldn't hear the *whoop* anymore, but on his earphones he heard the "Gas! Gas! Gas!" and a *"Damn!* I hope I don't do a zizz-wheel now," I hope I don't spin like a children's toy, and Young put the screwdriver under the ring. He twisted it slowly, a surgeon doing a delicate operation, *slooooowly,* the ring became almost round, then it *click!* cracked apart, it changed to a C-shaped and Young thought, *I'm in deep shit,* he'd have to write about this to Mouse. Young had some talent: he played the viola, painted, but he was uneasy with words, he'd often written to Mouse but still hadn't said, "Dear Karen,"

> *Karen,*
> *It's raining. I think we brought the rain with us. . . .*

> *Karen,*
> *I'm in an Arab tent that smells like a camel's butt. . . .*

> *Karen,*
> *Be glad you aren't here. I smell like a camel's butt. . . .*

and tonight he didn't write her, "Your ring just saved me," "Your ring's getting bigger," or *"Chérie! Ta belle bague—"* no, Young thought and thought and decided on,

> *Karen,*
> *I just broke the wedding ring. We were just gassed and—*

no, Young saw that that wouldn't do.

He decided to confess on audiotape. By now, *hip-hip, hooray,* he'd learned that C wasn't gassed, that a dog (or a rat, snake or scorpion) had urinated on the metal instrument, the instrument had detected it, and the *whoop!* was a cry of wolf, nothing more. The captain's dog, Ace, for the ace of spades, wasn't dead, it was sleeping and probably dreaming of corned beef hash, and the captain now radioed, "False alarm." C now breathed easier, *literally,* it took its masks off and fell asleep, but Young sat awake and stared

at his C-shaped wedding ring. The next day, he borrowed a tape recorder, sat as though in an electric chair, hit the red button, REC, and
did an unprecedented thing: he tried to pour out his heart to Mouse.

"Uh," Young began. The word was a moan, a pool of molasses
down in Young's stomach. "I'm sittin' in Saudi Arabia," Young
said. He sighed, then *tick,* then *tick,* five seconds went by. "Uh,"
Young said, then "Boy," Young said, then *tick,* then *tick,* the tape
made sounds like a razor blade chipping paint, like a distant cricket
in Syria. "What could I tell you?" Young said, then, sighing again,
he started with the local geology. "It's *flaaaat,*" Young said. "God,
it's *flaaaat.* It's flatter than anythin' I've ever seen. *Weeeell,*" he
suddenly blurted, "what's been happenin' with me? Uh, not
much," then *tick,* then *tick,* then Young bit the bullet and said,
"Uh, I slammed my hand in the loader's hatch." In his throat was
the *r*-word, *ring, ring, ring,* but he still couldn't say, "I smashed
it," "I squashed it," "I squoshed it," and he sat mute as, count
'em, twenty seconds went by. He turned the tape recorder off—a
truck rumbled by, and he turned the tape recorder on. "You can
probably hear the truck going by," Young said, then Young digressed onto Saudi cigarettes. "I kinda like 'em," Young said.
"They got more *kiiiick* than my Marlboros do," and Young never
returned to the rift in Mouse's ring. "Don't worry about me," he
told her. "Come hell or high water, *Iiiii'm* comin' home."

Well, Young had tried. He turned the tape recorder off, put
the tape in an envelope, put the *mahakana* label of a Pepsi can for
the Arabs in, didn't put a stamp on (in Saudi, a soldier didn't have
to), wrote an address on, and gave his *billet-doux* to C's first sergeant
to send to the Sunflower State.

B y now C was *getting* mail too. It was for Any Soldier, but
every day when the first sergeant brought it, C tore into it. Some
letters came from schoolboys,

Is it very hot?

and some from schoolgirls twelve years old,

Do you smooch?

but some were from college girls,

When you're back we'll show you a real good time,

and C, which hadn't even seen a BMO (a Black Moving Object: a Saudi woman) here, went wild, it saw a sorority full of Playmates and saw itself drinking its Bud and *yes!* and smooching with Miss January, Miss February, saying, "And then the Iraqis." On getting letters like this, C often thought, *On to Baghdad! Then on to the U.S.A.!* One day C got mail with names, ranks, and serial numbers on it. It came from the wives, brides and girls in Kansas, and C of course seized it as though it held hundred-dollar bills. Young had a letter from Mouse,

> *Dear Michael,*
> *Yes. My name is Karen. But don't you love me? Can't you say Dear Karen? You don't write often, and when you do it's just about camel butts,*

but Mouse also wrote, *"I love you."* The good Sergeant James had an Opium-perfumed, yellow-papered, violet-flowered letter from Teri, his wife,

> *Dear Norman,*
> *We miss you, but I know that God is taking care of you. Don't never doubt that He'll bring you back,*

and Lieutenant Russell, Tom's father, had a plain-paper letter that, of course, wasn't from Tom (or Tom's mother) but from the dough-nut dolly in Kansas, the one who Russell had told, "Please write me in Saudi." Her letter could have been to Any Soldier,

> *Dear David,*
>   *Let's see now, I'm twenty years old and I plan on becoming a flight nurse. Right now . . .*

but for Russell, who recalled her red parka, red-crossed armband, and red JENNIFER pin, her two white earmuffs that hung like ear-phones around her red-parkaed neck, and her pretty and playful smile, the letter might have been from Héloïse to Abelard. After reading it, Russell rode twenty miles to the closest phone and, for ten dollars, called up the girl in Kansas. He got her answering machine. "Hi, this is Jennifer," it purred into Russell's ear. "I'm either," I'm *ai*-ther, "unable to come to the phone right now, *or*," it continued playfully, "I know who you are and I *really* don't want to talk to you!" The machine then went *beep!* and Russell said, "Well, this is David Russell." He thanked her for her "Dear David," said C was safe, said goodbye, and rode twenty miles back to no woman's land.

In time C was practically papered with mail. The one boy who didn't get any was Specialist Gebert, who'd married into the War Resisters League. Gebert didn't know why, but his count-across-stitching bride (and her father and mother) either didn't write him or maybe, just maybe, her letters full of "I love you"s were in mailbags in Cairo, wherever. Specialist Walters, the boy who'd alley-ooped the girl at Bushwacker Bar, in Kansas, carrying her to her bed, got very exuberant letters from her from Arizona,

> *Dear Eddie!*
>   *There are horses here! Pretty cool huh! I'll probably fall off and kill myself! Ooo! Bad thought! We also went paddle-boating! The water was freezing! Brrrr!*

but she also wrote, *"I love you!"* Sergeant Medine, half Irish, half
Sioux, who'd once scanned the pen-pal column of *Stars and Stripes*
and chosen a sweet-sounding girl in England, the border of Scotland, and lately proposed to her, got letters that only an English
girl could write,

> *Dear Scott,*
>   *I am so anxious to meet you. And yet the meeting which*
> *I know will happen,*

will will will happen, triple-underlined,

> *fills me with great anxiety. I am reluctant to give full rein to*
> *my feelings because . . .*

On reading this, Medine said, "Gee. The way the British talk." At
his tank he gazed at the letter proudly, then said to some buddies
in C, "It's got perfume on it."

"*Whoo!*" someone cried. "Lemme get a whiff of it." He
smelled it and almost swooned from the White Linen, and C then
crowded around like bloodhounds.

"Yeah, there's a faint trace of it!"

"Closest I've gotten to a girl this year!"

"It's still over my head," said Medine, impressed by his eru-
dite fiancée. The girl kept writing but Medine stopped reading,
for he was riding a truck one day, the truck hit a rut and a vertebra
hit his spinal cord, he could still blink his eye (one blink for *yes*
and two blinks for *no*) but he was otherwise paralyzed, the first real
casualty in C. An ambulance took him off, and the peach-colored
letters from England stayed in the first sergeant's vehicle: his low,
wide, cockroach-looking hummer.

The most momentous letter to C was to Specialist Penn, the
boy who'd been saved by the intercession of Sergeant James. It was
faxed to Arabia, then radioed to the desert, and Penn was on his
tank in his sleeping bag when at eight at night he was told about

it. "Hey, Penn!" a boy shouted up, but Penn didn't hear him: his Walkman was on, his earphones were on, his head rocked and rolled, and his nose rubbed the bag's interior while he listened to *Pollywanacraka*, by Public Enemy,

> *She wants a lover,*
> *But not no brother!*

"Hey, Penn!" the boy shouted.

> *A man gotta havva lotta money,*
> *To get under her cover!*

"Hey, Penn," the boy said softly, having climbed on the tank and lifted off Penn's earphones.

"What's happenin'?"

"The first sergeant wants you," the boy said, and Penn unzipped his bag, put on his boots, hopped off, and hurried to the first sergeant's hummer.

In the dark, the vehicle was a man-eating cockroach from Mars. Inside was the double-chinned sergeant, who was holding a red-lensed flashlight and was writing the names, ranks and numbers of all his soldiers in a large loose-leafed book. The sergeant left lots of space for the W's, meaning wounded, the M's, meaning missing, and the X's, meaning dead, that he'd need to fill in in Iraq, and as Penn arrived, saying, "What's up?" he put his arm casually on this account book so Penn couldn't see it.

"Come here, boy," the first sergeant said. In the starlight the pockmarks on Penn didn't show, and Penn looked almost angelic. One month before, he'd married the pregnant girl in Kansas, she now was eight months and the first sergeant said, "You just had a baby boy."

"All right!"

"Seven pounds, eleven ounces."

"How's *she*?"

"They said she's doin' okay."

"All right!" said Penn. His eyes were wet. Around him the only light was the first sergeant's flashlight, the rest of C was asleep and its tanks were black silhouettes: bodies, turrets and cannons against the many-starred sky, and Penn simply went to his sleeping bag, crawled in, and fell asleep. In the morning he went to the far-off phone, called up Kansas, came back to C, and said, "I heard him! She had him cry for me!"

"What did she do? Slap him?"

"No," Penn said. "She played with him!"

"She say he's got your eyes and ears?"

"No, she said he's got my feet!"

"He'll be a clumsy motherfucker."

Penn and C then high-fived. This being Saudi, Penn didn't have any Dom Pérignon (and Penn couldn't drink it, being saved) but he put some orange, cherry and grape powder into his Al-Ghadir Bottled Water and C shared it, C celebrated, C was elated that girls, that babies, that life still existed where dark was day, and C raised its canteen cups, *bottoms up!* and toasted the newest person who it was fighting for.

One more day, and C would roll to the Iraqi border. And like some coach for the One Big Game, the scar-faced lieutenant colonel showed up and C assembled around him. It was late afternoon: the sun was low, and its light swept across the desert like wind till it smashed on the colonel's face. His face became red, as though he were staring into a forest fire.

"Smoke if you want to," the colonel, whose name was Fontenot, a Cajun from Louisiana, began. In his hand was a Carlton, and he pointed it toward a map of Iraq that he'd chalked on a vehicle behind him: a Bradley, a thing like a Brink's truck with tracks. "We're doing a frontal assault. I'd have preferred to flank 'em," the colonel said candidly, "but I've not been allowed to. I told the general, 'Roger, sir,' " and the colonel saluted, meaning *I'm in the army, I do as I'm told,* and C laughed, feeling camaraderie with him. "So," the colonel continued, and he pointed his Carlton again, "this is Omaha Beach, this is Pickett's Charge, this is charging up the Valley of Death. It's clumsy," the colonel admitted, "it's I'm-better-than-all-you-motherfuckers shit," and C now smiled at the implication that it was better than all the Iraqi motherfuckers. "So this could be a long day," the colonel said, and C nodded, impressed that it now belonged in the grand tradition of Omaha Beach.

Its predecessors in A, B, C, D had been to Omaha often. "We aren't," the colonel said, "some Johnny-come-lately, ain't-done-piss-ever fuckin' outfit. We have a proud record in World War II, we went to Vietnam, and you are the sons and grandsons of the GIs then." It was literally true, for one of C's tank mechanics in Cu Chi, Vietnam, was the father of Lieutenant Russell—of Russell who, hearing the colonel, thought, *I mustn't fail or I'll let my father down.* The boys who Russell commanded were C's second-raters: the Samoan, the Laotian, a Jamaican, maan, a boy who boop-boop-a-dooped around to the music of Shabba Ranks, the commanders of Russell's three other tanks were a recruiting sergeant, another recruiting sergeant, and a Hispanic who'd never commanded a tank till now. It must have been better in Cu Chi, Vietnam, but the colonel insisted, "You need to live up," and Russell and C agreed.

Of course C was scared. "You *will* be afraid. If you're not," the colonel continued, "there's something wrong with you," and the colonel admitted, "It's happened to me." He was still dreaming, his tanks still exploding, but he told instead of his near-disaster in Germany, 1977. "My tank caught fire. It wasn't a fire," the colonel said, "it was a fuckin' ape-shit conflagration, and I was sorely afraid." C laughed uneasily, and the colonel said, "You'll know when you're afraid, guys. You'll need to urinate, you'll taste a half-dozen nails, number-ten nails, in your mouth, and you'll find you can't slam a nail up your ass with a Sledge-o-Matic." C laughed and the colonel said, "It's okay to be afraid, guys. Cope with it, deal with it, face it, look at it, examine it, but do *not* let it dominate you."

C understood. On the nights of the "Why act now?" and the "Gas gas gas!" it had been afraid, all of C had but Specialist Young. Young hadn't needed to urinate, defecate, hadn't had the metallic taste, had even announced to C, "I'm never afraid." Even in Texas, Young had dressed up in cuisses, brassarts, in knight-in-shining-armor stuff, had carried a sword and, with other romantics, had tried to relive the Crusades—he *clank!* had been hit in the gorget, *clank!* in the genouillères, he'd dropped like an office safe and *"You,"* a referee had shouted, *"you're dead,"* he'd been carried away like C3PO, but Young hadn't felt, *I'm afraid.* He'd never seen a psychiatrist but, if he had, the man might have told him, "Yes, you're afraid. So very afraid, you've blown all your fuses out and you don't know you're afraid. Why do you always talk with a trumpet mute in your mouth? It's because you're afraid if you pulled it out, the words behind it would be *I'm afraid.*" "I'm not talkin' scared," the fire-faced colonel said now. "I'm talkin' no-shit, you-believe-you're-gonna-die, afraid. It'll *happen*," but Young thought, *No. I'm a natural soldier. It won't happen to me.*

The rest of C, sitting, kneeling, standing, believed what the colonel said. "The best way," he said, "to get over it," over being afraid, "is to fire one round. As soon as you do, you'll know what to do, which is *aim* and *fire* and *advance*. So don't worry," the colonel said, and like some inspirational coach he came to the go-and-gettem part. "I don't want to fight fair, guys," the colonel said. "I've nothing against the Iraqis, I don't even *know* an Iraqi. For all I know, Rashid and Fatima are a helluva nice couple, the kind you'd have over, but I know this: Rashid and Fatima are wantin' us *dead* and we ain't gonna give 'em their wish. We're gonna—" The colonel stopped, and he started again with a peroratorical ardor. "We're gonna *beat* these guys!"

C believed him. The colonel wouldn't lie, well, would he? and C had had corroboration from a reliable source: the Bible. One day in Saudi, C's pastor pro tem, Sergeant James, had gotten a letter from Kansas that said, "See Jeremiah 50," and as James studied this in his Bible, he'd underlined it in ballpoint black,

Thus saith the Lord: I will punish the king of Babylon,

well, Babylon was Iraq, James knew,

Thus saith the Lord: A people shall come from the north,

um, from the north? maybe south?

They shall ride upon horses against thee, O Babylon,

well, that must be D-Day in Iraq,

Her foundations are fallen, her walls are thrown down: for it is the vengeance of the Lord.

On reading this, James had said, "Praise Him!" He'd felt he'd just seen *Stars and Stripes* and had just read, "IRAQIS DEFEATED!" and he'd shared the news with his gunner, loader, driver, and the rest of C. All but the Buddhist were Christians, all had been heartened by James/Jeremiah, and today when the colonel predicted, "We'll beat these guys," a lot of C thought, *It's true. It's in God's plan.*

But the Bible left something out. "We'll beat 'em," the colonel said, "but it won't be free," he meant that a lot of C (the official estimate: forty-five) would be killed or wounded in Iraq. The colonel was heartsick about this. Night after night he'd sat on his cot, had chugalugged coffee and Diet Pepsis, had chain-smoked as though he had emphysema and Carltons were oxygen tubes, and, on a SECRET map of Iraq, in washable ink, had drawn the invasion routes for his Companies A, B, C, D. Then with a rag he'd erased them, then he'd started again, till his tent was a place full of Pepsis, of empties with Arabic labels, *ma-hakana-hakana,* his lines on Iraq were like Arabic too, they turned, twisted, doubled back as he sought to put his soldiers where, *knock, knock,* the Iraqis wouldn't think they'd be. "I'll do my goddam best," he now said to C, the sun setting, his face turning gray, "not to waste your lives. I'll probably make mistakes and you will too, and," the colonel admitted, "the mistakes will cause some of us to get hurt," to C he clearly meant killed. "All you can do is have faith."

It was dusk. A chilly wind came, and the colonel came to his closing words. "That song, that army song," the colonel said, and he quoted it,

> *It wasn't always easy,*
> *And it wasn't always fair,*
> *But when they called,*
> *We were there—*

"well, that's who we are," the colonel said. "This isn't the Izod-polo-shirt Weejuns-loafers crowd. There's not a whole lot of kids here whose dads were anesthesiologists or justices of the Supreme Court. We're the poor white middle class, and the poor black kids from the block, and the Hispanics from the barrio. And we're just as good as the fuckin' rest." The colonel looked at C's faces and said, "I'll be honest with you. You're who I want to go to war with, and you will do just great." He then walked off, and C walked back to its tanks as though to a Sousa song, C was prepared and yes, was *proud* to follow that man, that truly good man, to wherever he told them, even to the Gates of Hell.

The next day C started packing. C was in wild high spirits, for the sooner the war began, the sooner the war would end and the sooner everyone would be back in Kansas. In everyone's ear was a Walkman, and C put its clothes in its olive-green bags to the

The Star-Spangled Banner, by U2, or to its improvisations on *The Power,* by Snap,

> *Get lost, Iraq!*
> *Cause I will attack!*
> *And you don't want that!*

C had some surplus soft-boiled eggs that it threw at the engineers, yelling, "The yolk's on *you!*" and the engineers revenged themselves with Al-Ghadir Bottled Water, the plastic bottles coming at C like Indian clubs, then *splat!* then *splat!* the sounds of the first known water fight in Arabia. Some boys used air in hoses to blast the dirt from their motor filters, and one boy, a private, a boy who'd been told to check out the tanks for soft spots, used a steel sledge hammer, *bang!* to do it. "How will I know when I find 'em?" the gullible boy (who in Kansas had gone for the cannon report and the keys to the Cadillac) asked.

"They'll sound hollow," his tank commander explained. "You'll hear the *bang bang bang,* then *bong:* that'll be one of the soft spots."

"Then what do I do?"

"You write up a 2404."

"A maintenance report?"

"And they'll weld it."

"Okay," the boy said brightly, and he added his *bang*s to C's other bustling sounds.

At last C was going to war, and as though going off to their first summer camp, the boys speculated about it. How scared would they be? How collected? Could they just, *boom!* without compunctions, shoot at another human being? If the man burst apart like a bag of blood, could they shoot at the man behind him? For that matter, would the Iraqis be men or just kids conscripted in Baghdad? The colonel had spoken of Fatima—well, would the Iraqis be women, too? On one tank a boy tried to picture it: an Iraqi trench, and an Iraqi teenaged girl in, what? a helmet? a headdress? a veil?

in a belt of bullets certainly, and he wondered if he could just bump her off. A driver, he sat in his small compartment, his head, shoulders and arms were out, he oiled his mean-looking rifle and said to the loader near him, "You. Would you shoot her?"

"Hell yeah," the loader said. "That quick."

"Yeah, I would too," the driver said, but he wasn't happy, he'd been brought up not to rob, rape or murder someone of the opposite sex. He put a cloth at the end of his ramrod, ran it into his rifle, and said, "Well, what about rapin' her?"

"Hell no," the loader said. "I don't wanna *demoralize* her." He meant he didn't want to corrupt her morals and said, "If you figure, well, for the hell of it, that you're gonna rape her, it's a violation of her body that she's not allowin'."

"Of her corpse," the driver corrected him.

"Of her body, cause you're not gonna kill her *before* you rape her."

"Oh, but I can still kill her," the driver said ruefully.

"Yeah. You can kill her. You aren't here to rape her."

The driver reflected. He couldn't understand the code of ethics that let him put .22 bullets but not his penis into a teenaged girl. In practice, he wasn't about to drive to Iraq, to stop, to open his hatch as *zing!* as lead went every which way, to climb out, to take hold of Fatima, to pull off his fireproof suit, his gasproof suit, and his Jockeys, to put on a Trojan, and then and there to debauch her, but he said pensively, "Well, if I'm gonna kill some bitch, I'm gonna fuck her."

"That's your prerogative. But if—"

"Why not get yourself some pussy?"

"Well, why not do a civilian too?"

"A civilian ain't tryin' to kill me. But," the driver reflected, "if she had a gun she might try, and I'd rape her and kill her too."

"Well, we just think differently," the loader said. "If that's what you're gonna do and if I'm not around, that's cool, but for me, I'm not here to take some chick's virginity."

"Hey, they're none of them *virrrgins,*" the driver protested. He stretched the word *virrrgins* to show its utter absurdity.

"That's irregardless."

"You tryin' to tell me an Iraqi soldier's," *I-rack-ee* soldier's, "a *virrrgin?*"

"All right. Let's say she's not," the loader argued, "and you go and rape her, and she don't want you to. In a way that's a kind of a torture, cause if she don't want you to do it—"

"She don't want me to *kill* her!"

"But that ain't torture!"

"Tell me it ain't!"

"*Haha!*" From behind them, the boys heard the tank commander, the black lieutenant, and they appealed to this neutral party.

"Sir?" the driver asked him. "The worst thing that I can do to someone is kill her, right?"

"Mm-hm," the lieutenant said.

"So then what's a little dick?"

The lieutenant laughed. He saw that the boys didn't understand about war—well, neither did he, but he guessed that the driver would be too engrossed in killing, killing, and not being killed to attend to a lesser imperative. "Yeah," the lieutenant kidded him. "You give her American dick. She'll probably say, 'Oh, sucky sucky! Turned on!' "

"Wrong country," the loader muttered. He'd once served in Korea, and to him *sucky sucky* seemed oriental.

"Yeah, you'll be hockin' 'n' hockin'," the lieutenant laughed. "And she'll say, 'Ten dollars, please!' "

The driver thought about this. In his aviator glasses, his rifle before him, his cannon above him, he looked like an advertisement for Be All You Can Be. "Well, maybe, now that you mention it," he said completely seriously, "maybe I'll ask her first."

" 'Can I fuck you?' '*No!*' " the lieutenant laughed.

"I mean, I'll tell her I'm gonna kill her and—"

"Hey!" the lieutenant laughed. "Go ahead. Rape some bitches. Do it for the *Achille Lauro*," the Mediterranean ship the Arabs had hijacked once. "You got my permission," the lieutenant said, and he started walking away.

The loader called after him. He too took this seriously, and he said disdainfully, "Sir? Does this mean that we can take heads?"

"I don't give a fuck!"

"Put 'em up on the antenna?"

"Just don't put 'em in my compartment," the lieutenant laughed, then he walked away.

All over C the topic of conversation was war, was war. C debated: Would the Iraqis stay in their trenches waiting for C? Or would they attack it or ambush it? Would the Iraqis be novices just like C? Or would they be ten-year veterans of the Iran-Iraq War? C would have sat pro-and-conning until, the next morning, it rolled to Iraq, but in the army it's hurry up, wait, hurry up, and in midafternoon a *crackle!* came on C's radios and a major said, "Guidons," meaning all A, B, C, D, "we move out at 1900," at seven that night. C wondered, *What's going on?* its first sergeant said, "What's going on?" its captain said, "I'd give a wooden nickel to know what's going on," and C now went into hyperspeed, it tossed its olive-green bags full of brass-buttoned uniforms and of T-shirts with pictures of Bart onto trucks headed down to the Gulf, it poured its last bottles of water into a vat and *zap!* it stabbed a hole in each bottle bottom to let out the water faster, it climbed on its tanks and *arrr!* it started them up. The sun was an orange nine ball on top of the pool-table desert as C rolled out. In their turrets were Young, James and Russell, the specialist, sergeant, lieutenant, the last of them looking back at his grass: his Memorial Meadow, his symbol for Tom, and whispering to it, "Goodbye." C turned northwest, and a fizz went through it, its blood felt like soda water, the bubbles were partly pleasant, partly unpleasant, as the major now radioed, "Stay on my frequency! If I can't talk to you, I don't need you! Stay on my net!" the major radioed. "We're going into combat!"

3

Iraq:
The Border

The sun set like a stone, and the far horizon—orange above, black below—was as flat as the end of the planet earth. In minutes the orange disappeared, the clouds became black, the line between heaven and earth was like in Ad Reinhardt, the sky was India ink and the ground was too, the shadings, if any, were clear to a cat but not to C. Up front was the captain, proceeding at five to ten mph, tuning to the satellites to calibrate where he was in Saudi and steer northwest to Iraq, to his rear like circus elephants was the rest of C, as black as coagulations in black bean soup, the drivers using their night sights (their $10,000 sights, where a firefly looked like the sun) to stay with the tanks ahead. All around C the world was a tunnel full of horrendous sounds, *arrr!* but C went through it for two hours, for fifteen miles, then it stopped and got out its sleeping bags. To the north in Iraq was some of God's light: was American lightning, and C lay down in the sleeping bags in this familiar world. The *boom!* got to C in one, not two, minutes and thirty seconds, and C fell asleep.

It woke up at 4:45. The stars were out and Scorpio stood on its tail rampant, and by the north star were pulsars, were lights on American bombers, *on, off,* the lightning beneath them. At half past six the sky became bluer, then on the flat horizon a dot, then a spot, then a semicircle appeared and the red sun rose like an atomic explosion. The sun went higher, the captain said, "Move out," and C went northwest again. The desert was flat, was *flat,* and C seemed to be on some treadmill, for the same dirt, same pebbles, seemed to pass under it every ten, twenty, feet. At last C came to a rise as slight as one on a golf course, to C it looked like Mount Ararat and someone said, "Look! A hill!" On the other side was a sand trap and yes! was sand! and C gaped at that fabulous stuff as Lawrence had at the Hejaz, saying, "Look! It's sand!" At ten o'clock, C saw some clothespins, they lay on the desert like chicken bones, and at noon it saw something sensational: one, two or three miles ahead was—*what?* a city? a camel caravan? it shimmered and C couldn't identify it. The captain said, "What the *fuck* is in front of us?" his driver said, "Damn! And my camera's packed!" the tall brown objects got closer, closer, the captain said, "Are they trees?" the driver said, "No, they're bushes!" the captain gasped, and C passed some pale gray bushes, wastepaper-basket high. Not disappointed, the captain said, "Bushes!" and C, as it gaped at that miracle, life, real life, said, "Bushes! Bushes! Look!"

The day wasn't hot: it was sweater-weather cold, but C was acting sunstruck, acting as if its brains were frying, were going zzz, as if it had staggered across the Sahara forty days. At one point the captain held up his microphone and, not turning it on—the Iraqis could hear him—said, "This is Captain Burns. I've turned on the FASTEN SEAT BELT sign," then he returned to his solemn-as-Rommel self. In the tanks behind him the rest of C sang weirdo songs like

> *I'm so glad we*
> *Had this time*
> *Together*

or told dirty camel jokes, "He thought, *Well, I'm on the desert. No one can see me. I'll fuck that camel . . . ,*" or told other animal tales, "The camel spiders, they're nasty," "The camel spiders?" "Big fat furry spiders. They bite you and *eat* you," "Shit! If I see 'em, I gonna shoot 'em!" For lunch, C brown-bagged it, it took out its MREs, Meals Ready-to-Eat, and with its Swiss knives (or its bayonets) it cut the metallic bags, pressed out the pork in barbecue sauce or meatballs in spicy tomato sauce and, still rolling, the dust rising, the dust twenty stories high, the Iraqis presumably seeing it, ate what essentially were C-ration sandwiches on Reynolds Wrap. Or it used plastic spoons, till at three in the afternoon it stopped and the 2500-gallon fuelers rolled up. The first sergeant stepped from a hummer, got on all fours, put a stick in the crook of his fingers, said, "Far corner pocket," and shot a white pebble toward the Persian Gulf. C was quite balmy now and stopped for the rest of the day, which (even if C had forgotten) was Valentine's Day.

The sun set. Up north the lightning began, and the *boom!* got to C in just thirty seconds. Up north there were also sparks, they rose from Iraq like from welding rods, then faded around the Big Dipper, and "Hey," a commander cried, "that must be the Iraqis," the Iraqis' antiaircraft rounds. Then in Iraq came a lightning flash, there were no sparks anymore, the Iraqis were dead, presumably, and "Oh," the commander said, "they must be hatin' it." And *then* like a fly that won't be swatted, the rounds rose from a different part of Iraq, the Iraqis were resolute men but the commander said, "Oh, they're stupid motherfuckers."

"Yeah, they're stupid," his driver said, but his loader said nothing. He stood on the turret thinking, *It's like the Super Bowl,* the 49ers and Bengals, the 49ers throwing a bone-breaking tackle, a Bengal going upside down and his leg going *crack:* his leg breaking like a celery stick. *It'll be a rough game,* the loader thought, then he got in his sleeping bag and C fell asleep.

It woke up at four saying, "Oo! What is it? Thirty degrees?" it put its dark parkas on, and when the sun came up, it started to roll northwest again. By now the ground was like seashore sand, a couple of bushes aspiring like at Sea Island, Georgia, and C exclaiming, "Another bush!" At noon C saw the edge of Iraq: the berm, the legendary berm, the mound of ground along the Iraqi border, shimmering, singing siren songs, and C continued until it was three thousand meters (about two miles) away, just out of Iraqi range. Then, C spread out: a mile to its left, a mile to its right, the tanks lining up like at El Alamein, the cannons pointing at Iraq. Today wasn't D-Day and C stopped and ate its MREs, Meals Ready-to-Eat, but the captain climbed into a hummer and, his seat shaking like an earthquake, *slap! slam!* continued to the end of Saudi: to the Great Wall of Iraq. As advertised, the Wall was six feet high and made of sand, sand, and stones, but in back of this berm was a berm that was *twelve* feet high. Not happy about it, the captain got out of the hummer and, to the scar-faced lieutenant colonel, who'd come in an earthquake himself, said, "Sir, this is taller than I'd thought."

"It ain't shit," the colonel replied. "It won't stop a tank," and as though to belittle it, he climbed up the six-foot berm, then climbed down the other side, then crossed a ditch that at least wasn't full of fire, then *clump!* then started up the twelve-foot berm and out of Saudi Arabia.

The captain accompanied him. *All* the four captains did, and the four were an all-American lot: the black captain of A, the Hispanic captain of B, the tall white captain of C—Captain Burns—and the red captain of D, the buffalo-shouldered descendant of Cherokee chiefs. At 220 pounds, this man was a runaway locomotive, all Oklahoma fleeing before him, and as he climbed the Wall, he practically battle-cried, "We need the fuckin' map! Lieutenant!" to someone behind him. "Bring us the fuckin' map! *Now!*" The Indian's face was big, his lips were big, his teeth were as big as piano keys, *plink! plunk!* they could probably pound out *Great Balls of Fire,* and the Indian grinned extravagantly lest the lieutenant assume that he was the roaring asshole that he pretended to be. "Goddammit, lieutenant!" the Indian whooped. "How'll we fight the fuckin' war without the fuckin' map? You you— You *dickweed!*" He then turned to the colonel yelling, "We are surrounded by *dickweeds!*" and, his teeth rattling, as if they were being pounded by Jerry Lee, he started laughing, *"Hahaha!"* the colonel laughing, the captain of C, Captain Burns, well, relaxing, and the lieutenant bringing a map of this part of Iraq—*Iraq,* not Greater Iraq, not Kuwait, for Companies A, B, C and D (and 250,000 other boys, also girls) had, in three dizzy days, done an end run to their left, to their west, and were now at the lion's den, at Iraq itself.

By now the four captains stood on the twelve-foot berm and lo! through binoculars, looked at the land where civilization began, where the Garden of Eden was, the Hanging Gardens of Babylon were, where the hand of God, wielding chalk? wielding chisels? chopping away in cuneiform? wielding a can of red spray paint, perhaps? wrote His graffito to Nebuchadnezzar, "Weighed. Weighed. And found wanting." To look at, Iraq was like Saudi: *flat,* and the captains saw a vast pancake, that's all. They couldn't see the wire, concertina wire, or Iraqi trenches, for the Iraqis were miles away, but six hundred meters from them was a shantytown shack, an Iraqi outpost. The captains were out of its rifle range, but in the shack the Iraqis (if any: the captains couldn't spot them) were surely on radios saying in Arabic, "We see Americans! They're white, they're black, they're brown, they're red like in *Fort Apache!*" and the Iraqi mortars, artillery, rockets, would be on this equal-opportunity outfit soon. "We're silhouetted," the colonel observed, and he started down the twelve-foot berm: down the *Iraqi* side, and the four captains went with him. *"Hahaha!"* the Indian shouted. "We are now walking into an Iraqi minefield!"

And *clump!* But there were no mines there, and at the bottom, inside of Iraq, the captains used the binoculars (rubber-coated, in case of a sudden impact) to peer at the shantytown shack. The four were bunched like a square-dance square, and the colonel observed, "We are subject to incoming artillery. I mean," the colonel explained, "even Rashid knows where the berm is." He started back to Saudi, but the Indian pulled out a little gadget: an Instamatic, and the colonel said, "You got your fuckin' *camera* out?"

"Lieutenant!" the Indian yelled, handing the Instamatic to someone behind him. "Take this picture!" and the Indian's *joie de vivre,* like a gale, blew a grin to the colonel's lips.

"This is my boy," the colonel said, huddling up to the Indian like an old Legion buddy.

"Iraq! *Hahaha!*" the Indian roared, twisting his index finger over his and the colonel's shoulders.

"Hey, Mom, look, we're here," the colonel said.

And *snap!* The lieutenant said, "Here you are, sir," and handed the Instamatic back, the Indian told him, "Smile, goddammit!" and *snap!* and shot him, too, the captain of C, Captain Burns, said, "All we need now," the captain was *smiling,* had thirty-two *teeth,* "is tracers in the background," the wind was whistling, *whoo!* and four gray pigeons flew from the shack, the colonel said pensively, "Pigeons," he tried to light up a Carlton, *whoo!* the wind blew his Bic out, the black captain shielded the Bic for him, the Indian howled, "Ugh! What a cheese-eating thing to do!" the colonel said, "Hey. If *you* were an LTC," a lieutenant colonel, "*you'd* get the treatment too," the Iraqis, if any, in the shantytown shack said, "Aim for coordinates 550! 227!" the wind was a herd of horses stampeding by, the captains turned away from it, the hoods of their parkas up, the colonel said, "Let's load up this fuckin' tourist group," and the safari returned to Saudi before the Iraqis could zero in.

C was still two miles back. But the next day the wind died down, the fog moved in, and C rolled up to the Great Dirt Wall. In the twelve-foot part the engineers cut a few notches, and C put a tank at each of these embrasures, the cannons pointing into Iraq, and (though today wasn't D-Day) it attacked its first target: the shantytown shack. At three in the afternoon, the boy who'd kissed the little girl's hand in Kansas, saying, "I'm in love with her too," and who drove a 60-ton tank in Saudi, drove through a notch in the Wall into Indian country, and the commander, who was C's solemn Captain Burns, put his head, neck and shoulders out to address the Iraqis, if any, in the shantytown slanty-roofed shack. In his pocket, Burns had a *Soldier's Guide to Saudi Arabia,* but the Arabic phrases there for "Good morning," "Good evening," and "Please call the U.S. Embassy" were inappropriate here and, his body exposed, his hands like a megaphone, he called out in English, "Hello! Hello! Is anyone there?" On getting no answers (or rifle rounds) the captain called out, "Last warning!" and told his I-love-her driver, "Okay." The boy changed gears, the tank backed up, Burns radioed, "Send it!" someone said, "Fire!" and the engineers fired a six-inch-wide round, a round so fat that people called it an oil drum, watermelon, football, can. It practically flapped like a pelican as it huffed and puffed to that hapless shack, then *boom!* it missed, then *boom!* a second round hit, the shack was a big black cloud, it went up fifty feet and the driver thought, *Wow! It's like movies!* The boy was elated (and envious) as the engineers on his radio shouted, "Got that fucker!" "Blew the fuck out of it!" and "Hoo hoo!"

That night C celebrated, C had hot ham, gravy, vegetables, and a pound cake drowned in warm raspberry sauce. C was at last in lightning land: the bombers, the ones called the buffs, the big ugly fat fuckers, went over C and *boom!* and dumped on Iraqi men? women? kids? in the still-invisible trenches, the helicopters went over, then *boom!* the mortars (like steel stovepipes: a boy dropped a mortar round in and the round popped out) went *boom!* the cannons went *boom!* the rounds whistling over C as in movies of World War II, it was night but the very next day the rocket launchers came from C's rear, from Oman perhaps, from a raft in the Indian Ocean, and the rocketeers in their well-washed clothes hit a button and *boo-boo-boo-boom!* from twenty-seven rocket launchers came 324 rockets, trailing fire, the rockets passed over C, the sky—*the whole hemispherical sky*—was the brightest of beaded curtains, was the real pearly gates, and C stared at the sky transfixed. "It's fuckin' impressive, sir," a sergeant said to Captain Burns.

"Just remember," said Burns, who was combing his inch-long hair in a hummer's rearview mirror, "that what goes up must come down. I bet the OPs," the Iraqi outposts—"I bet the OPs perked up."

"Yeah," another boy laughed. "There's probably an Iraqi PFC, he's cold, he's hungry, he's sittin' in an OP and he's got to send out a spot report—"

" 'Spot report!' " a boy laughed, pretending to be the Iraqi soldier. " 'I saw it and you'll be hatin' it!' "

The two boys laughed and Burns smiled. But then the rocketeers hit the road before the Iraqis, triangulating, could try to deliver tit for tat, and one boy in C, now imperiled, yelled at the fleeing rocketeers, "Yeah, ruin the fuckin' neighborhood!" He and C waited anxiously, but the Iraqis didn't fire.

By now, so many things were going *boom!* along the Great Wall of Iraq that C was glad to escape unscathed. In midmorning, a group of Iraqis appeared just out of C's 2000-meter range, the Iraqis waving a big black flag as if doing wigwag, left, right, as if spelling out, "Nuts to Company C," and C at once radioed its mortarmen, saying, "Coordinates 543! 236!" A mortar round went from the stovepipe, then *boom!* it missed, it exploded near C and someone said, "Uh-oh. That looks awful close."

"We oughta bombard 'em with leaflets," another boy said. " 'If you don't give up, we're gonna get accurate.' "

"Yeah," still another boy. " 'If you don't give up, we're gonna get our shit straight.' "

But that wasn't all. A few hours later, the artillerymen fired at Iraq, the rounds left the cannons, then *boom!* one hit a bird, a butterfly, a mite in a mote of dust above C, it exploded, it formed a black nimbus cloud, and a shower of jagged-edged rain fell on C's territory. A few hours later, the colonel was reconnoitering, his tank was a mile inside of Iraq when a voice on his radio said, "We have movement at 575, 260, we want to shoot artillery."

"No, goddammit! You *can't* shoot artillery, that's *me*!" the colonel radioed.

"Roger," the voice replied, and the colonel rolled back to Saudi as hot as his engine exhaust, nine hundred degrees, and he called all his majors, captains and lieutenants together. All forty officers stood on the desert well out of A, B, C and D's hearing range.

"What *language*," the colonel began, he seemed to be speaking from out of his four-inch scar, it was red and wet and he seemed to be snarling through it—"what *language* is the primary language spoken in the U.S. Army?"

"English," an officer answered.

"Well, *if*," the colonel continued, his helmet was off, it lay on the sand upside down like a crude spittoon, and in his knife-fight-suggestive scar and his razor-blade haircut he looked like a man on death row—"if one uses *English* one can communicate *accurately*, and if I tell you, 'I am at 126, moving *north*,' what do I expect reported to higher headquarters? 'He is at 126, moving *north!*' Not 'He's at 126!' Is anybody having trouble grappling with this?" No one did, and the colonel concluded, "If not, let's start doing it!"

"Yes sir," the officers said.

The most serious *boom!* at the Wall was at one o'clock on a wild, windy, sandstorm-seething night. C was in its tanks, asleep, when someone who wasn't in C saw two Iraqi tanks and, on his radio, called for the helicopters: the big black angle-edged bugs like a Martian armada. Now, A, B, C, D and the Big Red One were also in tanks that at night when the pilots couldn't see the insignia, the /\s that meant *friendly, friendly,* looked like Iraqi ones. Not taking chances, the pilots didn't radio down, "There's two big Iraqi vehicles," but "There's two big vehicles, coordinates 915, 270."

"Yeah," the boy on the ground radioed up. "Those are enemy. Go ahead, take 'em out." The pilots paused and the boy said, "It don't look like you're doin' a damn thing. Go ahead, take 'em out."

"I tell you," one pilot said. "It's hard to pull this trigger."

"Do the mother," a second pilot told him.

"Okay. I hope they're enemy—"

"Go. It's all right."

"—cause here it comes." The pilot hit the red trigger, a missile went into the night, it hit what alas! was a Bradley, a Brink's truck full of American infantrymen, the Bradley and its own missiles blew up. C, to the west, was mostly asleep, but one-fourth of C was watching out for Iraqis, and it saw the pillar of 100-foot-high fire.

"I guess that hit it," the second pilot said.

"I'll shoot the second vehicle," the first pilot said.

"Let's do 'em," the second one said. "This Bud's for you."

And *zoom,* another missile went out. It hit the other vehicle, which also was full of Americans, and another fire-tornado rose. "Oh!" said the pilot, impressed.

"All right! He's dead too!" the second pilot said.

"Hoo-wee!" the first pilot said.

To the west, C had its radios on. It heard someone say, "Be advised. Two ambulances are going through," and, off the air, C said, "What happened?" "I don't know," "I hope no one's seriously hurt." Not until morning did C learn that six Americans were mutilated, two Americans dead, and the most distressed person in C was its Captain Burns. Burns hadn't been in a war before, but at nineteen he'd encountered death in Missouri, he'd been in the woods with a Colt rifle, *splat!* and the heart of an eight-point deer was an oak-tree ornament, the blood was the contents of every curled leaf. *It's dead,* Burns had thought. *It never will run. It never will get its ninth antler,* and though he hadn't stopped hunting, he'd thought of how very long *never* is, of how a deer never emerges from it, and when he'd come to Saudi, he'd resolved that the smallest—*smallest*—fraction of C would succumb to that dead-ended status, death. In his pocket he carried the 91st Psalm,

> *A thousand shall fall at thy side, and ten thousand at thy*
> *right hand, but,*

and each day in Saudi he read it,

> *but it shall not come nigh thee,*

and, like some penitent, read it,

> *but it shall not come nigh thee,*

and read it and read it and interpreted *thee* as every last boy in C. And today when he learned that Americans were *hoo-wee!* were crippled, killed, when he saw that he couldn't control all the TNT around C, he resolved that, if nothing else, he'd ensure that the words on C's tomb wouldn't be "We have met the enemy: us." "We," he announced to C, "are a greater danger to ourselves than the Iraqis are," and he said to C: No ammo. No loaded weapons. If he didn't approve it, authorize it, no shooting at the Iraqis. None.

C was appalled. Why, there was a goddam war on! By night and *day* the Iraqis were creeping up, the Iraqis got two thousand meters away, they looked at C with binoculars, wigwagged their flags, and *dit dit!* tapped out in Morse, the Iraqis had guns, mortars, vehicles, had rounds that as yet—*as yet*—hadn't hit anyone in C. All around C the army went *boom!* the mortarmen, artillerymen, rocketeers, *boom!* the engineers sat on TNT, they played a dumb game called Uno, the cards were red, yellow, blue and green, the engineers shouted, "Uno!" then *boom!* then sent a pelican at the Iraqis, but C still played its "No, you didn't say *May I*" with Captain Burns. Often, C saw an Iraqi and radioed up, "Black six," Burns's radio code, and "May we engage him?" and Burns, well, *practically,* radioed back, "Where is he? What is he wearing? Are you sure he's not an American? That he's not the colonel? That he's not a PFC who's lost? Can you see if he's wearing dog tags? Can you ask him who won the Super Bowl? Are you *sure* he's not one of us?"

"We're sure!" C said.

"I'll double-check."

C thought, *The captain's crazy.* To look at, C was real soldiers, was Willie in World War II, it needed a bath very badly, water was short and C hadn't washed since—*when?* it looked at its grungy clothes and said, "Gee, there's things growin' there without Latin names," it acted like soldiers too, saluting haphazardly, saying its weird little passwords like "Suitcase," "Sprocket," and "Bearskin," "Soapbox," and "Pizza," "No, that isn't right," it carried its rifles convincingly *but:* its rifles, machine guns, cannons were empty, they had no rounds and C, poor C, had never gone *boom.*

The result was, no one in C was killed or wounded along the Great Wall of Iraq but C became nervous, *nervous.* "The best way," the colonel had told it, "to get over it," over being afraid, "is to fire one round," but C didn't fire and C was always afraid. One boy played on his Walkman his *Killing an Arab,* by The Cure,

> *I'm starin' down the barrel,*
> *At the Arab on the ground,*

the boy now thinking, *I wish,*

> *The sea is in my mouth,*
> *But I hear no sound,*

and one boy with idle energy started digging, his shovel stabbing the sand, *crunch!* the hole coming up to his hips, his waist, the rest of C asking, "You diggin' to China?"

"No, the United States." The boy then added obscurely, "I don't believe in God."

"You are one crazy soldier."

"Yes, I am goin' crazy. A man who says he ain't goin' crazy—" the boy looked at C judiciously, like the gravedigger in *Hamlet*— "is goin' crazy." His own head ached, his hands craved his rifle, his black machine gun, his cannon, his fingers itched—the Iraqis were out of his range, that's true, but the Iraqis alarmed him, the Iraqis could kill him and *oh,* he wanted to shoot at Iraqis! To shoot!

So did all C. It didn't, it was nervous, and just as some people will kick the cat, it got itself surrogates, instead. One boy wrote to a creditor in Louisiana,

> *Well, here's your damn $110, and excuse me if my being in this war fighting for your slugass so you can continue doing whatever it is slugasses do interferes with . . .*

and one boy wrote to a tank-part manufacturer in Indiana,

> *It's a shame that you sell inferior products to the U.S. government when at certain times and places it could mean life or death to a U.S. serviceman. We . . .*

and one boy who'd gotten mail to Any Soldier answered,

> *Yes! A lot of people here are mad,*

but most of C picked on whoever was closest, starting on Captain Burns. Though not to his face, it called him Gus, Bullet Bob, the Four M'er: the Mutant Micro-Manager Mogul, and C picked on privates, too. One was the homeliest boy in C, his face was an anvil, *clang!* a man could repair a horseshoe there, and C now appointed him an Honorary Iraqi. A girl had written him, "I love you lots," and sent him her photograph, but someone in C asked, "Do you two have an emotional attachment?"

"No. . . ."

"That's good, cause she's fat and ugly!" All of C laughed, and the joker continued, "She'd lose some weight if she cut off her head!"

Another Honorary Iraqi was the boy who'd once said, "I don't wanna *demoralize* her." A loader, the fattest soldier in C, he smoked his Dorals in a tank with a ton of explosives, then on the floor he dropped his ashes, his wrappers of MREs, and his first drafts of "Dear Mom, I may not be coming back." His gunner was Sergeant Spence, the boy who'd made crazy love using Dippity-Do, who hated him and, one day, who asked the first sergeant to sack him, sad-sack him: to kick him off the otherwise cozy crew.

"No, you can't fight with a three-man crew," the wise first sergeant said. "You ain't goin' 'gainst plywood tanks and paper people. You goin' 'gainst shootin'."

"Maybe," said the *demoralize* boy, a party to this proceeding, a big brown blur in the fog on this cold morning—"maybe I need to see a shrink, but *he,*" he nodded at Spence, "drives me *nuts,*" then he crumpled an empty pack of Dorals and dropped it into the fire they were huddling around.

"What this is, is a personality conflict," the good first sergeant said.

By now C's lieutenants were all Honorary Iraqis. The black one was very well liked, but one day a PFC incredibly called him "You nigger," and the one from West Point was the nicest person in C, but one day he called out, "Oh, sergeant," and the sergeant exploded, yelling, *"Don't yell at me, sir!"* The lieutenant, whose name was Jones, said, "You're causing problems."

"How am I causing problems?"

"You're hard to get along with."

"I'm hard to get along with?"

"Well, that's what I hear."

"I'm quitting!" the sergeant shouted, and he went stomping south as if in ten minutes he wouldn't have to come stomping back.

The lieutenant that C, all bulletless, shell-less, scared of Iraqis, most often dumped on was Russell. One night Russell saw an Iraqi just inside of Iraq and radioed up, "He's running, then dropping, then running again. May we engage?" At that time, Russell and his four tanks were west of the rest of C, were "attached" to Company D and were taking orders from the Cherokee Indian. *"Roger! You may engage!"* the Indian radioed-roared, and Russell told his Samoan gunner, "Okay, engage."

"No, LT," the Samoan said, LT being slang for lieutenant. "You do it. Go ahead."

"No. Go ahead," said Russell.

"No, LT," the Samoan said, for he believed in the Sixth Commandment. "You'd rather do it. Go ahead."

"Okay," said Russell, he hit his red triggers, *tatatata,* a row of red tracers went into Iraq, and the Iraqi fell down, dead, wounded, or lying low. "I think I got him," said Russell, but now the Samoan despised him.

A worse case was his Laotian loader. The boy who'd smiled like a chorus boy was like a Kabuki character now: his lips, eyes and eyebrows pointed down, and if Russell went near him, his nostrils widened like Yuranosuke's in the eleventh act of *Chushingura*. The boy, like Russell, was writing a daily diary, but it was a bill of indictment against the LT,

Already the LT scares me. . . .

What the hell is he talking about. . . .

I don't know what's wrong with the LT. . . .

I don't know how long I can even hold on. . . .

and almost poetically,

> *Because I'm a private nobody cares,*
> *Because I'm a private they want me*
> *To be STUPID.*

One day, Russell sat sleeping in the Laotian's compartment, and the Laotian, his face going black, his eyebrows doing their Kabuki thing, "I'll kill you, oh, Moronao!" went to a sergeant and said, "If if— If this happen again, I won't put up with it! Because— *uhhhh!*" Too angry to formulate sentences, the Laotian exhaled violently, then said, "Every time—*uhhhh!* The next time this bullshit happen, I'll load a round and—"

And what? the sergeant thought.

"And and— And shoot in the *sky,*" the Laotian said, "and I'll get all the people attention!"

Well, he'll get Russell's, the unconcerned sergeant thought.

So far, C hadn't shot at C, but much of C had designs on the man who'd left it naked to the Iraqis: on Captain Don't-Shoot-Till-I-Say-So-and-I'll-Never-Say-So Burns. "I don't think anyone likes him," a boy wrote to Kansas. "The bet is that someone will kill him," and one day a sergeant suggested how to do it. "What I'll do is," the sergeant told C, "is I'll say *Gizmo! Gizmo!*" and Burns's innocent gunner, loader and driver should duck as C opened fire on Burns. The sergeant, of course, was jesting, well, wasn't he?

C's heebie-jeebies would end if, *charge!* if C could roll into Iraq, its guns spewing steel at Iraqis. C was still waiting, for C had heard that the Soviets had a peace proposal and the Iraqis' leader, Saddam Hussein, had surrendered, or rather he *might* surrender if Saudi did, or America did, or no, if Israel surrendered what's west, no, east of the Jordan, or no! The truth is, C didn't know, for C's one radio, Sergeant James's, just received the BBC, and ninety percent of the BBC was *"Crackle."* But one day as James sat twisting his two-foot antenna, he heard the BBC say, *"Crackle* announcement from Saddam Hussein."

It was six in the evening. The wind had been an express train, then the caboose had gone through, the air was suddenly calm, even warm, and C, some of C, was standing near James's tank. One boy had caviar, a recent present from Kansas, he'd spread it on Keebler Crackers but C had stared at it warily, as if it had issued from some dead fish. One boy had tasted one, yes, one little smelly black ball, he'd rolled it between his tongue and teeth, directing his consciousness onto it, and one boy who'd once eaten caviar at Boccaccio's, in Houston, had said, "Eat the cracker, too," then James said, "He," meaning Saddam Hussein, "is goin' to make an announcement."

"I hope," someone said, "the announcement is 'Fuck you all! Come get me!' "

"Yeah," someone said. "He brought me here, and I want to kick his ass."

C was for war. In part, C was mad at Iraq for dragging it out of its Klub Kamilles, but C also felt that the war was just. "I don't want peace," the oldest soldier in C had said to James recently. "I have a fourteen-year-old, and I don't want him in this bullshit years from now. I'm forty-one," the soldier, who C knew as Grandpa, had said, the moon as thin as a fingernail behind him, the black clouds in front of it, the moon setting over Arabia, over America. "If there's any blood to be shed, I'd just as soon bleed for *him.*"

"Yeah. Put them away," the Iraqis away, said James, who now slid his radio to and fro like a vacuum cleaner, trying to pick up the BBC. The radio hummed like, well, like a vacuum cleaner, then it reached the right geomantic spot and the BBC distantly said, "Saddam Hu *Crackle* has just said, *'Crackle.'* "

"I think he's giving up," said someone in C.

"I don't think so," said James, staring at the dial as though lip-reading it.

"He *crackle*," the BBC said. "He has just said, 'Our people will *crackle*.'" One boy twisted the antenna, which by now could be used for fishing in sewers, and the BBC said clearly, "'Our people will continue to struggle.' We are not sure if this is an outright rejection of the Soviet peace proposal, but—"

"Pretty safe," someone said.

"—but it would seem to be."

The next day C met with Captain Burns. It assembled at Burns's muddy tank, and Burns (whose father, an attorney, had come home every evening saying, "Hi, Bob," shaking hands) was as solemn as always, speaking as though to the Roman senate, emanating *gravitas*. "Peace," he announced, "is not breakin' out. We're going to LD," meaning going to go to the Line of Departure, then to Iraq, "the day after tomorrow. The news," he continued, "is, the Iraqis have accepted the Soviet peace proposal," well, it was certainly news to C. "So why are we LD'ing? Bush hasn't accepted it. Bush called up Sergeant Medine," and Burns now looked at Medine, the boy who'd hit a rut, been paralyzed, and been ambulanced out, but who, recovering, had recently hitchhiked back to C, "and Medine said, 'Don't take shit.' So we're going to let Sergeant Lemon," and Burns looked at another sergeant, "attack. Sergeant James," and Burns looked at his preacher-in-residence, "is a very religious man, and I hope the Iraqis he's going to kill won't bother him. I hope they believe in Allah."

Standing around him, C was as pensive as Burns. One boy thought of the girl he'd loved in the seventh grade, and one boy thought of his bride in Kansas. Medine didn't think of his English fiancée but of a Domino's pizza: cheese, onions, mushrooms, sausage and pepperoni, along with a Mountain Dew.

"At 0538," Burns continued, "we'll cross the berm," the Wall of Iraq. "We know in our hearts we don't want to do this, but we know in our heads we got to. So our sons—" and Burns interrupted himself, "Well, I don't have any sons but I have a cat," not smiling, "so my cat won't have to do this two years from now."

C chuckled. One boy said, "Sir?" and asked him if Saudi, Syria, Egypt—if the Arabs were cooperating or if C was fighting them, too.

"Nobody's backed out. Nobody's backed down," Burns said. "The Brits are still saying, 'Don't take shit.' "

"Go get 'em, lobsters," someone said, and Burns quickly wrapped it up.

"We should have done this— What? Today is the 22nd? We should have done this yesterday. So fuck it," Burns concluded. "Let's do it the 24th." He then put his hands palms down and slid them apart, meaning "Dismissed."

He felt relieved. No one in C had asked him, "What do we do the 25th?" or "What do we do the 26th? the 27th? the 28th?" or "What do we do from then to New Year's Day?" and Burns hadn't volunteered that C was supposed to do zero, zilch, for C was supposed to have nine dead, thirty-six wounded, and the generals had no further use for C. Not mentioning this, Burns walked away, but he disburdened on the lieutenant from West Point. "Deep down inside," Burns told him, "I don't want to do this. But," sighing, "we're going to do it."

The lieutenant thought, *What can I tell him?* The lieutenant's profile was aristocratic, his nose, lips and chin were a perfect crescent, his lips were thin and he used them hesitantly. "The scariest thing about this," he said to Burns, "is, we may not be here for the memories."

"Mm," Burns said, and he walked away.

C stayed behind, scribbling its "Jim"'s and "Joe"'s in the captain's autograph book. The black lieutenant wrote,

You've been like a father to me,

and wondered, *Will I ever see him?* "Hey, sergeant," he called to James, the boy in C most abreast of God's intentions. "Will this be the Battle of Armageddon?"

"No, I don't think so."

"Do you think we'll *die?*" The lieutenant said *die* as if hitting a punch line, *haha, I'm not really serious.*

"No, I don't think so. But," James went on, "the important thing if you die is, you die in Christ. Then there'll be somethin' better."

"Yeah, sometimes I wish I was saved."

"Sir, you can be saved right now."

Now, McRae, the lieutenant, was someone who never reflected, he said whatever leapt to his tongue-tip, but James was reminded of Specialist Penn, the boy who'd been saved in Saudi, and James thought, *Well, hallelujah! He's comin' to Christ!* The lieutenant was Christian, yes, he'd gone to a Christian High in Ohio, he carried a *Big Red One Bible,* but James knew the Bible said,

Let the words of my mouth be acceptable in Thy sight, O Lord,

and James felt the lieutenant's addiction to *fuck, fucker, fuckin',* and *motherfucker* wasn't acceptable to Him who'd created man in His image. What's worse, C was now christening tanks, christening them the *Stranger,* the *Wolverine,* and the *Phantom Lord* ("How about *Satan's Ship?*" "No, God wouldn't bless you," said James, whose tank was *Crusading for Christ*) and C was now painting these names on its cannons for God and His angels to see in Iraq, and James was aghast at the black lieutenant's—*his* lieutenant's—selection. The lieutenant had had a British *Playboy,* a British soldier's gift to C, he'd said, "What bitches," someone had said, "They're coke whores. They sell themselves for coke," the lieutenant had said, "Well, fuck it, we'll call it the *Coke Whore,*" and, to James's horror, he had painted that on: that and a girl in an I-wanna-be-in-*Playboy* pose. Pornography was forbidden in Saudi, but Captain Burns had said, "Oh my God, I don't see it," and now it devolved on James to make the lieutenant repent-and-repaint lest C, in thirty-six hours, go to Iraq behind a banner abominable to God.

"Sir, you can be saved right *now*," said James.

"No," the lieutenant said. "I'm too far gone."

"Sir, you can be saved no matter *what*," and James pulled his Bible out and read the same passage from Romans he'd read to Penn. "Do you want to repeat it with me?"

"No," the lieutenant said, and a new concept leapt to his tongue-tip. "No, I'm not like Penn, where I think I'm gonna die and I say, 'Oh, God, I love you,' 'Oh, God, please help me,' 'Oh, God, if You do, I'll go to church on Sunday.' No, I been livin' bad," the lieutenant continued, a man on a sax commencing a red-hot lick, *waaa!* "and jus' cause I'm scared, I ain't gonna change. If I die, then I die."

"If you die, sir, you're going to *hell*."

"Well, if I go to hell, then I go to hell."

"Sir, you shouldn't play with your *life*."

"But sergeant, I *want* to!" the lieutenant said—*waaa!* the sax was now horizontal, the ceiling was cracking, the plaster was coming down. "My philosophy is, I like *cussin'*, and I like my life like it *is*," well, more than the life of a God-mouthing Sergeant Saint James.

"Sir! You should let God *change* you!"

"*Sergeant*," the lieutenant said. He was deep into this solo, and he couldn't change to a minor mode and say, "Sweet Jesus. Save me." "I read the *Bible*," the lieutenant said, "and I don't *drink*, and I don't do *drugs*, and I don't cheat on my *wife*, so jus' cause I don't praise *God* all day don't mean that I'm going to *hell*!" He then seized the captain's autograph book, scribbled in,

Your son, Bennie,

turned back to James, said, "Anyway, I'm gonna live. So *fuck* it!" and strode to the USS *Coke Whore*. Behind him James was aghast, as though the lieutenant had just defected to the Iraqis. It's good to believe in God if God's on your side, but it isn't if God's against you, and James was afraid that God wouldn't smile on *Crusading for Christ* if it went into battle behind the *Co,* the *Co*—he couldn't even say it.

T he next day, its last in Saudi, C got ready for D-Day. It filled up its gas tanks and, at a vat labeled POTABLE WATER, filled up its own canteens, shaking the vat as though it were labeled SHAKE WELL and, at the last two drops, saying, "Whoo! That's the last water we'll get!" C blasted the dirt from its filters, and it zeroed its cannons by pointing its index fingers up, down, left or right, and by making fists: *right on,* the cannons now accurate (or so C hoped) to one half-foot at a one-mile range, at a 1600-meter range. For the zillionth time the lieutenants said, "Listen up," and reviewed the invasion plan, and, who can blame them? the nervous crews got it totally wrong. "We punch out of here tomorrow," the lieutenant from West Point began.

"It isn't tomorrow, sir," a tank commander said. "It's the next day."

"No, it's tomorrow," the lieutenant continued. He pointed to a map of Iraq and said, "We go through the berm," the Wall, "and we spread to the right."

"No, we go to the left," a driver said. He was sitting on top of a tank, looking at the map upside down.

"No, we go to the right," the lieutenant said.

"No, sir, the berm is *that* way, right?"

"Yeah. . . ."

"So we're comin' in and shiftin' *left.*"

"No, you're looking at it upside down."

"Humor me for a minute, *would* you, sir?"

"Well, we'll talk about this later. . . ."

In the afternoon most of C wrote to its wives and girls in

Kansas. Its captain didn't, lest the love letter get to his wife when she'd already heard that he'd died. One boy who'd written his wife saying, "Say hi to Sara Ann," meaning "I'm in Saudi Arabia," now wrote her saying, "Say hi to Irene," meaning "I'll be in Iraq." The black lieutenant wrote to his bride, then he built a fire, burned all the envelopes from her, and kicked the ashes around lest the Iraqis should kill him, get her address, and write her, "The camels are eating him." Lieutenant Russell, who didn't have a wife or girl-friend, wrote in his diary to Tom,

> *Well, we're going in, and if it means my life so be it. My faith is in the Lord.*

With twelve hours to D-Day, Russell didn't write about Tim, the man who pretended to be Tom's father, but Russell's little diary/ diatribe was now full of I-don't-like-Tims and I-don't-like-your-mothers,

> *She was pregnant and was going to abort it. . . .*

> *The wedding dress was the one I had paid for. . . .*

> *Tim is using her. . . .*

> *Tim is twisting her. . . .*

> *For someone so "proud" she sure kisses ass to Tim. . . .*

for Russell had never recognized that the entries might not be best for Tom.

At sunset, Russell put the diary in Nomex: in fireproof fabric, then into .50-caliber and 20-millimeter ammo cans, then from his olive-green bag he pulled an American flag he'd bought for $1.50 at the Fort Riley PX. The flag, like pornography, was *verboten* in Saudi Arabia, but Russell felt, *If I can die for it, I can fly it,* and he put the four-inch-high flag on his radio antenna. On another tank Specialist Young, who thought, *I'm a natural soldier. I won't die,* took camouflage cord (a cord to tie camouflage with) and tied it to his machine gun, intending to put in a knot whenever he killed an Iraqi, and on *Crusading for Christ* the crew formed a circle, holding hands, and Sergeant James said, "Thank you, Jesus," commencing his nightly prayers.

But tonight was the dark one of James's soul. He'd once loved the desert: the sand below, the sky above, and nothing to distract anyone who, like Christ, chose to contemplate on God. James, too, had been in the desert exactly forty days, but in between sand and sky tonight was the *Coke Whore,* and James was afraid that God had decamped. Not letting on, James held hands on top of *Crusading for Christ* and said, "Thank you, Jesus, for bein' here," well, James could certainly hope. "You was there for Elijah, for Hezekiah, and," James continued, squeezing his soldiers' hands, "we thank you for lettin' us know that in the mids' of destruction and the bombs all fallin' aroun' us, you'll be there for *us.* We ask you to bless us, Jesus," said James, and he pumped his arms as though pumping a gallon of faith into his circle and, in the end, into himself. He then said, *"Ah-men,"* and his all-white crew said, *"Ay-men,"* the sun set and James climbed into his tank, then into his sleeping bag, then he fell asleep.

All of C fell asleep. The guns were silent, but at one in the morning there was a *boo-boo-boo-boom!* for the rocketeers were at C again, and C almost leapt from its bags as *one! two! three! 324!* as the yellow rockets went over and as, on the yellow soil, the shadows of the tanks stampeded south. C watched, then most of C fell asleep but James stayed awake, aware that today would be D-Day. He needed assurance, and in some inner ear he heard someone say, "Read the Bible," and "Read I Samuel 17:45," and, using his blue-lensed flashlight, he turned to this verse in the David-and-Goliath story. Of course, James had often heard this verse at his father's church in Virginia. Unconsciously he may have chosen it, but he felt he'd been guided to it by God, and, by the blue light, the Bible all blue, he read the words of David to Goliath,

> *Thou comest to me with a sword, and with a spear, and with a shield: but I come to thee in the name of the Lord of Hosts,*

and James thought, *Thank you, Jesus!* Clearly, God meant that He hadn't skipped out, that He was still here, that James wouldn't go to Iraq in the name of the *Co,* the *Co,* but of God Himself. James underlined all of I Samuel 17:45, then someone or Someone told him, "Now turn to II Kings 7:3," the siege of Samaria by the army of Syria, and James did and read,

> *And there were four leprous men and they said, Why sit here until we die? Now come, and let us fall unto the host of the Syrians. And they rose up,*

and *thank you, Jesus!* for James had also heard about this in Virginia. A preacher (not his own father) had read the four-leper verse and *hey!* had jumped to the aisle, shouting, "They *thought,*" the congregation repeating, "They *thought,*" the preacher continuing, "they hadda *die!*" the congregation repeating, "*Die!*" The preacher had turned, had twisted, his body a question mark, shouting that the lepers had won and the Syrians lost. "So get *up!*" the preacher had shouted, sweating, his handkerchief at his brow, "cause while there is *God* on your side, you're *not* gonna die! Get *up!* Get *up!*" the preacher all but demanding, "Get up and *dance!*" the congregation—among it, James—backing the panting preacher up, saying, singing, "Get *up!* Get *up!*" the meaning to James tonight was "Get up and go to Iraq! for *God's* going with you!" and James was undaunted now, James was confident now, James whispered, "Thank you, Jesus!" and put the Bible behind him. Up front, the air force's flares were over Iraq, they beckoned like the Star of Bethlehem, they said, "All ye faithful, *come,*" and James fell asleep in *Crusading for Christ,* a Christian soldier in camouflage dreaming of Onward, On.

At four o'clock, C woke up and acted as if today weren't different from all the previous ones. On one tank a sergeant chewed out a private, "Hey, soldier, shine your boots."

"No, I'm not gonna," the sleepy private said.

"You no-time-in-grade 'cruit private," the sergeant teased him. "I'll put you over a gun tube," a cannon, "and I'll have my way with you."

"Sergeant," the private yawned, "it'll take you and a whole nother company like you."

On another tank, a boy crawled out of his sleeping bag and, rolling it up, said, "It must be gettin' pregnant. It's harder and harder to roll it up," and on *Crusading for Christ* the driver climbed out and said, *"Oo!"* for the wind was a gale, it hit him at forty mph and carried a skin-chilling rain. "It's miserable out," the driver reported.

"No," said James, and James was like Jeremiah now, his eyes incandesced like Saint Elmo's fire. "The weather's from God! It's *cool,"* James explained, "and the tank works best when it's cool. The *rain,* it holds down the dust, so they," the Iraqis, "won't see us, and the *wind's* from the south, so they can't use gas. The weather is nothin' but *God!"*

"You think so?"

"I *know* so!"

At 4:30 C was still dressing. On top of its shorts and T-shirts it put its warm sweaters, then fireproof suits, then suits full of charcoal to soak up Iraqi gas. The charcoal, like newsprint, got on C's hands, chins, cheeks, and C soon looked like the dogfaced soldiers of World War II. C put its boots on, then booties against the gas, then gloves, then on its heads the earphones for Walkmans

and, over these, in its helmets, the earphones to listen to Captain
Burns. By coincidence Specialist Young, Sergeant James and Lieutenant Russell weren't using Walkmans today. Young had a tape
of Bach's *Violin Concerto in A Minor,* Bach would divert him but,
alas, his Walkman wasn't working. James had a tape of "Get *up*!
Get *up*!" but as C's pastor he didn't want to play it if C couldn't
share it, and Russell, a junior officer, was obliged to listen to Captain Burns. Over everything else, C put its camouflaged bulletproof
vests.

At five o'clock C ate its MREs. It started its motors, *arrr!* but
it still heard the big fat fuckers, their *boom!* their *boom!* it felt this
against its celluloid goggles, then it heard a red-crossed chopper,
raaa-raaa-raaa, descending a half-mile from C to pick up a boy
who'd tripped while on top of a tank, falling, cracking his skull.
At 5:30 the sky was still black, but the wind and rain eased as C
started rolling behind the Wall. On *Crusading for Christ,* James
twisted the "key" on his helmet to ask his gunner, loader and
driver, "Do you want me to sing for you?"

"Yes," "Yes," and "Oh, yes."

"All right," said James, and he sang in his cotton church-
choir voice,

> *Be not dismays,*

he meant *dismayed,*

> *Be not dismays,*
> *Whate'er betide,*
> *God . . .*
> *Will take care of you.*

He sang very slowly, as though he had all the time there was,

> *Beneath his wings,*
> *His love abides,*

God . . .
Will take care of you.

He was like someone's mother singing, "May angels attend thee," and his crew, hearing this in its earphones, was pleased that God, angels, Allah, anyone, would care for it in Iraq. C now turned north. In the Wall was a fifty-yard gap, the engineers had created it, and as C approached it, James sang slowly and softly,

> *Through every day,*
> *O'er all the way,*
> *He . . .*
> *Will take care of you,*

and at 5:38, on schedule, as C started through the gap, the six-foot and twelve-foot berms at its sides like the Gates of Hercules, the song came straight from James's heart and James embroidered every note,

> *He will, yes, He will,*
> *Take care, take care,*
> *Yes, God . . .*
> *Will take care of you,*

and James and C (and fifteen companies east of C) rolled into Iraq, the land of Nebuchadnezzar, the land of the fiery furnace, the land of, *dear God, be with us,* of Shadrach, Meshach, Abednego.

4

Iraq:
The Breach

★

The sand of Iraq stretched on, endlessly on, an empty extrapolation of Saudi, no sand hills, no sand pits, *hmm,* no Iraqis, as James and all C invaded it, *arrr!* at ten steady mph. At last C was loaded: in guns, rifles, cannons it yes! it had rounds, golden cylinders, it could go *bang* as soon as its wary captain said, "Now." Like Patton, the tank commanders in C had their shoulders out, at their hands were giant machine guns and at their thumbs, giant triggers, the rounds were as big as hot dogs and, link by link, they rose out of cans with hundreds more. On top of some cans were cornflakes boxes to keep the disastrous sand out, and at sunrise, seven o'clock, the red of the *Kellogg's* gleamed on C's muddy tanks.

C was still rolling, rolling. It saw no Iraqis, heard no Iraqi *boom*s, it listened instead to its Walkmans, keeping cool. The boys who liked music by Mozart had left it in Kansas, it wasn't in Sand-in-the-Sprockets Land, and C played pop as it pushed into Castle Iraq. On his Walkman the Samoan had *Lau Lupe (My Lovely Dove)* and the Laotian *Lac Yin (I Overheard)* but most of C had more stirring things like *Fight the Good Fight,* by Triumph, *Dirty Deeds Done Dirt Cheap,* by AC/DC, and *Appetite for Destruction,* by Guns N' Roses, and like kids doing homework it listened to these devotedly. On one tank the gunner's pet number was *Some Heads Are Going to Roll,* by Judas Priest, but today he was playing the deadweight music of *Dying to Meet You,* also by Judas Priest. He was deadening himself for the slaughter ahead,

> *Then with an arm raised*
> *The slaughter is started,*
> *One or two crack up*
> *And start to cry,*

the music on him like sacked cement,

> *Selfishness breeds in*
> *A cesspool of sorrow,*
> *Every few moments*
> *Friends die,*

the weight of the music crushing him,

> *Synchronized watches*
> *Flash in the sunlight,*
> *As into the battle*
> *We all are led-d-d-d,*

like lead, he was dead underneath it, *left,* he was part of his gun tube, *right,* was part of his gunsight, *left,* he scanned for Iraqis.

At eight o'clock C was still rolling. The name of its straight-arrow route was Axis Saturn. Back in Saudi, a major in Operations had named it Axis Pig, the scar-faced colonel had told him, "I'm sorry. I don't attack on Axis Pig," the major had said, "Well, hell, I'll name it Axis Thucydides," the colonel had said, "No, we needn't go to extremes," and the major had changed it to Axis Saturn. At nine o'clock the Axis started to slant uphill (a hill in Iraq being fifty feet high) and C stopped, for the berms, ditches, wires, mines and Iraqis, sitting in trenches, squinting through sights, saying, "We're waiting, Satans," would be on the downhill side, and the colonel now radioed to A, B, C, D. A man who'd taught history at West Point, the colonel knew that a battle isn't as Delacroix painted it, that, in the words of *The Art of War,* written 2400 years ago in China, a battle is usually fought with a sword that's sheathed. He knew that the Jews under Gideon, confronting the Midianites, blowing on trumpets, shouting, "The sword of the Lord!" had never unsheathed it but that the Midianites had lost their morale and fled. He knew that the Greeks under Epictetus, the Greeks in white ostrich plumes under Alexander, the Romans under Pompeius Magnus, had always aimed at a man's morale, that the English under King Arthur had galloped at the Romans, who (said Geoffrey of Monmouth) had run like sheep from lions, that the English against the French, the Spanish, the Russians had been outmatched except in morale, morale, that Napoleon had said that morale is to all other factors as 4:1, that even the Sioux under Sitting Bull had appeared like the dawn, almost synchronously, on the ridges above the Americans, the palefaces turning paler. "Everyone. Go on line," the colonel now radioed to A, B, C, D, "and come onto the ridge like the Sioux Nation."

"Roger," said A, B, C, D, and two thousand tons of tanks hit the ridge simultaneously and—*at last*—started to shoot at Iraqis, two thousand meters (or one and one-quarter miles) ahead. It wasn't raining now, and C, through binoculars, saw the Iraqis running like ants in a Raid attack, the Iraqis crissing and crossing as if anywhere in Iraq were better than here. They probably thought, *Oh God! It's the Mother of Battles,* for one minute later someone in C called out, "A white flag!"

C was suspicious. It couldn't tell if the flag-waving man was signaling, "We surrender," or signaling, "I surrender, and I don't know about anyone else." At the man's sides the Iraqis, not putting their hands up, were running every which way, and C didn't know: were they getting more flags? more guns? some mortar rounds full of gas to three, two, one, to shoot at C? were they getting their rice? their toothbrush and Crest for their trip to the POW camp? and C, not knowing, kept shooting and hoping to not hit the flag-waving man. One tank commander, who with Lieutenant Russell was still attached to Company D and its Cherokee, was jamming his trigger, relieving a one month's itch, and at the same time jamming to Pink Floyd's *Dogs of War,*

> *We can't stop*
> *What has begun!*
> *Signed and sealed*
> *We deliver oblivion!*

On the commander's radio the Indian shouted, "Cease fire!" but the commander didn't hear him, for the Walkman he'd bought at a Sears in Kansas was working but his radio, thirty years old, was not. "They're givin' up! Wait!" the Indian cried, but the boy only heard the *Dogs of War,*

> *We all have our dark side*
> *To say the least!*
> *Dealin' in death is*
> *The nature of the beast!*

and *tatatata,* he hit an Iraqi who, alas, was the flag-waving one. "Cease fire!" the Indian roared, and Russell, the boy's lieutenant, shouted this too, but the boy was still grooving on

> *Dogs of War don't negotiate!*
> *Dogs of War won't capitulate!*

and his red tracers were grooving the sky. "I wish we'd move up," his gunner, wired to the Walkman, said, for the Iraqis were out of his range, "so I could shoot too." "Mmf," said the rocker-and-roller, emitting his red-tailed lead,

> *We will take,*
> *But you will give!*

You will die,
So that we may live!

Then *crackle!* the radio worked, and the voice of Lieutenant Russell was a Caruso 78. "Cease fire!" Russell cried, the boy at last heard him, his thumbs and his *tatatata*s let up, and a group of Iraqis started to walk to C. "I got approximately ten," a boy radioed, meaning "I see approximately ten."

The ten had white flags. They also had guns, and C wasn't sure: were they an Iraqi dirty trick, an Iraqi kamikaze crew, an Iraqi detachment coming at C? A month ago the Iraqis had pulled that one on the Saudis, and scarcely a minute ago, near C, an Iraqi had come with a kilo of TNT. "And when he was captured he blew himself up," the colonel radioed now, and C was all anxious as the Iraqis, approaching, became an Arab human wave.

"I got nineteen now! twenty!" the Indian radioed. "I see— *Hell!* I see a whole damn company now!"

And *crackle!* On the radio someone said, "Another soldier," another Iraqi near C, "came with a Claymore," a kind of mine, "strapped to his chest." The man on the radio said to beware of Iraqi surrenderers.

"I count fifty-three now!" the Indian radioed.

"Looks like about twenty more!" a boy radioed him.

"Roger! We got about eighty now!" the Indian radioed.

By now the Iraqis, brown-skinned, black-mustached, looking like a crowd of Mexicans advancing on a California vineyard, were at C's tanks. C shouted, *"Qif,"* the word for "Stop" in the *Soldier's Guide to Saudi Arabia* in the chapter on Saudi limousine drivers, and the Iraqis stopped, C gestured, and the Iraqis dropped their guns and Russian bazookas. C had them undress and, not finding any TNT, it *whew,* started breathing, saying, "We're like Sergeant Fuckin' York," for C was satisfied that the Iraqis (*these* Iraqis: many, many more were ahead of C) were truly surrendering.

C had them dress again. It used their red-and-white head-dresses to tie their hands behind them. It thought, *We won't have to kill them now,* and it was grateful to these two hundred sensible men. "You tell Saddam," a sergeant told an Iraqi who sat like Job on the wet-with-rain sand, "we are comin' to kick his ass," and Russell talked baby-talk to an English-speaking captain. "Tank. You know tank? Is tank," said Russell, pointing at his *My Hillbilly Babe.* "Iraqis have tank?"

"Yes," the Iraqi said, frowning. "But your English isn't very good."

The most talkative man in C's area was the captain of D. His name, honest Injun—Cherokee Injun—was Bushyhead, though people in Kansas had often told him, "You're putting me on."

"No, I'm really John Bushyhead."

"I'm Donald Doe." Or whatever.

"Doe? Like in Do Re Mi? Like in *Tic Tac Dough?* Like in *Ain't got no money, ain't got no—* No!" the Indian had bellowed. "You're puttin' me on! *Hahaha!*" His teeth had been headlights, and, no less dynamic, he now went among the Iraqis saying, "Don't worry! Don't worry! We won't hurt you!" He patted his shoulder and said, "We're Americans," patted the Iraqis, too, put his palms in the Indian-from-India salutation, saluted. He said to the English-speaking man, "We'll feed you! We'll get you water! We'll abide by the Geneva Convention! We'll treat you well!"

"Thank you, sir."

"Don't worry!" the Indian said. His compassion was real, for he was descended from POWs too. In October, 1838, the U.S. Army had invaded the Cherokee lands in Georgia, had told the Cherokees, "Hasten," had herded them like the buffalo onto the Trail of Tears, the wind was whining, the snow was blinding, the old men, women and children dying, his own great-great-great-grandfather comforting them, the Cherokees going eight hundred miles to Oklahoma, the birthplace of Captain Bushyhead, U.S. Army. "No, we're Americans," the Indian told the Iraqi.

"Please thank you, sir."

"No problem!" the Indian said. "We got a leg wound!" he radioed now, and a chopper took an Iraqi away. "No, take that off

him!" he shouted, and a boy took a red-and-white blindfold off an
Iraqi. "Hey! Knock that off! It humiliates them!" he ordered, and
a boy put down a candid camera that he had aimed at the Iraqis.
"Don't do it," the Indian reconsidered, "unless the Iraqis don't see
you. *Hahaha!*" he suddenly roared, then he went fifty paces, turned,
took out his Instamatic ("Smile, goddammit!" he'd said at the
Wall) and when the Iraqis didn't see him, *snap!* he did the you-
push-the-button bit and Kodak would do the rest.

At noon the Iraqis, a crowd of Mexicans after a long, hard
day at the vines, were driven to Saudi, and C like CNN corre-
spondents took out its tape recorders to communicate this to its
wives, brides and girls in America. "We got prisoners, babe," a
boy announced in a Sony. "They all got smiles, got smiles," he
continued inventively. "They're gonna get food now, and that's all
they care about, bye-bye." In fact, about half the Iraqis were still
in their trenches waiting for C, and now the army started to reason
with them. For thirty minutes, C heard the *boom*s of the bombs,
the bomblets in fire-tailed rockets, the ten thousand, count 'em!
cannon rounds, it seemed as if giants were on the desert railing at
one another by means of enormous tom-toms, *We're better than you!
No, you're not!* and C in its tanks, its plugs in its ears, said, "Jesus
fuckin' Christ! They," the Iraqis, "must be hatin' it," and announced in its Sonys, "You can listen, babe." At 2:45 C's solemn
captain said, "Three, two, one," and C turned its motors on. A
driver stared at the KIM, SHELLEY, MOM he had scratched on his
hatch to look at while dying. A gunner, tears in his eyes, stared at
his two-year-old, three-year-old, and adoring wife: a photo on his
cannon barrel, and told them, "I love you. Goodbye," and Russell
stared at a photo of Tom, his black-eyed (due to the flashbulb) son.
"Gentlemen," the captain radioed. "Be careful. We pose a greater
hazard to ourselves than he," an Iraqi, "does." An engineer thought

of his wife in Kansas, he'd met her at a poetry class, she'd recently sent him a poem by Thomas Campion. She had taped it and he'd often played it,

> *The man whose silent days*
> *In harmless joys are spent,*
> *Whom hopes cannot delude,*
> *Nor sorrows discontent . . .*

"We go about five miles an hour," the captain radioed now.

> *That man needs neither towers*
> *Nor armor for defense,*
> *Nor secret vaults to fly*
> *From thunder's violence . . .*

"Good luck, fellas, shoot to kill," the captain radioed.

> *He only can behold*
> *With unaffrighted eyes*
> *The horrors of the deep*
> *And terrors of the skies.*

"God bless you all," the captain radioed—*arrr!* he rolled out and C rolled beside him.

Russell went fastest: ten mph, for he was leading all A, B, C, D to the horrors and terrors ahead. At dawn today the Samoan, his gunner, the boy who believed in "Thou shalt not kill," had finally told him, "I'm not gonna shoot at Iraqis," the Samoan's voice like a phonograph record a thumb was on, "Iii'm nooot gonna shooot," and Russell had told him, "Okay," for he'd thought the Samoan meant "I'll let them surrender, instead." Ahead, the sand looked like Ralston, wet from the rain, and as Russell rolled over it, half a league, half a league onward, it seemed to be *steaming,* seemed to be *smoking,* and Russell deduced that the chemical corps was now in Iraq making smokescreens, but Russell couldn't see the Iraqis either, them or their berms, ditches, wires, even sand, and his commanders couldn't see *him* in all the Svengali smoke. "Go slow!" one commander cried, and as his driver, at one mph, avoided the mother of all rear-enders and as his own cannon vanished, a wing in a cumulus cloud, the commander radioed, "We can't see shit!"

"Cease smoke!" the Indian radioed.

"The smoke is blowin' into us!"

"Cease smoke!" the Indian radioed, the chemical corps laid off, the cloud drifted off and lo! in front of Russell there were no berms, ditches, wires, for he had apparently done an end run around them on Valentine's Day, but there was an Iraqi trench. Russell shot into it left to right like a man with a garden hose, but he didn't hit any Iraqis, for none were there. A boy threw grenades but the Indian radioed, "Stop it! There may be chemicals there!" that's what the POWs had said, and the Indian radioed, "Get the Ace." A dozer, bulldozer, its blade of estate-gate size, appeared, and an engineer drove it along the Iraqi trench. In front of the dozer the sand spilled down, and in back there emerged a flat, barren, innocent desert.

By now the rest of C was rolling by Russell, rooting up Iraqi mines, shooting at Iraqis ahead: but Russell stayed put, for he'd done his job. At the officers club in Kansas once, he'd watched a practice attack on Iraq: a lieutenant had charged through the club, the bridge chairs falling, officers fleeing, but at one purple chair he'd stopped, he'd stood there like Mr. Clean as four more lieutenants charged past him, and Russell today was Mr. Clean, for the rest of C passed him and Russell just "overwatched" it. He relaxed. He discovered that he wasn't dead, and he reflected that he might survive this war and see Tom. Night after night in Saudi he'd worn a Walkman and listened to Tanya Tucker, to *Would You Lay,*

> *Would you go away*
> *To another land?*

Walk a thousand miles
Through the burning sand?

and he'd wept when he thought of Tom, far away in Texas. In his diary he'd written to Tom, "I can't wait to see you, son," "I can't wait to see you, son," "I love you, son, and I'll see you," and today he almost believed it. He felt he'd been in an electric chair and a governor had said, "I might pardon you." He decided that if he survived he'd go to Texas every, no, *twice* every month, in summer he'd go in June or July, he'd stay with Tom at the air force base, no, the Holiday Inn, go hunting or fishing with him, and if Tom's mother and Tom's pseudo father refused, well, Russell would get the best lawyers for $10,000, $20,000, get DNA tests and say, "Your Honor, I am Tom's father," would fight for Tom as he'd fought for Tom in Iraq. Was this the best thing for Tom? *Of course,* Russell thought.

He checked his Casio. The time now was 1515, was 3:15. His body was in his tank, his shoulders were out, his thumbs on his wicked machine gun. His eyes were on C but his mind was on Tom and on what he'd write in Tom's diary,

Well son! It's been one busy day. . . .

One mile ahead, the rest of C, its plows in the sand like bulldozer blades, its captain carefully saying, "At *my* command. Three, two, one. Fire," its cannons responding, *boom!* was closing on the Iraqis. So far C was uninjured, undead, but it wasn't happy now, for Burns was now jamming its Walkmans. The man had been strict in Saudi, but C felt that he was now stiff as the stern-faced leaders in *Dying to Meet You,* the music by Judas Priest,

{We're} led to positions
By stern-faced leaders
Who never let one smile
Depart from their face.

"Be careful. Be careful," said Burns, Nervous Nellie, Worrywart Willie, on C's crackling radios now, and his voice was a drizzle on C's little picnic. Was someone in C going faster than five mph? "Slow down," said Burns. Was someone in C going teenily, weenily, off his course? "Don't cut in front of me, man," said Burns. Was there a dirt road in front of C? "Stay the hell off it. It could be mined," said Old Mister Party Poop. Were there any—*eek*— any anthills in front of C? "I don't know what these are but they could be mines," said Burns, who didn't seem to understand he was pissing off C, which didn't think it needed a six-foot-two mom (a mom with a mustache) to tell it, "Do this. Do that." "We're getting a little too cocky," said Burns. "So slow down and think about what life and death is about. . . ."

Oh, how C hated him! Burns, C felt, was acting as if some strings in his fingers led to each soldier in C: to puppets, to baggy-legged sacks of straw that he either jerked or they wouldn't dance. C didn't see that Burns was obsessed, *obsessed,* with the life of each soldier in C, that he'd have felt reckless if he'd said nothing but *"Charge."* At five fussy mph he got to a trench with Iraqis in it, C used machine guns to "hose" it and the bulldozer blade to erase it, he then went another quarter-mile and, to conform to the intricate lines on the colonel's map of Iraq, did a 180: a left about, and he attacked the Iraqis from behind. *"We* are confused," the colonel had told him in Saudi, "so let's confuse the enemy, too," and C was now rolling south, *arrr?* its cannons pointed at Russell and Russell's cannons at C. "This is the shittiest part," the colonel had said, this was an invitation for friendly fire, for C inadvertently shooting at C, and the colonel had candidly said, "I hope it works." In fact, C had already shot at its buddies today. Ten minutes earlier, it had shot in Russell's direction, *boom!* it had missed a sergeant, a boy who'd promptly radioed, "I'm receivin' fire!"

"Goddammit! Shift fire!" a second sergeant had radioed.

"Shift left?" the Indian had asked them.

"No! They need to shift right! They're firin' right at me!"

"Roger," the Indian had said, then he'd appealed to Captain Burns and Burns had told C, "Be *careful.*" And now, all his cannons aiming at Russell's, a lot of Iraqis between them, and (hey, enough's enough) the colonel's radio out and the colonel incommunicado, the finical captain of C was especially finical. *"Please,"* said Old Mister Fuddy-Duddy. "Verify targets, particularly looking south."

C only groaned. "Now everyone shit," a boy in C grumbled, though not on C's open radios. "No, you have to shit orientin' east, no, you aren't shittin' right, no . . ."

It was almost inevitable. At about 4:20 a round landed right in the midst of C. It landed ahead of Burns's tank, Burns saw the yellow flash, heard the *boom!* felt the blast on his goggles, and Burns's driver, the boy who'd kissed the little girl's hand and said, "I'm in love with her too," said, "Sir! There's a round landing there!"

"I saw that," said Burns in an I'm-in-control-here tone. "Don't worry. It's our own mortars," meaning that the mortars were "softening up" the Iraqis ahead of C. Then *boom!* a round landed at Burns's left, and Burns's driver said, "Jesus Christ! Sir, that was damn close!"

"Don't worry," said Burns, and he radioed the number-two man in C: the executive officer, an unobtrusive lieutenant whose name was Light. "Tell the mortars lift fire," said Burns. "It's comin' in close."

"Roger," the XO, executive officer, standing up in his tank, replied, and he tuned to another channel. "Cease firing the mortars," the XO said.

"The mortars aren't firing," a boy on the XO's radio said. "Not for ten minutes now."

"Roger," the XO said. He got back on channel number one but Burns was already on it.

"*Please,*" Burns was telling him, and Burns's voice was like acid now, for the pressure that all of C felt didn't burst out of Burns, it just dripped, "*please* do that quickly, I'm *tired* of getting shot at."

"The mortars aren't firing," the XO said.

Burns didn't remonstrate with him. Burns, if anyone, knew he was under mortar fire, and he radioed the mortar commander himself. "Are you firing?" said Burns.

"No, we aren't firing."

"Well—" Burns began.

And *boom!* a round landed in back of Burns. His driver felt like in Ohio when he'd been drinking and driving and *waaaaa!* the cops had been chasing him, and his gunner felt like in Missouri when *he'd* been drinking and driving and *craaash!* done a Chappaquiddick, crashing into the Jack's Fork River. He'd almost drowned, but he'd never told his mother, and he was thinking now, *Damn! Lift those mortars!* and also was thinking, *I'll never tell Mom!* Meanwhile, Burns, who was looking to the north, east, south and west for the source of the *boom boom boom,* had a sudden insight: the mortar rounds might not be made in the U.S.A.

"We're takin' *enemy* mortar rounds," he radioed to C. "Back up," he said to his driver, and the driver rapidly did. In seconds they were safe, but the driver and gunner were furious at Burns, who'd often told them, "We are our own worst enemies," but who'd forgotten that the Iraqis were enemies too—the Iraqis who'd tried to kill them while he was frostily telling them, "Don't worry." *Jesus,* the driver and gunner thought, a guy can die here because of Burns! And even Medine, loyal Medine, who was Burns's loader, who'd slept with no cot, no blanket, no sleeping bag, no food but a can of Mott's Apple Sauce as he'd hitchhiked to C and to Captain Burns ("Don't think we forgot you," said Burns, almost showing emotion)—even Medine thought the name of this tank should be *Three Men and a Baby* and not *Saint George.* He thought of the sergeant who'd told him, "I will say *Gizmo,*" who'd told him to duck as C opened fire on Captain Burns, and Medine thought, *Well, I wouldn't blame 'em.*

The mortars stopped and C started rolling west. It continued to shoot at Iraqis, this time from their flanks, and the boy in the dozer continued to bury them instantly—sometimes, in fact, before they were dead. In the *Coke Whore* the black lieutenant, who, in the past, had hollered that the Iraqis were towel-headed motherfuckers, that C shouldn't shilly-shally with them, that, no, "We should fuckin' slaughter 'em," and (to the beat of *The Power,* by Snap) that *he* would do murder and mayhem on 'em,

> *Maniac, brainiac,*
> *Winner of the game,*
> *I am the tanker*
> *Who will maim—*

the lieutenant was using binoculars when five hundred meters ahead an Iraqi rose like a paper target, waving something white, and the lieutenant hollered, "I'm goin' to get this guy!" In spite of all prior hollers, he meant that he'd capture, not slaughter, the man, but in the gloom below him the gunner, the boy who'd made love to Miss Dippity-Do, Sergeant Spence, now saw the Iraqi and thought, *No, I'll kill him.* Spence hated all the Iraqis, who'd dragged him from Kansas, but, even more, he thought he'd return to Kansas, strut into Bushwacker Bar, and tell all the *heyyy*-saying girls, "We got the first kill, we are *baaad* motherfuckers," *the girls will look up to me,* Spence thought. But then the lieutenant told him, "Don't shoot!"

The black lieutenant wasn't the sum of his *fucker*s and *fuckin'*s. The 'hood he was from was Ohio, his father was an air controller

in Dayton, and his full name was Bennie James McRae III. He'd
gone to college at Bowling Green, his major was English Literature,
he'd read his *The Secret Agent*, his *Moby-Dick*, his *Richard III*, he'd
recited his *Canterbury Tales,*

> *At nyght were come into that hostelrye*
> *Wel nyne and twenty in a compaignye,*

and his words had Ohio accents, *compaignye* like in Company C.
But every day his King's English had been challenged at Phi Beta
Sigma, the black fraternity house, where the brothers got "buzzed"
on Bud and got "back" from the kickin' flygirls: the good-looking
girls at Zeta Phi Beta. The not-yet-lieutenant might say "It's good"
when he evidently meant "It's baaad," and the brothers would scold
him, "Oh, nigga, you a *banana*," a banana was colored but not
inside, until by his senior year he was as kickin' as all twenty brothers at Sigma. And now in Iraq he was fluent in Basic Black but
still was a conscientious kid from Ohio: he wasn't kill-crazy, he'd
prefer it if abracadabra, all the Iraqis would disappear, would turn
to a puddle of butter, oleo, oil. Or would surrender like the Iraqi
five hundred meters ahead.

"Don't shoot!" the lieutenant hollered and Spence (who himself had decided, *I shouldn't kill him*) didn't hit the buttons under
his thumbs, and the Iraqi ran toward them. So did three others,
and the lieutenant radioed-hollered to Captain Burns, "There's
more comin'!"

"Okay. Be cool," said Burns.

"Somethin's flappin'!" the lieutenant hollered. "A white handkerchief!"

"Okay. Be cool," said Burns.

"Roger!" the lieutenant hollered: oh, he just *loved* to holler,
but he was cucumber cool and told himself, *Be alert, an Iraqi may
blow himself up.* He put his hand up: *halt!* like a traffic policeman,
and the Iraqis stopped, then he bowed on his tank like an Arab
praying, and the Iraqis fell on the sand salaaming. "We have them

down on the ground!" he hollered to Burns. "Their heads are covered!" meaning "Their hands are on top of their heads." "They're on their knees! They're twenty meters away! I got the main gun on 'em! Over!"

"Okay. Be cool, I'm coming," said Burns, and far from concluding that the Iraqis, confronting a ten-foot cannon and a gargantuan gob of TNT, were under control, he *arrr!* he came roaring up. Climbing out, Burns and the black lieutenant went to the Iraqi worshipers, Iraqis with palms together, chins on their chests, *please don't kill us,* but Burns wasn't taking risks and he took his Beretta out. At that the Iraqis started wailing, concluding that Burns meant to execute them.

"Speak English?" said Burns, and one Iraqi nodded. "You," said Burns, pointing at the Iraqi, "tell," pointing at Burns's own mouth, "them," pointing at the other three men. "You tell them: No harm."

"Harm?" the Iraqi said.

"You're safe."

"Safe?" the Iraqi said.

"Yes."

One foot away, the lieutenant squatted, staring into the Iraqi's eyes. Back in Ohio he'd often stared at his miniature schnauzer and said, "Hey, Button. How are you doin'? You happy today? You sad?" and he stared at this brown-eyed man as he'd stared at Button. The man was thirty or so. His eyes were wide with fear, and the lieutenant sensed that he had a home like *him,* wanted to be there like *him,* was out on this desert like *him—my God,* the lieutenant thought. *This motherfucker is someone like me. He's human.*

"You tell them: You're safe," said Burns.

"You're safe?"

"Roger," said Burns, and the lieutenant climbed back on his tank amazed, though he didn't show it. "If he," the lieutenant said to his crew, referring to Captain Burns—"if he told that guy, 'Suck my dick,' the guy would repeat it." The crew laughed, a boy took away the Iraqis, in the trenches were more Iraqis, dead, the boy with the dozer buried them, sand unto sand, r.i.p., and as Burns climbed onto his tank to radio to C, "Now don't become complacent," *arrr!* the astonished lieutenant drove off.

S ay this for Burns: at sunset no one in C was scratched, though other boys in the area who'd felt the Iraqi mortar rounds or Iraqi mines were bleeding, becoming blind, dying. At sunset C stopped, ate its MREs, rolled out its sleeping bags, and in the chilly drizzle curled up like larvae in the soft, snuggly bags. C wasn't safe yet, for to its west were more Iraqis and all around were Iraqi mines, and half of C was awake looking for Iraqis (ten o'clock, twelve o'clock, two: the eyes of the boys were warm butterballs) and listening to C's droning radios, "Radio check," "I hear you." One understands, but a number of sentries fell asleep, among them the boy who'd said, "I don't wanna *demoralize* her," who'd smoked his Dorals in the *Coke Whore* a foot from the TNT, and who now was awakened by Sergeant Spence. "You better fuckin' wake up," Spence told him at reveille, four o'clock, shoving an elbow into him. "And wake up the others, too," and the boy, the fattest in C, climbed off the *Coke Whore*. He started to walk—well, waddle, as if he were chafing and he hadn't talcumed himself—to the still-sleeping half of C as Spence on the *Coke Whore* muttered, "The motherfucker."

"The fat stinkin' motherfucker," the black lieutenant agreed. "If I see him sleepin' again I'm kickin' his ass off this fuckin' tank in the middle of this fuckin' war. And if—" BOOM! The lieutenant was startled, for there was a thunderous BOOM! as sudden as a sonic boom, and the lieutenant cried, "Incoming mortars!" Somewhere the fat boy was screaming, and the lieutenant cried, "What's wrong, motherfucker?"

"Help! Help!"

"What's wrong?"

"I need help!" The lieutenant couldn't see, but the boy was lying on the ground sixty feet from the *Coke Whore*. A moment ago he'd been walking along when BOOM! he'd seen a bright light like a strobe, had flown through the air, and had hit the ground. *"Oh shit!"*

The noise woke up Specialist Young. He'd been asleep in his drizzle-resistant tank, but he now jumped up, and, his head out the hatch, he heard the hubbub and thought, *It's Kostic,* was PFC Kostic, his pool-playing pal at the Klub Kamille and his best friend in C. "Help me! I stepped on a fuckin' mine!" said Kostic, then added equivocally, "Don't come here! There's fuckin' mines!"

Not even thinking, Young chose to help him. "Give me the fuckin' aid bag!" Young shouted to his commander, *shouted,* he had just woken up and hadn't put on his trumpet mute, his voice for a moment wasn't as flat as Iraq. "I'm comin'!" he shouted to Kostic.

"Help!"

"No, you can't go. There's mines," said Young's commander.

"Help!"

"I ain't gonna step on the fuckin' mines!" shouted Young.

"No, stay where you are!" said Kostic. *"Help!"*

Young had predicted this. In Kansas when Young had gazed into the pitcher of Bud, he had foreseen that one of the ten dead, forty wounded, soldiers in C would be Kostic, "He's going to lose it," Young had divined, "he's losing it even now." Even in Saudi, Kostic had lost his gas mask *twice,* and often he'd gotten orders and said, "I won't do it." Kostic was loader for Sergeant Spence, who hated him and, one day in Saudi, had even reported him for pissing into an empty bottle of Al-Ghadir.

"I *told* him," said Kostic, defending himself to C's first sergeant, "that I have a bladder problem, which, when I've got to go, I've got to go then and there, and I *told* him——"

"You piss in a bottle?" the first sergeant had said.

"I piss in a bottle but *he*——"

"I piss in a bottle too," the judicious first sergeant had said to Spence—to Spence who at four in the morning now was going on tiptoe in Iraq, his feet in his flashlight light, his feet doing detours around the pebbles, the anthills, the tiny twig piles, his feet more or less debating, *no, here's where the mine is, no, here,* then wavering in midair like the hands of a hesitant gambler, *no, I'll bet on 12, no, 24,* then (light as a spider) dropping onto the hazardous sand as Spence, who was nearer than Young, progressed to the night-shrouded source of *"Help!"*

His loathing for Kostic was nowhere in Spence's mind. It had just—*disappeared,* like the sines and cosines he had once learned in school, and he was thinking, *Oh God! When I get there what will I see? A leg off? A stump where the leg used to be?* Spence had gone sixty feet when, by his flashlight, he saw the screaming boy sitting, his right foot on top of his left one, his right boot a bag of blood and bones, and he said to Kostic, "It's not that bad," and patted him on his shoulder.

"It hurts!" Kostic cried.

"The medics are on their way. Stay still."

"All right!" Kostic cried. He was thinking, *Why me?* but also was thinking, *I'm glad that it's me,* if Young had been out on this drizzling night it might have been *him,* his best buddy, and Kostic was thinking of Young's close call as a red-crossed vehicle came and as Spence and the medics carried him on. "The pain! The pain!" Kostic cried. A medic injected some morphine but Kostic cried, "I know I'm a pussy, but I need more!"

"No, you're not a pussy. You're doin' real good."

"Oh God! Oh God! I need cigarettes!" Kostic cried, and Spence jumped onto the tank, reached in, and tossed him down his Dorals. The medics turned the motor on, Kostic still cried, "It hurts! It hurts!" and thought, *It'll hurt forever,* and he rolled into the darkness to—where? No one in C was told.

Spence thought, *One loader down. Who's next?* and Young was now pondering too. Young was upset by this accident and by his own response, the shout of "Give me the aid bag" that had roared out of him like out of Pandora's box, and he wondered how he could report this to Mouse, his unblushing bride in Kansas. The previous day he'd taken his ballpoint pen and written,

> *Dear Karen,*

for Mouse didn't like it if Young said *Karen,*

> *I bet you can't guess where I am. Well, we punched a hole in Saddam's defenses—*

but Young had thought no, the letter had less-than-zero emotion, it was as flat as "Please pass me a Pepsi, dear," he'd torn it up and this morning he started again. He didn't write, "It happened to Kostic, next it could happen to me," for Young didn't believe this, he was a competent loader and Kostic wasn't, competent people didn't step on mines, but Young took his pen and wrote,

> *Dear Karen,*
> *Frank blew his foot off. We shouldn't be getting hurt this soon. We are doing things totally fucking wrong. We—*

No no no. Young tore the page from the pad, the gloom-and-doom-loaded sentences weren't for Mouse. But what sort of sentences were? Still thinking, Young took an MRE and used a Swiss pocket knife to cut the shiny brown bag. He took out the brown bag of entree (of omelet, or tuna with noodles, or pork with rice: he wasn't watching) and, as always, put it on top of the grill at the back of the tank that the engine exhaust came out of. He turned on the engine, and, as the food warmed up on his $3,500,000 range, he thought he might write to Mouse, "Well, Frank was taken away," no, "Well, God knows where Frank is," no, he thought and thought and at six in the morning, dawn, he still hadn't written her, "Dear."

At six C started shooting. C was again at full strength, for as though completing a scorecard, *slash,* a hit for the visiting team, the first sergeant had written a W, meaning wounded, at Kostic's name in his Doomsday Book and had radioed to Personnel, and a PFC from Nebraska (Kostic was from California) was the new loader in C. And now C shot at Iraqis, *boom,* all of C did but Specialist Gebert, the boy who'd married into the War Resisters and who now shot inadvertently at the American MPs. Gebert for months hadn't heard from his bride, her father, her mother, he hadn't gotten a letter, a card, a "Wish you were here," he'd phoned them in Texas and gotten a *"Ring ring ring."* He'd become worried. He'd dreamt he was on the desert and the first sergeant told him, "Your wife is dead and you'll be in Saudi forever," and he'd sat up in his sleeping bag saying, "No!" What happened to Gebert's confounded mail?

"I bet there's an Arab," a sergeant had told him, "and *Gebert* is the Arabic word for *The hell with Allah,* and when the Arab sees your mail he burns it."

"Well, I'm goin' down to Riyadh," Gebert had seethed, "and I'm gonna aim the cannon at Schwarzkopf," at General Schwarzkopf, the Allied commander, "and I'm gonna tell him, 'I want my fuckin' mail!' "

"Why don't you write to Any Civilian, Any Post Office, U.S.A," the sergeant had suggested, "and tell him, 'Please write me'?"

Gebert had smiled, but he'd become anxious, also he'd lost his sleeping bag and was sleeping in the sentries' bags: in musical sleeping bags, and he was the groggiest boy in C. At seven, at sunrise, his cannon was pointing south at a group of MPs and Gebert was sitting amid his wires, cables, circuits and switches, his hand on his red master blaster, his master trigger. In front of him on a gold chain was half of a coin, a Christmas gift from the dead? unconscious? unloving? girl he was married to. It was the left half, which said,

THE

WATCH

THEE A

EVEN W

ARE A.

The girl herself had the right half, which said,

LORD

OVER

ND ME

HEN WE

PART,

and when, in Texas, Gebert and the gentle girl had put the two halves together, they'd had a golden quote from Genesis 31:49,

THE LORD

WATCH OVER

THEE AND ME

EVEN WHEN WE

ARE APART.

At seven o'clock in Iraq today, Gebert was resting his hand on his red master blaster when *boom!* the cannon went off and a round whistled toward the MPs.

And *boom!* it fell short. It didn't hit the MPs, but a mile away the colonel of A, B, C, D was master-blaster red. "What's going on?" he yelled on his radio, which was working again, and he raced across the desert to Gebert. On his arrival, he didn't yell at that specialist but at his tolerant sergeant, a man who hoped to retire

in June, to buy some plum trees in Tennessee, and to make mountain dew on his $975 pension—he also yelled at Lieutenant Russell
and at the Cherokee captain, saying, "Goddammit! Someone is going to get *killed* here!" The colonel, like Captain Burns, believed
that C's worst enemy was C.

It clearly wasn't the Iraqis. By eight o'clock all the Iraqis who
weren't in POW camps were dead, even buried, or, in their tanks, were
on the road north to fight another day, and C could scarcely believe it:
C was now camped in Castle Iraq, its mission completely accomplished.
The ground war was one day old and C (and the other companies) had
created a ten-mile breach that now, with the mightiest *arrr!* the sound
of ten thousand horses, the rest of America's army (and Britain's, too)
was rolling through. "It was easy," a commander in C announced. "It
was like the Pistons playin'—" He thought, but he didn't know a bad
enough team in the NBA. "Playin' a high school team."

"Yeah," a gunner put in. "Like the 49ers playin'—" The
gunner thought too. "A *junior* high school team," he announced,
then he and the commander high-fived, their hands in their gloves
going *slap!* like a swatter on a bothersome fly.

"Yeah," the happy commander said. "We're goin' home!"

If wishes were horses. C didn't know it, but at this moment
there was a meeting in Saudi, and the generals learned that they
still had a Big Red One. It still was alive, they could tell it, "Go
here," "Go there," and from their files they pulled a fat contingency plan. The top page said SECRET, then it said something
suggestive of God's awful words in the Bible, in Jeremiah, "Behold,
I will punish the king of Babylon. I am against thee, O thou most
proud. . . ." The top page said OPERATION JEREMIAH.

Not knowing this, C didn't do something sensible: *sleep,*
but sat and told stories about the war. On *Crusading for Christ* it
listened enchanted to Sergeant James, who preached to it of God's

power. "I woke up," said James, referring to one night earlier, "and God was mentionin' to me, 'Read the Word,' and I told Him, 'Lord, I don't want to read right now,' and He kept mentionin', 'Read the Word,' and He took me to Second Kings," and James then opened his Bible to II Kings 7:5, the four lepers versus the Syrian army. At James's church in Virginia the preacher had shouted that God had made scary sounds, "It sound like a *horse*, it sound like a *buzzard*, when God get started translatin', *God!!!* know how to do it!" He'd shouted that, to the Syrians, the lepers had sounded like the Egyptian army and lo! the Syrians had fled! and James was also inspired today. He read to some soldiers in C,

And when they,

the lepers,

were come to the uttermost part of the camp of Syria, behold, there was no man there,

and James said, "Well, that's what happen' to *us!* We got to Three-Niner Kilo," to the first trench in Iraq, "and there was no Iraqis there, the Iraqis was gone! Now that was the doin' of God!"

The boys in C nodded. "You say what my grandmama does," said one, who now thought of coming to Christ.

"Your grandmama's right," said James, then, looking up, he saw the black lieutenant approaching. The boy, the worst sinner in C, was taking the route of a drunken sailor, zigging and zagging, walking on top of the tank tracks lest, by straying to unspoiled sand, he'd hit an Iraqi mine like Kostic and, who knew? get his foot fragged, leg amputated, die. The lieutenant veered to his left, right, left, like a checker becoming a king, till he came to James and said, "Well, that was fucked up. About Kostic."

"No, that was a blessing," said James, somewhat Pangloss-ically. "We *all* had been walkin' aroun', it could've been *all* of us."

"It could've been me," the lieutenant agreed. He didn't shout it: he sighed it as if reciting it in Ohio in English Literature. The previous day, he'd heard the anthill alerts, "I got some anthills," "It looks like anthills," "There's twenty anthills," he'd even seen the anthills himself, little dunes in front of the *Coke Whore,* and he'd thought, *Yes. They look like mines.* On his tank there wasn't a plow but on James's there was, and he'd almost said to James, "Go first," then he'd remembered that James had a daughter, son, that Specialist Penn on James's tank had a son a month old, *the kid'll be needin' his dad,* the lieutenant had thought, *and if Penn—oh, fuck it,* and the lieutenant had told his own driver, "Go forward." The anthills were anthills, apparently: that or the scars of American rounds, but as his tank flattened them, he'd known he could die, and from what happened to Kostic he knew he could die even now in Mission Accomplished Land.

If he died then he'd go to heaven—*not.* Even in Kansas, James had said, "Sir, you're goin' to hell," and the lieutenant had laughed and said, "Yeah, I'm goin' and I'm takin' over!" but hell had a certain immediacy now, and he had been brooding about it. Hell, Hades, Pandemonium: the lieutenant didn't know where it was, it lay in the fourth dimension perhaps, just past the end of outer space, but he knew what was *in* it: an ocean, the water was lava, the flames were a flaming ammo dump, were *Apocalypse Now,* and in this lava, treading, were millions of people like him. And *splaaash!* the lava rolled over them, over *him,* he went under, was ten feet down, in his mouth was a sizzling fire, *don't panic,* he paddled up, up, *oh, God, I can't breathe,* he surfaced and saw the Nazis, the Arabs of the Middle Ages, the Romans who'd crucified the Lord, all bobbing and burning and *splaaash!* he was drowning again, *oh, God,* he'd be here forever, be here in the year 1,000,000, and he'd been brooding and, yes, considering coming to Christ as, zigging and zagging, he'd come up to James.

James may have sensed it. "Do you think if Kostic dies," James said, "that he'll go to heaven or hell?"

"I don't know. I don't know if Kostic's saved," the pensive lieutenant said. "I know that if *I* died, I'd go to hell."

"Why's that?"

"Cause I'm bad. I'm always cussin' and God wouldn't want me."

"No, God will forgive any sin. Except," said James homiletically, "if you murder yourself—if you murder yourself, that's it."

"That's true," the lieutenant said.

"Jesus forgave Mary Magdalene," James went on. "She had the seven devils, but she kneeled at Jesus feet, and Jesus," and as this pastor went on, went on, the lieutenant decided that yes, a sinner would go to hell but a Christian like James was already there.

"So what does the radio say?" the lieutenant interrupted.

"It says Saddam says, 'The war's goin' just as I planned.' "

"Oh, yeah!" the lieutenant laughed. "He planned to get his *ass* kicked!" The lieutenant didn't come to Christ but James thought, *He's still a Christian, he's bein' rebell'us, he'll come aroun'.* The drizzle intensified, the lieutenant walked off, and James saw him do his damnedest not to drop into the bottomless pit: saw him zig, zag, and walk on the tank tracks until *hallelujah,* he climbed safe and sound on the *Coke Whore.*

"Guidons!" At four in the afternoon the colonel went on the radio to A, B, C, D. On another channel, he had just talked to the full "bird" colonel, who'd talked to the two-star general, who'd talked to the wooden-legged three-star, who'd talked to the four-star in Riyadh, Saudi Arabia, and the colonel of A, B, C, D had learned of Operation Jeremiah. "We're moving!" he radioed now and C, which still hadn't slept during this R&R, this Rest and Recreation vacation, wasn't upset, it was raring to go on behalf of PFC Kostic. A day ago Kostic had been an Honorary Iraqi, a boy the captain had said to, "Bluntly, I think you're borderline," but C was a band of brothers now: the Iraqis had hurt one and the

Iraqis must pay. As C saddled up (as C filled its gas tanks, cleaned out its filters) it didn't quite say, "Let's win one for PFC Kostic," but one commander said, "It's time for our payback now," and his crew, climbing on, said it was time to turn on the lasers, get the Iraqis' range, and shoot the Iraqis. "Hell, yeah!" said C. "Let's lase and blaze!"

And *arrr!* At five o'clock C rolled out. As it did, it saw something surrealistic, like a scene in a Swedish movie. In the drizzle were four Americans, the wind made their ponchos go *whap!* as if they were condors taking off, the four people stood in a circle like in a solemn ritual, where are we? at Stonehenge? who are they? the Druids? and in their hands in white cotton gloves they held a lot of white papers that like a jury's verdicts, *guilty, guilty, guil—* they somberly passed around. In their midst, where the altar would be, was a black plastic bag, it also went *whap whap whap!* and on top in wet camouflage clothes there lay an American boy. The boy didn't move. He was dead, very dead, his face was so pale that, to look at, he must have been dead all his life, hadn't been in this grand invasion or even the Klub Kamille, raising a Bud, saying, *"Whoo."* In fact, he'd just died today, the target of friendly fire: his own, for against regulations he'd picked up a little white ovoid that lay in Iraq like an Easter egg: an American bomblet, American dud. To see what's inside it, he'd cracked it (an egg on a frying pan) smartly against a tank, and *boom!* he'd lost his hands and half his face, then someone had radioed but, in the rain clouds, the red-crossed chopper couldn't find him. The boy was in A, the black captain's company, but a sergeant in C had sent up a flare and had radioed frantically, "Do you see the red flare?"

"Negative," the helicopter pilot had said.

"Do you see the orange one? Do you see the white one? Do you—" But all thirty flares had entered the clouds like candles being blown out, and in a whisper someone had radioed, "You don't need him now."

"We don't need him?"

"Roger. We no longer need you," the boy had radioed, and

now, an hour later, as C started rolling to Basra? to Baghdad? the secret target of Operation Jeremiah, one of the Druidlike people knelt at the black plastic bag and, in his white gloves, *zip!* he zipped it, and six soldiers lifted it (three on the left, three on the right, like a pallbearer party) and as the soldiers sank in the mud they carried the cumbersome bag to one of C's hummers. They put it inside by some duffel bags, then they got a second bag and a second dead boy, one who'd been watching the egg-breaking one, and a sergeant in C went south with the casualties as the rest of C, not talking, just thinking, *One day old. The war's only one day old,* went north.

Iraq:
The Battle

★

The sun set, the moon rose, and in its light the sand of Iraq was like snow, *jingle jingle,* a person almost heard the sleighs. The fog was almost romantic, but in spite of the night sights (the $10,000 sights) the drivers couldn't see the Easter eggs till *boom!* they exploded innocuously and, like lightning, lit up the fog. At midnight C stopped. It was groggy but it didn't sleep, for the drizzle persisted and C had to scrunch in the hot, humid tanks, then at 3:30 it sat up, had MREs, turned on its motors, *arrr,* and at 5:30 continued north. By seven the drizzle was rain, the sun rose behind seven veils, the sky was a cardboard color, and the wet sand was like at low tide, but C rolled on.

At eight it saw an Iraqi, then twenty, then twenty more, then at 8:30 an army, advancing across the desert at C. Not shooting, the Iraqis were surrendering, waving things like the parachute parts of Iraqi flares. A few Iraqis had nothing white and C tossed them the *Jayhawk News,* an army newspaper, and the Iraqis, astonished that C hadn't slaughtered them, held up a "V" and a *Jayhawk News* and perhaps said in Arabic, "Extra! Extra! We surrender!" Not stopping, C shouted, *"Go south,"* but the Iraqis patted their lips like Indians going "Woo woo," and C, interpreting this as "We're hungry," tossed them a carton of MREs or, somewhat mischievously, a bag of MRE pork ("But that's against their religion, isn't it?" "Yeah!") or a bottle of Al-Ghadir or, with little regret, a Waha Natural Mango Drink, a tongue-numbing product of Saudi. As the food hit the sand, the Iraqis just dove on it, dove like on fumbled footballs, dove in front of C's roaring tanks, and *"Hey!"* the commanders shouted, *"watch out!"* The drivers swerved, the Iraqis stayed three-dimensional, and the commanders tossed them more MREs.

In time C was tossing out MREs as if it were fleeing from wolves. The bags of beef stew, chicken stew, of pears, peaches, applesauce, of maple cakes, cherry cakes, and even of Tootsie Rolls were C's letters to the Iraqis, "We didn't want to kill you, and now we don't have to. Thank you." C, as the colonel had said, was from the block and the barrio, and it had sympathy for the Iraqi unfortunates. One black commander who, as a boy, had more or less lived on biscuits dipped in molasses, his mother telling him, "Don' go stuffin' yourself," saw the Iraqis as people who but for the grace of God were *him,* and he asked his gunner, loader and driver, "Y'all want to give 'em the MREs?" His gunner, a Peruvian immigrant, remembered the people who'd told him, *"Dame dinero.* Give me some money. *Para comprar comida.* To buy some food," near the border of Ecuador. The loader remembered the people in Mexico, *"Yo tengo hambre.* I'm hungry," and the driver remembered someone at a McDonald's, "May I?" who'd snapped up the remnants of his Big Mac. All three soldiers said, "Yeah! Give 'em the MREs!" and tossed them until the commander showed the Iraqis his empty palms, meaning "I've nothing left."

One boy in C was weeping. When he was five, his parents had left him, and he was thinking of Saddam Hussein, *He left the Iraqis stone cold.* The boy, a medic, rode in a red-crossed vehicle that the Iraqis were herding around, patting their lips and, like Barbary pirates, trying to climb aboard, and the boy was Saint Bridget in his largess with his MREs. Weeping, he handed them out, but the Iraqis squabbled, cursed, and pulled the MREs from their buddies' pockets, and he had to pacify them by tossing more. At last someone in C said, "We'll be beggin' like *them,*" the driver accelerated, the Iraqis chased after him, and the saint tossed the last of his MREs, still weeping.

His conduct grated on C's oldest soldier: Grandpa, who rode in this vehicle too. Grandpa, a sergeant first class, a man with three chevrons, two rockers, had served since the 1960s, when the sergeants had *screamed* at the 'cruits like him. His own fat sergeant, wearing a Smokey-the-Bear hat, had once hit his chest on Grandpa's, then hit his *head* on Grandpa's, then hollered, "You dickhead! You fuckin' civilian!" and Grandpa had pulled out his genital organ and said, "Hey, *this* is a dick, do I look like this?" Ah, those were the days, Grandpa felt, but sergeants were scoutmasters now and privates like Saint Bridget gave meatballs in spicy tomato sauce to the Iraqis, going boo hoo. Grandpa couldn't take it: he glared at Bridget's tears and, like the sergeants of long ago or General Patton, hollered, *"You motherfucker!"* and cocked his hand back and slapped him. "These are your goddam *enemies,* man!"

The boy, who was black, said nothing.

"These," Grandpa hollered—*"these* are your fuckin' *enemies,* man!"* my God, he thought, what should a sergeant do? sew swastikas on the Iraqis' arms? hammers and sickles? stencil on the Iraqis' foreheads, "FUCK UNCLE SAM," tell Bridget, "Either we stop 'em or they'll be in Harlem," *how* should a sergeant motivate an Age of Aquarius boy? C, he believed, hadn't seen an Iraqi *soldier* yet, the Iraqis so far were fuckin' civilians, drafted in Kuba carpet bazaars, the *soldiers* were in the Republican Guards: the Tawalkana (or "Go with God") Division, the Saddam SS, the men who'd used gas in Iran and who C (the colonel had radioed) would be fighting tonight, *tonight,* today was no time to cry, baby, cry! "Your *enemies,"* said Grandpa, practically spelling it, *e-n-e,* the tips of his mustache twitching, but Bridget said nothing and Grandpa stopped hollering, thinking, *I can't prevent it. People in C gonna die.*

A ll that day C rolled north, C and other companies, battalions, brigades: one mighty division, the Big Red One, and other divisions, too: two thousand tanks like a space armada, unstoppably bound for the Death Star. All day the Easter eggs, like party poppers, went *boom!* they shredded some tires and vehicles hobbled along like in *Mother Courage,* but C went at Rommel velocity: at ten or more mph in a stop-sign-less, red-light-less, and cop-less environment, relentless as an uninterrupted hum. C became dopey and, to stop dozing, sang *The Star-Spangled Banner, God Bless America,* and *God Bless the U.S.A.,* or it listened to Walkmans and stirring things like *Have Mercy,* by Richard Marx,

> *We're laughing in the face of*
> *A loaded gun,*
> *But it won't be in the papers*
> *When the D-Day comes,*

but the day was warm, sixty-something, the tanks were hot, and C's heavy heads rolled forward till *bop!* they bounced on C's bulletproof vests.

The weather was a process in a mad chemist's flask. At first it rained, then in the sky appeared a weird circle, pale as a 40-watt bulb: the sun, then the scud disappeared and the swooping swallows were a reminder of Kansas, then like a slap in the face came a sandstorm, a gale from the south, and the empty brown bags of the MREs (the gifts to Iraqis) caught up to C, passed it, and hurried on, as if anxious to tell the Tawalkana Division, "C's coming." The wind then died, the yellow sun set, and a moon just a sliver short of a full moon rose, it was dead overhead at ten o'clock, a hole in a soot-black dome: a halo around it and, around that, an array of black, jagged-edged, sinister clouds like in old horror movies, bolts of white lightning (quiet as moonlight) dropping to C's black horizon. "I think that Allah is telling us something," someone said on C's radios.

C was still rolling, rolling. It was bone-tired, its drivers were falling asleep, meandering, almost colliding, its rattled commanders were crying, "Go left!" and "Go right!" and waking the wayward drivers up. C's tired captain, Burns, fell asleep, his loader shook him and Burns said, "Okay," and fell back asleep. The colo-

nel, commander of A, B, C, D, was worse than asleep: awake, for
he hadn't slept for forty hours and was thinking, *I'm dreaming,* for
to his right a tank was on fire, it glowed like a red-hot coal, its
cannon was on the sand but at intervals, *boom!* the rounds in the
tank exploded, *boom!* the tank was Iraqi but, to the colonel, it could
be one of the ones he'd dreamt of ("Alfa!" "Bravo!" "Charlie!").
The colonel didn't want to fight the Tawalkana, not tonight: he
still hadn't "softened it up" with mortars, cannons, and big fat
fuckers like at the Iraqi border. His soldiers had never rehearsed,
for the colonel didn't have a map of the Tawalkana's—*well, what?*
its trenches? its tunnels? its forts like the French Foreign Legion's?
The colonel didn't know where the Tawalkana exactly was, or
where the Americans to his right were, or where—*or who*—the
Americans to his left were, or, most perilously, if any Americans
were to his front, he could always say, "Fire!" but who would die?
The colonel didn't want to play blindman's bluff with the Tawalkana tonight.

No matter. The colonel had orders: *attack,* and at 10:30 he
radioed them to A, B, C, D. He said, "Okay, guys, good luck,"
and then on another channel radioed his full-colonel boss. "There's
lots of things about this I don't like," the colonel said dryly, "and
if I'm alive tomorrow I'd like to talk to you about them."

"Ditto, I don't like this," another lieutenant colonel radioed.

"You're right," the full colonel radioed back, "and if I'm alive
tomorrow we'll talk about it." He too had orders: the general,
sitting not in a tent but a tank, jolting along at ten mph, holding
a red-lensed flashlight, consulting a map so small that his fingertip
hid his 18,800 troops—the man had ordered a midnight-and-
moonlight attack on the Tawalkana, hoping to find it more confused than his own far-roaming, bone-tired boys.

By now C and everyone else were on a black desert called Al
Qarnain that C called Norfolk Objective, and, as C urinated there,
its pastor got an intriguing new message from God. "I know this
seems weird," said Sergeant James, "but He told me to do it," and
as his crew watched, he climbed to the top of his shadow-topped

tank, in a bag was a small plastic jar of oil, not motor but olive oil: the oil the preacher had blessed at the Church of Deliverance, in Kansas, and James took it out and climbed back in. "Hey, guys," he resumed, "I'm goin' to *anoint* you," and, opening the plastic jar, he dipped his middle finger in and painted a glossy cross on the gunner's, loader's, and driver's brows, saying, "In the name of Jesus." Then James led the three in their nightly prayer, saying, "We ask you to bless us, Jesus. We ask you to send us twelve legions of angels," that's 72,000 angels, he'd often explained, "to keep all hurtin' things from us. We ask you to bless our enemies, too," he continued, "to tell them that what they're doin' isn't right and you don't approve of it, Jesus," then James said, *"Ah-men,"* and his crew said, *"Ay-men,"* the full colonel radioed, "Let's roll it," the order went like a hot potato to the colonel, captain, lieutenants, to the sergeants, specialists, teenager privates, and C entered into the biggest tank battle in all of American history, call it the Battle of Al Qarnain.

*T*atatata! A row of red tracers went in front of C, right to left, coming from who? the Iraqis? muddled Americans? no one in C could tell. As the bullets went by, the boy who'd said, "I'm in love with her too," and who, the past hour, had watched the lightning like the sky cracking, thinking, *It's like in Psycho,* shouted, "Hey, bullets bullets!" waking up Captain Burns.

"What what what?"

"Sir, we're here!" The boy, Burns's driver, meant that C was close to the Tawalkana.

"Gunner! Start scanning!" said Burns. "Gunner! Gunner!"

"What?" said the gunner, waking up.

"Start scanning!" said Burns, then he radioed to C, "Start scanning!" In theory the Tawalkana was east of A, B, C, D and all four companies were rolling east, but the night (as one soldier said) was as dark as a cow's insides and a gunner who thought he was aiming east might be aiming southeast or— *Boom!* from the south there suddenly came a *boom!* and a Bradley, a Brink's truck full of American infantrymen, exploded. "Oh shit, a Bradley's been hit!" a commander radioed as, in the company south of A, B, C, D, a pillar of orange fire rose from the Bradley. "Cease fire!" the captain of that woeful company radioed. "You shot my Bradley!" the captain's colonel radioed to A, B, C, D. "That's bullshit! We aren't shooting!" the colonel of A, B, C, D radioed back. "That's right! He's not shooting!" the full colonel radioed, and, as the boys in the Bradley lay dying and as the living wondered, *Who did it? A, B, C, D? someone else? the Iraqis?* and as, in the lightning, the blackness near C seemed to crack, here, there, like a castle collapsing around it, C went east at five nervous mph.

C did but B did not. As C watched, aghast, thinking, *What are they doing?* the tanks and Bradleys of B, to the right, seemed to turn south, then west, until, as the Tawalkana appeared in C's night sights and as C's gunners cried, "I see hot spots!" it seemed that B was turning tail and fleeing to Saudi Arabia. "Bulldog!" the colonel radioed the Hispanic captain of B, a Chilean named Juan Toro. "What the *hell* are you doing?"

"What do you mean?" said Toro. His accent was California: was Standard American.

"You're heading in the wrong direction!"

"Negative negative. I'm heading east."

"Wait one!" the colonel said, and he radioed to Captain Burns of C. "Are *you* heading east?"

"Wait one," said Burns. It's surprising, but Burns didn't have the technology to determine where east was. The stars weren't out, the moon was a blot overhead, the compass on Burns's wrist was a top in his steel-sided tank, and in their wisdom the Senate and House hadn't bought him a gyrocompass, saving the American taxpayers $4000. "Do *not* hit the trigger," said Captain Cautious to C, then he climbed out, climbed down (*and into Iraqi fire?* he wondered) and walked fifty feet. He looked at his compass and lo! it was *he,* not Toro, who'd somehow gone in a semicircle tonight, and the "hot spots" in the night sights weren't the Tawalkana but the Big Red One: the 26-ton ammunition trucks and 2500-gallon fuelers that, like a prince's retinue, had trailed him a hundred kilometers across Iraq, each flaunting the English word FLAMMABLE that, in the heat-sensing sights, the gunners of C couldn't see. Burns walked to his tank, climbed on, and radioed the colonel, saying, "Boss? You ain't going to believe this, but we are facing due fuckin' west."

The colonel didn't flip his lid. "Roger, I want you to fix it," he said to Burns calmly—*calmly!*—and Burns then radioed the Cherokee, the captain of D, who also was facing west, to try to untangle their forty tanks and Bradleys.

"The deal is," Burns said, "we're pointed west. I just confirmed it."

"I'll come up on your right," the Indian said but he really meant left.

"No," the colonel interrupted. "You *can't* come up on his right. I'm confused."

"I'll come up on the *left*. My fault," the Indian said. He too was confused, for the north wasn't on his left anymore, it was now on his right.

"I'm *really* confused now," the colonel said.

In the dark was the Tawalkana somewhere, looking at C through sights. Now war, any war, is utter confusion (see the third verse of *The Star-Spangled Banner*)—it's one great supersnafu, and Burns wasn't mortified tonight, he was just *horrified* by the prospect of friendly fire, of C shooting at an American. Back in Missouri his friend had once shot himself instead of a deer, dropping dead, in Texas his troops, confused, shot a round at the gentle village of Florence, in the Civil War a Confederate soldier killed General Stonewall Jackson, in World War II the British killed General McNair, in Vietnam not one, not two, but *thousands* of Americans died at American hands, in Saudi the happy pilots said, "This Bud's for you," and killed two American boys, in Iraq an American pilot killed nine British boys, even Kostic, yes, Kostic, had stepped (so the medics suspected) on an Easter egg made in America, and

Burns didn't want to preside at C's mass murder tonight. By now the colonel was sending up flares, *attention! attention! this is east!* the desert was like Royal Stadium, in Kansas City, the Tawalkana was shooting but Burns said to C, "I remind you: we are on weapons hold," meaning that C couldn't defend itself till Burns said, "Yes, you may."

And *tatatata* went the Tawalkana! The targets in C became anxious, *anxious,* and one boy in C started shooting too. An infantryman, a Bradley commander, he was attached to C and his name was Second Lieutenant Homer, from Michigan. He was quite slight and, in his glasses, looked like a mathematics major, a boy who knew pi to five places, a perfect nerd, but as a child he'd had to use fists, sticks, darts, even bicycles, against his much older, beer-drinking, bullying brother, and he was quite scrappy too. In Saudi he'd often stood up to Burns, saying, "You tankers! You sit there in sixty tons of steel! You tankers are *pussies,* sir!" and tonight, having seen some Iraqis (they *were* the Iraqis, weren't they?), he hadn't thought twice, he'd hit his machine gun, *tatatata,* and Burns had to radio him, "Cease fire!" The lieutenant reluctantly did, and Burns reminded him, "You need *permission,*" and the colonel chewed him out too, "We're turned *around.* We're facin' fuckin' *west.* Let's turn east before we start shootin' people, *please.*"

The lightning was dropping like crashing planes. It now was 12:30 and C had gone east, then north, then west, and at Burns's command of "Left wheel march," it now went south, and it was going southeast when in a trench fifty meters ahead it saw the van of the Tawalkana: a group of Iraqi infantrymen. The group had a Russian bazooka that on an Iraqi's shoulder could kill an American tank.

What happened, happened in two seconds flat: an Iraqi stood up and stared at Burns as if telling him, "We been waitin' for you." The driver of Burns's tank gasped, and the gunner said, "*Hey!* There's a guy there!" and put his fingers on his red triggers, waiting for Burns's command of "Fire!" But fate was frowning tonight, for C was going southeast and a half-mile past the Iraqi was Company B, the ultimate destination of any hot bullets from C, and Burns addressed his driver not gunner and said, "Run him over."

The driver was glad to do it. He was the "I'm in love with her" boy, and his name was Specialist Anderson, from Ohio. A good-looking guy, he had a dapper mustache and he was the only boy in C (not counting the captain, lieutenants) who'd gone to a college: to Southwest Texas State U, Sweet Sue. To pay for it he'd been a driver: a valet parker, he'd hit the walls sometimes, he'd never hit any human beings, but as soon as Burns said, "Run him over," Anderson said, "All right!" Like all of C he was scared, but he alone could do something about it: he twisted his throttle and *arrr!* roared toward the Iraqi.

"I'm running *over* this guy!" Burns radioed to C.

And *arrr!* On the throttle the hand had a strangler's grasp, the guy was now forty, thirty, meters from Anderson, in the sight he was Day-Glo green, was a character in a Nintendo toy, was now twenty meters, ten.

"I'm going to *kill* him!" Burns radioed to C. "Back me *up!*" In his heart, Burns didn't want the Iraqi, Americans, *anyone* to bite the dust tonight, he hoped the Iraqi would—*what?* would radio him, "Black six! Black six! I surrender!" but the Iraqi didn't wave a white hankie and Anderson drove over him. The tank seemed to hit a speed bump, the treads presumably turned the man to a bag of white pebbles, white gravel, the tank rolled on. "You got him," said Burns. "How do you feel about it?"

"It was awesome," said Anderson, who, watching the staring man go white, green, white, in the lightning, a photo in strobo-scopic light, a Mario in Sarasaland, hadn't considered him some-thing real.

"You shouldn't feel that way," said Burns.

"Sir?" said Anderson, not understanding.

"You're killing a guy with a 60-ton tank."

"Okay," not wanting to argue with him.

"I feel like shit," said Burns, then suddenly thought, *But maybe I didn't kill him!* Maybe the man had ducked, maybe by now he was standing up, was aiming a bazooka at Burns's grill, the slits that the engine exhaust came out of, maybe his trigger finger was— "Watch my grill door!" said Burns to C, and damn! well, speak of the devil! the Iraqi or *an* Iraqi stood up in the trench with a Russian bazooka, aiming at Burns's vulnerable grill. Then *boom!* the Iraqi fired it.

In back of Burns in a Bradley was the scrappy lieutenant, the boy who'd jousted on bicycle-back in Michigan, who'd fought with a 250-pound soldier in Honduras, who'd said to Burns in Saudi, "Sir, you really screwed up," and who ten minutes ago had muttered when Burns said, "You need permission." The lieutenant, the Bradley commander, had his head, neck and shoulders out, but the gunner was fully inside, his eyes at his night sight, ears at his Walkman. The gunner, till now, had been playing the Rolling Stones but had put on Led Zeppelin, *Black Dog,* and had been listening to

> *Hey, hey, mama*
> *Said the way you move,*
> *Gonna make you sweat!*
> *Gonna make you groove!*

then he'd seen the Iraqi point the bazooka at Burns. The gunner hadn't fired, for an order's an order, but he'd shouted out, "RPG!" meaning "Rocket-propelled grenade launcher!" or "Russian bazooka!" and as the Iraqi, *boom!* shot at Burns's grill, missed, and loaded another rocket, the lieutenant succumbed to common sense: he held up his rifle, *bang! bang!* and shot at the Iraqi bazooka-bearer.

The bullets hit Burns's tank. Inside it Burns heard the *ping,*

ping, the BB-like sounds, but he couldn't see the Iraqi and, in the tumult, forgot that he'd just said to C rather vaguely, "Watch my grill door!" "Put your head out," he said to Sergeant Medine, his loader, "and see what that is."

"Hell no," said Medine, laughing at Burns's impertinence, and Burns radioed to C.

"Who's shooting? Who's shooting?" Burns said, well, snorted as though in "Who's dared to defy me?"

The scrappy lieutenant didn't tell him. He didn't have time to, for he was still going *bang!* and his gunner, who was listening to

> *Oh, oh, child,*
> *The way you shake that thing,*
> *Gonna make you burn!*
> *Gonna make you sting!*

—the gunner was shooting too, was shooting the narrow cannon that, like a little erection, stuck comically out of the Bradley. Its rounds were an inch across, that's all, but four of them left the cannon per second, *boo-boo-boo-boom,*

> *Hey, hey, baby,*
> *When you walk that way,*
> *Watch your honey drip!*
> *Can't keep away!*

and *boo-boo-boo-boom!* they missed the Iraqi and landed a half-mile ahead on Company B. "I'd greatly appreciate it," the Chilean captain radioed to Burns, as politely as if he were telling him, "if you would please pass me an MRE," "if you would redirect your fire." Other rounds landed on Burns's tank, the sound of them clanged inside it, and Burns radioed to C, "Be *careful!*" One round hit the Iraqi, *boom!* he exploded in so many parts that a boy in C, watching, wondered, *Why are they shooting that rag?* and the gunner, still tuned to his Walkman,

> *Didn' take too long*
> *'Fore I found out*
> *What people mean*
> *By down and out!*

—the gunner concluded, *I got him.* The gunner stopped shooting but Burns was now apoplectic.

"God *damn* it! Get under *control*!" cried Burns, who still hadn't seen the Iraqi rag. "I *told* you to ask *permission* first!"

In the Bradley the gunner turned down the Walkman. "Tell that asshole," he said to the scrappy lieutenant, "the guy had an RPG."

"*Explain* to me," Burns cried. "What the *fuck* are you doing?"

"I covered your back door," the lieutenant said unflinchingly, but Burns was obsessed by the murderous friendly fire on him and on Company B.

"I have *told* you to ask *permission*!" said Burns. "Now that is the *last* fuckin' *time*!"

In the gloom below him sat Anderson, Burns's driver, thinking, *My God! We'd have eaten a rocket before you said, "Fire."* Anderson wanted to shout to Burns, "Do you know what you sounded like? A fuckin' bloomin' idiot, and the whole company heard you," and the gunner and loader were scandalized too. The gunner thought, *No, I'll never tell Mom,* and Medine, the loader, thought, *Hell—if I were Lieutenant Homer, I'd never cover Burns again.* Medine was getting resentful of Burns and his "own worst enemies" creed. One minute earlier, when Anderson ran the Iraqi down and Burns said, "I feel like shit," Medine had snickered and, standing up, had asked the hypersensitive captain, "Sir, can I get out?"

"What for?"

"To take the Iraqi's picture." Just teasing, Medine had held up a Kodak Explorer and Burns had fallen for it.

"No! That's disgusting!" Burns had told him, seizing his collar, pulling him in. Medine had laughed but he didn't laugh now, for he'd almost died from Burns's authoritarian "Ask permission"s. He did his second job: manned the radio, but he looked at Burns discontentedly, thinking *asshole* and, to his mild surprise, thinking *gizmo, gizmo.*

C continued its 180. It went southeast, then east, then at one in the morning it headed for the Tawalkana. Its drivers were more than sleepy: were sound asleep, they lay like on Barca-Loungers, enjoying their *zzz*s till they woke up at ten-foot ditches and at a commander's cry of *"Hey!"* C's finical Captain Burns was like Balanchine leading the *corps de ballet,* saying, "Go left," "Go right," "Are you left?" "Are you right?" "Someone just crossed in front of me," *"Stop,"* "Well, we're going to try this *one* more time," but to his north was the Cherokee, to his south was the Chilean, and in between were just one hundred yards, and Burns's slaphappy drivers were *clunk!* were sideswiping now. At about 1:30 a lightning bolt fell, and C saw the outer edge of the Tawalkana: a Russian truck, and C, its hearts in its throats, reported this to Burns. "One truck! Range 1150! Over!"

Burns didn't say "Fire." He said, "Going higher," meaning that he was tuning out C and tuning the colonel in to ask if the truck could conceivably be American. The colonel said no, and Burns tuned again to C and the black lieutenant, saying, "Okay. You have permission to volley fire." He meant that all the lieutenant's tanks, rhinoceros tanks, were to fire on the truck simultaneously: a sure success, and Burns now acted as though in command of a spit-shined firing squad at Fort Riley. "At *my* command," he said as though a drum were rolling and the Iraqi truck had a blindfold on. "Three. Two. One. . . ."

Burns had learned this in Germany. A second lieutenant, he'd been hunting one day and he'd seen how the German forest-masters guarded against friendly fire. "*Laden.* You may load up," a German had said to Burns autocratically, then on his bugle he'd blown the load-up call. "*Wo ist Ihr hut?* Where is your hat? You may not shoot without your hat," the German had said, and Burns had put his green hat on. "*Ihr hemd.* Your shirt," the German had said, still acting like Göring. "It doesn't match your hat," and Burns had changed it. "*Nein.* You still may not shoot. The heart's on the other side," the German had said, and Burns had passed up a stag that was facing right. At last the German had said, "*Schiessen.* Shoot," and Burns had killed a left-facing stag, and the German had said, "*Entladen.* Unload," and had blown the applicable call. The German had been, well, *despotic,* but no German hunters had died that day and Burns would prefer him to the impetuous boy (an American boy) who thirty minutes ago had shouted out, "Fire!" "Fire!" "Fire!" and hit a Bradley, Bradley and Bradley. The boy, immediately south of A, B, C, D, had killed four Americans: one who'd been married at Christmas was now being shoveled up, another who'd been the best man had red-hot steel in his skull, another was in one piece but his feet and his boots were still in a Bradley, another was nothing but soot, and, in addition, eighteen boys were on the ground groaning, one without ears, lips, fingers or long-range goals.

"Three. Two. One," said Burns in his measured, hello-I'm-your-robot-commander voice. "Fire," said Burns, the four gunners did, the truck (which indeed was Iraqi) exploded, turned to a steel skeleton, and Burns said robotically, "Cease fire." But now all of C was fighting for Burns's attention.

"Truck! About 600 meters!"

"Truck! To your left at 900 meters!"

"More trucks! At 1300 and 1500, respectively!"

"Okay," said Burns. "Be careful." He chose the closest truck, but he still hadn't said, "Three two one," when *boom!* someone shot it, and Burns behaved like a teacher when someone is throwing spitballs. "White!" he scolded, using the radio code for the black lieutenant's unit. "Don't *ever* send another round without getting clearance!" A chorus of voices came back at Burns.

"We're not firing!"

"That's Wolfpack!" Meaning "That's Company D!"

"That's not white!"

Then *boom!* another round hit an Iraqi truck. "Now, *somebody* in my sector fired," said Burns, still petulantly.

"That's Bulldog!" Meaning "That's Company B!" for the Cherokee and Chilean captains were going like gangbusters now.

"That's not us! That's Bulldog!"

"That's Bulldog! To my right!"

"Thank you," Burns said coldly.

Oh, how C detested him! In Kansas, C had rehearsed, rehearsed at the $20,000 computer game, in Kansas it was the Nintendo Wizard, "Tank!" "Where is it?" "Behind that rock!" "On the way!" "Attaboy!" the Iraqis were smokin' hulks in four seconds flat. The mission in Kansas was get the *draw,* get the Iraqis before they get *you,* get faster, get faster, the captain himself had said, "Do it," "Don't fiddle-fuck," "Lase 'em and blaze 'em." Sometimes in Kansas, C had been *too* fast, sometimes there'd been a red-bordered explosion and *"No,"* a commander had said, "that's a Bradley," but never had C been like in Iraq, never said, "Tank! Hello, Captain Burns? We have what we think's an Iraqi tank. Do we have permission to shoot it? Pretty please?" And tonight C was looking at Madman Muntz, WE GOT TRUCKS! WE GOT 100 TRUCKS! the trucks could be full of Iraqis with rockets and Burns was saying wait, wait—

"I'm going higher," said Burns.

C cursed him. One boy muttered, "He's fuckin' stupid," and one said, "It's gizmo time." The black lieutenant saw an Iraqi Bradley, a BMP, and radioed-hollered to Burns, "On the left! You can see tracks and a turret on a BMP! I'm lookin' at a perfect shot on a BMP!" a BMP was serious stuff, but Burns's answer was *"Kkkkk,"* was static, for Burns was now on the colonel's channel, not C's. "We should *destroy* it!" the lieutenant hollered, then *tick,* then *tick,* the seconds went by, the ice age began in Armenia, spread to Iraq, the lieutenant had 144 incarnations in Assyria, Athens, Ohio, and Burns descended to C again. "Black six!" the lieutenant hollered. "Do we have permission to *fire?*"

"At what range? At what azimuth?" said Burns.

"I got a range of 1960, azimuth of—" In his tank the lieutenant's compass pinwheeled, and he made an azimuth up. "Eighty!"

"Okay. What's your target?"

"A BMP!"

"What's the target?"

"I say again BMP!"

"Can *you,*" Burns said to the scrappy lieutenant, double-checking on the black one—"can *you* identify this target?"

"I identify *two* and would like to engage sometime tonight."

"By all means," said Burns cavalierly, then to the black lieutenant said, "You may en— You may en— Heh!" He laughed, for somehow he couldn't pronounce the word *engage.* "If you can hit it, you can engage."

At long lovin' last! "BMP! Direct front!" the lieutenant cried. "Three two!" the lieutenant cried and, forgetting the "one," cried, "Fire!" and the BMP exploded, turned to a bonfire, then to a nighttime-colored shell.

"You hit it," said Burns monotonously. "You have the first kill that I know of." He added, "For us."

"I want a *tank!*" the lieutenant laughed, but he was uneasy about it: he'd waited twenty minutes, twelve hundred *tick tick tick*s, well, that's what it *seemed,* to take out one BMP, and he knew an Iraqi tank would be full of Iraqis shooting at C. What could happen in twenty minutes *then?*

To the north of C was the Indian's D: was Lieutenant Russell and Russell's four tanks. And *boo-boo-boo-boom!* his gunners were like at El Alamein, for the Indian didn't employ the "You may,"

"You may not," procedures of Burns, no, the Indian (who was one-eighth, but who acted twenty-tenths) stood in a Bradley radio-roaring, "Everybody engage!" "Everybody engage!" "Now *kill* the sonofabitches!" At two o'clock he surpassed himself, saying, "Keep *hosin'* these fuckers! I'm gonna read a fuck book! *Out!*" and with this carte blanche the gunners in Russell's unit went ape. On one tank the gunner turned on a Walkman and listened to AC-DC, to *Thunderstruck,*

> *Turned on the drums*
> *Beatin' in my heart!*

"Yeah, I'm turnin' 'em *on*," the gunner cried,

> *The thunder of guns*
> *Tore me apart!*

"No, it'll tear *you* apart," the gunner cried,

> *You've been . . .*
> *Thunderstruck!*

"No, *you* have been thunderstruck!" the gunner cried, *boom!* and an Iraqi Bradley, a BMP, blew up.

It became like the sun. "Wow! Check this out!" the gunner's commander cried, for the BMP was the rainbow: was orange, then yellow, then, at the edges, green, then blue, it grew to a seven-colored fireball, *it's beautiful,* the commander thought. "Go to daylight!" he cried, and the gunner turned off his night sight, where all was pale green, the color of IBM monitors, Honda speedometers, Supermario, signs on Interstate 70, and turned to his daylight sight.

"Wow!" said the gunner.

"Ain't that somethin'?"

"Yeah!" said the gunner.

"Let's find more of 'em!"

"Yeah!"

The boys high-fived. *All* the gunners in Russell's unit were jubilant now, all but in Russell's own tank. The boy whose face was an oblate ellipsoid, a soccerball someone was sitting on, a character in *Peanuts*—the Samoan was listening serenely to *Lau Lupe,*

> *My lovely dove,*
> *Will fly away,*

and was remaining faithful to "Thou shalt not kill." Six hours earlier, rolling pell-mell across Iraq, he or his once-a-monk loader or, just maybe, the hand of God had pulled on a yellow handle: the shutoff switch, and the tank had practically hit the Great Pyramid. It had been dead as a camel's corpse ("I wanted to push it," Russell had written to Tom, distraught) till the maintenance people said, "It's the shutoff switch," and Russell, at forty wild mph, had caught up to D—Russell who now implored his dove-loving gunner to kill the Iraqis before the Iraqis killed *him.* "BMP!" Russell cried.

"I don' see it."

"It's direct front!"

"I don' see it, lieutena'."

Russell jumped into the Samoan's compartment. "You see? It's *darker,*" he told the Samoan, pointing to the night-sight screen and the BMP. Aboard it, the Iraqis had apparently turned off the motor, *hello, GIs, there's nothing here,* but the acres and acres of burning things ("Get the fuck *away* from it," the Indian had radioed) had warmed up the BMP and darkened it on the Samoan's screen. "Do you *see* it?" said Russell, his fingertip on it.

"Uhhh," the Samoan grunted. His voice seemed to come from the small intestines, the site of the Stygian villi that in Kansas had feasted on boiled bananas and coconut milk, and he was still peering when *boom!* the BMP became black black *black,* for the *thunder* gunner had hit it. "Okay, lieutena', I see it," the Samoan said.

"Okay!" Russell said. He climbed up, climbed partially out, and peered through his night-sight binoculars. "BMP! Direct front!" Russell cried.

"I don' see it, lieutena'."

Perhaps the Samoan didn't. He also didn't *want* to see it, ("*Filelega.* You cannot choose to," a Samoan pastor had written him) and he still hadn't fired by 2:30, three or 3:30, when Russell suddenly saw an Iraqi bunker. A shapeless mass, it was one hundred meters ahead and Russell cried, "Do you *see* it?"

"No, I don' see it."

"You *got* to!" The tank was still rolling, the bunker and the Iraqis (Russell saw two Iraqis now) were eighty, sixty, forty meters ahead and Russell cried, "Use the co-ax!" meaning "Use your machine gun!" "Shoot and I'll talk you in!"

"No, I can' identify it, lieutena'."

"Shoot! And I'll talk you to it!"

"No—"

By now the bunker was ten short meters (just a first down) away. It was still shapeless, a lump in the black bean soup, until to its right, on a burning truck, a gas tank exploded, the night became bright, and Russell beheld that the "bunker" was an Iraqi tank, an Iraqi *tank!!!* its cannon in Russell's *face!!!* Russell, his head in a lion's mouth, thought, *Shit!* and cried, *"It's a tank!"* and, to his driver, cried, *"Back the bitch up!"* The driver speedily did, and Russell went *tatatata!* ineffectively as he shouted—no, *screamed*—to the Samoan, *"Engage! Engage!"*

"I don' see it, lieutena'."

"Goddammit! You see where I'm shooting? Just shoot!"

"I don' see it, lieutena'."

So far, and God knew why, the Iraqis hadn't fired. Perhaps the Iraqi gunner had said, "I don't see the Americans," or "I don't think that *they* see *us*," or "I'm praying to Allah, sir," but Russell couldn't count on the gunner's indulgence while in Iraqi range. *"Stop!"* Russell screamed, the driver did, and Russell dropped to his seat, seized his own Cadillac, started to turn it, and—*boom!*

heard a *boom!* for the *thunder* gunner had hit the Iraqi tank. It metamorphosed: turned to seven colors, the crew decomposed, and Russell screamed at his 20/2000 gunner from Pago Pago, *"Now* can you see the sonofabitch?"

"Yeah, I can see it, lieutena'."

"Well," Russell screamed, "that's a *T-72!"* the most powerful tank the Russians made. "At best I'm *dead,"* Russell screamed, "and *you* are now hatin' *life,* and at worst we're all *toast!* And *you,"* Russell screamed—*"you* have just killed us *all!"*

The Samoan said nothing. His back was to Russell, who wanted as never before to live and see Tom, dear Tom.

"Now *get* your head out of your *ass!"* Russell screamed.

Nearby was the *thunder* tank. It was doing an instant replay of the actions of Russell's tank, for its commander shouted, "Back up!" and its driver retreated, *arrr!* at twenty terrified mph. A few seconds earlier, to the music of

I thought, What can I do?
Thunder!

and to the gunner's own cry of *"Thunder!"* a round had gored the Iraqi tank. In moments the TNT had started exploding, the tank had turned red, red, *red* like iron in a forge and *pop!* the sound was like popcorn, *pop!* the turret had taken off like a UFO, like the rounds in *The Star-Spangled Banner.* "The rockets' red glare! The bombs burstin' in air!" the gunner had cried patriotically, then the turret had risen fifty feet, then, fiery red, it had hovered above them and God! it was now coming down! *"Back up!"* the imperiled commander cried, and, as the driver fled, the red UFO crash-landed where they'd just been. "Whoa!" meaning "Whew!" the fun-loving gunner said.

The boys didn't know, but in back of them was a supersnafu: was a Company D, a D that belonged to another captain, not to the Indian one. It wasn't in radio contact with him and, with thick black clouds in front of the moon, it didn't know that he was ahead of it. Unintentionally, it now rolled into the Indian's D. It got ahead of Russell's thunderous tanks, and the scar-faced colonel, seeing it, got on the radio crying, "Cease fire! Defiant," the other unit, "is going up the ass end of Wolfpack!"

"Cease fire!" the Indian radioed to D. "Defiant is movin' up right behind us! Acknowledge!"

"Roger!"

"Roger!"

"Red!" said the Indian. "Talk to me!"

"Roger!"

All three lieutenants rogered him, but the *thunder* radio didn't work and the *thunder* people didn't hear him. The gunner was now on Van Halen, on *Running with the Devil*,

> *Oh yeah! I live my life*
> *Like there's no tomorrow!*

and was now shouting, *"I see 'em,"*

> *Least I don't need*
> *To beg or borrow!*

and was now shooting, *tatatata,*

> *Yes, I'm livin'*
> *At a pace that kills!*

and the commander, hands on his own machine gun, observing the gunner's tracers, listening to "A pace that kills," was shooting at someone or something too.

"*Runnin' with the devil!*" said Van Halen.

"Cease fire!" the Indian cried.

"Runnin' with the devil!" said Van Halen.

"Cease fire! If you don't cease *fire,*" the Indian cried, "I will *relieve* your fuckin' *ass!*"

The *thunder* people didn't hear him. They weren't shooting at Defiant, for they were disoriented and, in fact, were shooting at Company C, at their buddies in C. The executive officer, XO, Lieutenant Light, was sitting on his tank attentively, his legs inside like a kid's at a swimming pool, when *tatatata!* the red-tailed rounds came at him like laser beams and he leapt inside, seized his microphone, and said, "Cease fire!" No way: the *thunder* crew saw the "Iraqis" and blasted away at the XO's unfortunate tank.

"Everybody!" the colonel radioed. "Get your ass down in Charlie! Keep your head down!"

"Roger," the XO radioed. His voice had a little chuckle, as if he were saying, "Yes sir, you needn't tell *me.*" "My head is down: *down,*" he chuckled, and the colonel then radioed to D.

"Cease fire!" the colonel ordered. "You got to *stop* that guy!"

"If you don't cease *fire,*" the Indian roared, "I'll rip off your fuckin' *head* and I'll shit down your fuckin' *neck!*" and Russell, the responsible officer, got out of his tank, intending to run to the *thunder* tank and do the rip-shitting himself. But the Indian's words (*cease fiiire,* as though from a 50-foot well) were audible now in the *thunder* tank, the gunner obeyed them, and in his ears the only sounds were Van Halen,

> *I found the simple life*
> *Weren't so simple, no,*

and the Indian's loud-and-clear "You fucked up. You were firing at Charlie Company. Thank you for bringing discredit on Delta Company. *Out.*"

In the tank the gunner just sagged. His hands dropped from the Cadillac and his head dropped to the headrest that, whenever the cannon recoiled, delivered a sort of short left jab. He now lay against it, thinking of his buddies in C, seeing them at Bushwacker Bar, the girls accosting them, *"Heyyy!* I'll write you in Saudi! I got new stationery! Red, orange, yellow! The rainbow!" the gunner thinking, *Oh shit! What if I killed them?* The gunner, aged twenty-two, was the chief mischief-maker in C, a boy who in Kansas had liked to put cherry bombs in C's wastepaper baskets, sardines in C's ventilation shafts. He had been breezy, free-and-easy, but he was catatonic now, his head bent, his eyes shut, his chain with a little glass whale (worn in the past on a white silken sweater at Bushwacker Bar)—his chain swaying to and fro, almost hypnotically.

His name was Specialist Gilliam, from Tennessee, he hadn't hit anyone in C but he'd made a new man of D's precipitate captain. The Indian still was Chief Big-Bear, was rarin' and roarin' but now was obsessed, *obsessed,* with the prospect of friendly fire, was now a devoted disciple of Captain Burns. After he'd said to Gilliam, "Okay. No one's hurt," and Gilliam, *whew,* had come out of his coma, the Indian never again said, "Everybody engage." He'd once heard that in Vietnam, the percent of deaths due to friendly fire was (was it true? quite possibly)—was sixty percent, a man didn't need the Iraqis with friends like *that,* and the Indian now radioed-roared to D, "We're doin' unsafe things!" "Don't fire till I tell you to!" "Back off! Back off! Who's firing across Charlie's front?" and once when someone in D went *boom!* at a BMP, "Cease fire! Enough is enough! The fuckers are *dead*!"

A t four in the morning someone on A, B, C and D's radios said, "Peanut butter time," and A, B, C, D took its PB or pyridostigmine bromide pills, as it did at four in the morning, noon, and eight in the evening every day. The pills, a prophylactic against the Iraqi gases, came in plastic like Contac, and Captain Burns of C now pulled off a glove, pulled off the plastic, and pop! at four

o'clock popped the pill like a robot getting its four-o'clock lubri-
cation. He then put the glove on and glanced at his cuff: it was
still green not red, the cloth on his cuff didn't detect any gas, and
Burns continued his slow, slow, juggernaut progress through the
Iraqi BMPs. "We're doing okay," he said to C in his "You can
just call me Hal" voice. "You guys got good kills. I like that."

He was pleased. A moment ago, someone had jumped on his
tank (someone in the American infantry) and told him, "There's a
lot of dead enemy here," and someone had radioed him, "There's
a lot of body parts here." In his night sight he'd seen the Iraqis
lying unsystematically like at a slumber party, their feet, hands or
heads nearby: lying supinely as C rolled over them, over the live
ones too, one driver going round, *round,* like a boy at a meat-
grinder handle, grinding the Iraqi in. Well, that was swell, but
Burns was more pleased that C was alive, that the Iraqis weren't
firing or, if they were, were firing wild, that C wasn't doing friendly
fire. Just south of A, B, C, D, another impetuous boy had now hit
American tanks, five American tanks, he'd killed an American who
whoo! had vanished except for a pelvic bone that now was an osso
buco, well done, he'd messed up another twelve but C was un-
scratched and Burns attributed this to his "Clear it with me."

It was now four o'clock. Not far from Burns, the black lieutenant saw a number of—well, were they BMPs? or did they have
cannons? then they were *tanks,* and the lieutenant radioed-hollered,
"I see four vehicles! I can't figure out what they are! The range is
approximately 1190! Over!"

"Give me an accurate azimuth," said Burns pedagogically.

"Four vehicles! Twelve o'clock!" the lieutenant hollered.

Burns thought, *No no.* Twelve o'clock, meaning straight
ahead, wasn't an accurate azimuth: it was east if the boy was facing
east, it was west if the boy was facing west (as C had been facing
earlier) and Burns said acidly, "I don't expect a grid, but I do
expect an *azimuth* and a *range.*"

All of C heard him, and most of C thought, *He's crazy.* C was
quite mutinous now, C was in kill-or-be-killed range of—*what?*

four tanks? of things it was fearful of, but Burns was the ultimate
bureaucrat, the clerk at the city hall, city court, the 911 operator
who tells you, "Last name? First name? Middle initial? Wait, I've
another call." Burns's own gunner thought, *It's like school. We need
a note from Mother,* and Burns's loader, Sergeant Medine, thought,
Someone should gizmo him. But who? Medine was the person nearest
him, but Medine was the quietest guy in C, in Kansas he'd stayed
in the barracks, written his pen pal in England, read classics like
Oliver Twist, and listened to *Don Giovanni* as C, rushing off to
Bushwacker Bar, said, "Jesus, what's that?" In Saudi, Good Soldier
Medine had hitchhiked back to Burns, who hadn't exactly hugged
him (he hadn't a hug-a-boy nature) but who'd leaned *toward* him
and, his eyes tearing, had said, "I'm happy." A lot of water had
flowed since then, and Medine (half Irish, half Sioux, and the Sioux
was ascendant tonight) stood next to Burns thinking, *If I don't kill
him, who will?* The last straw came when a startled commander saw
an Iraqi leviathan, an Iraqi killing machine, and said, *"Tank!!!
Direct front!!!"*

"What range? What azimuth?" said Burns, still like a prissy
professor at MIT.

"1300!!! Direct front!!!"

"That's bullshit," said Burns. " 'Direct front' is not an azimuth, send me a proper report or I won't accept it. Permission
denied." And then Burns said, "Out."

Medine thought, *The man's irrational.* Where did he think he
was, in a little girl's game of Simon Says? Go Back, You Didn't
Say May I? He was at *war* and a cannon was aimed at four of his
troops, four friends of Medine's, *It's their life or Burns's,* reasoned
this son of the Custer killers. Someone in C, he thought, should
do some triage: the captain should die and the sergeants and specialists live, someone in C should do as in chess: should give up a
castle and get two knights, *I'll kill him,* Medine decided, *and I'll
enjoy every moment of it.* On his chest was a holster, then a Beretta,
he grabbed the holster, unsnapped it, grabbed the Beretta, and—

And duty prevailed. He slowly let go. "I'm going higher,"

said Burns, unaware of this little brush with death, and Medine (his Irish still up, but his Sioux suppressed) returned to his rusty radio dial, as stiff as an old can opener, it put little dents in his fingers, *ow,* he tuned to the colonel's channel and Burns called the colonel's radio code, "Whiskey six." And now Burns couldn't listen or talk to C.

The commander who'd just said, *"Tank!"* and who Burns had told, "Permission denied," was a headstrong soldier from Michigan. He'd turned to his gunner and said, "Did you *hear* him?"

"Yeah!" the gunner had said. "If they," the Iraqis, "start shootin', we'll be fuckin' history!"

"I can't fuckin' *believe* it!" the commander had said. "It's fuckin' *unbelievable!*" He was still rolling east, was 1100, 900, 700 meters from the Iraqis, a second by Iraqi cannon round, tick of a Timex, beat of a heart, and he couldn't report this in triplicate, sign it, imprint it with someone's signet ring, seal it, and send it by cooing carrier pigeon to Burns. His lieutenant, the one from West Point, was shocked and radioed to Burns, "Black six!"

"He went higher," the cheerless first sergeant said.

Then things got hairy. A boy, a commander, saw an Iraqi tank and Iraqi *crew:* some green luminescent insects that, in his night sight, were scurrying toward their tank. "Let's shoot 'em!" his gunner cried, but the commander said, "No!" He was scared but, a black man, was also scared of the twenty percent unemployment in his hometown in Tennessee, and he radioed to Burns obediently, "T-72. At 970 meters. Eleven o'clock. I see people runnin' towards it. Can I engage?"

"Kkkkk." Just static, for Burns was still on the colonel's channel.

"They're crawlin' on the fenders now. Can I engage?"

"Kkkkk."

"They're in the vehicle now. Can I engage?"

"*Kkkkk.*"

"The turret's movin'. Can I *engage?*"

"*Kkkkk.*"

And the good first sergeant cut in. The sergeant was three years short of retirement, of $1104 per month, he didn't want a roasted commander but he didn't want to disobey orders and tell him "Fire!" He calmly told him, "Either you shoot 'em or they'll shoot *you,*" a staff sergeant then said, "Do it!" the commander said, "*Fire!*" and the gunner, a boy who'd done friendly fire in Idaho (he'd been an atomic reactor guard and his rifle had gone off)— the gunner hit the red triggers, *boom!* and hit the Iraqi tank. The turret left for Orion, Iraqis aboard, and the commander bowed his head, saying, "May God forgive me."

He then looked up. And lo! his sight was aglow, was aswarm with the Tawalkana, scores of Iraqi tanks, and the commander forgot about the unemployment in Tennessee. He cried, "*Fire!*" and his loader, who at this critical point was tuned to the Rolling Stones, *Paint It Black,*

> *I see a red door, and*
> *I want to paint it black!*
> *No colors anymore,*
> *I want them to turn black—*

the loader did a sort of twist-again to the Stones. He turned to the ammunition, *black!* and put one round in the cannon, *black!* as fast as he'd done it in Kansas, *black!* and the cannon went *boom!* and the night sight went black, and *boom!* and Iraqis exploded. "*Fire!*" the imperiled commander cried, "*Fire!*" and Iraqis disintegrated till a voice on the radio said, "Stand by," meaning "Stop."

The voice wasn't Captain Burns's. The captain was still on Olympus, and the voice was Lieutenant Jones's, the one from West Point, who'd been taught that an order (even a possibly dopey one like "Ask permission")—an order's an order, genuflect to it, fall on the floor before it, *do* it. As soon as Jones said, "Stand by," the mini-mutiny ended, the shooting stopped, and Jones tried to re-establish communications with Burns. "Black six," Jones radioed tensely.

"I see a BMP!" his own gunner said.

"BMP. Eight hundred meters. Eighty degrees," Jones radioed.

"I see people *movin'* on it!" his gunner said.

"Request permission to engage it. Over," Jones radioed.

"We're gettin' *closer,*" his gunner said.

And the radio answered, *"Kkkkkkkkk."*

Oh, great ghost of Caesar! Jones hadn't learned about this at the Point. He had arrived in July, 1985, he'd learned that an order is God's word, obey it, then he and 160 cadets had been told to fall in in alphabetical order from A to Z. The catch was, the 160 were plebes, who'd then had to "ping" to their destinations like in *The Parade of the Wooden Soldiers.* They couldn't look left or right, couldn't see if the boy or girl beside them was ASTOR, CASTOR or PASTOR, couldn't say, "Hello, who are you?" but as they pinged along going *crash!* in each other's ribs, the firstie (the senior) who'd given this idiot order had acted as if the 160 didn't know their *abc*'s. "You bonehead!" he'd yelled at Jones. "Did you eat dumb-dumb doughnuts today? Did you drink stupid juice?"

"No, sir!" Jones had snapped.

"You beanbrain! Who told you to *talk* to me?" the firstie (an Army linebacker) had yelled. "And who told you to *look* at me?" Jones had looked forward again, but the firstie had almost frothed and said, "And who told you to look *forward?*"

"Sir!" Jones had said. "May I look forward?"

"You *bonehead*! You *beanbrain*! You three-dimensional *zero*! Who said you can ask *questions*!" And now, six years later, the firstie (a captain in Operations) still was at Jones's rear, and Jones felt he'd be in eternal hell if he didn't say, "Captain Burns, may I fire?" and if Burns didn't answer, "When ready, Jones." But that didn't happen, for Burns's wandering ghost said, *"Kkkkkkkkk."*

"The BMP! It's five hundred meters!" said Jones's gunner.

"Request permission to engage it," Jones radioed.

"*Sir!* We can't just *watch* this!" said Jones's gunner. The gunner was 24.4 percent fat (the army's limit was 24, and he was being discharged in May) and he looked like a Southern sheriff sweating in a Southern summer, and the loader looked like the Southern sheriff's prisoner. He was *shaking,* his knees were *knocking,* one hit the switch to the ammo locker, the door then opening, closing, *whoosh!* like a guillotine blade.

"Sir! We need *somethin',*" the loader said, "in the damn *chamber!*"

A whirlpool was swirling inside of Jones. At age eight he'd had a bicycle, his father had told him, "Don't skid it," his sister had crashed in front of him, and Jones, not skidding, had ridden it over her neck, *crack!* nearly breaking it, tonight every neck in C was exposed and Jones was thinking, *But but! I don't have permission! What should I do?*

"The *turret's* turning!" said Jones's gunner. "Do *something!*"

HONK! A horn that meant *overload* went off in Jones. His head couldn't hold the *Should I do A?* and *Should I do B?* the two whirled like in a Waring, colliding, crumbling, the top of the Waring coming off, the food oozing out, and Jones aborted the inner conflict by turning the Waring off. He sighed like a man who's shooting a beloved horse and said to the Southern-sheriff gunner, "Go ahead. Take 'em out."

To the gunner, he sounded sad, but the gunner cried, "Roger!" and "Heat!" meaning "High explosive antitank!" The loader went *whoosh,* put in the round, closed the cannon door, *clap!* the gunner just flexed and *boom!* the BMP and Iraqis turned to a thousand sparks.

C had observed this. It didn't quite feel like the crew of the *Caine,* for Jones hadn't said, "I'm relieving you, Captain Queeg," but C's new leader tonight was the take-over boy from West Point. His first disciple was Sergeant James, who already trusted in God not Burns, who saw three ominous tanks and who radioed the black lieutenant, "Sir, either give us permission or we're gonna fire on our own."

"My ass'll get chewed. But fuck 'em, *shoot* 'em!" the lieutenant cried, then James went *boo-boo-boom!* then another commander cried, *"Tank!"* and the black lieutenant cried, "Shoot it!"

"Six," meaning Burns, the commander said, "might be upset if I shoot it!"

"He'll be more upset," the lieutenant cried, "if it shoots *you*!" At that, the commander cried, *"Fire!"* and the gunner (who was Specialist Young, who was sitting in)—the gunner went *boom!* and cried, "Hoo, I got one!" and C was now cannon-shooting, the sky was falling, it *boom!* it sounded like hundreds of oil drums falling, then bursting, the *boom!* the world was the *Hindenburg,* all exploding, in *boom!* in *boom!* in the sand were cracks and the fires of hell jetted out, the dead were dancing and Burns was *boom!* was down from the mountain now, was *boom!* was shouting as C was dancing around the Golden Calf, was *boom!* was on the radio shouting to C, "You have to have authorization! You have to—" BOOM! BOOM! BOOM!

B y five o'clock the Iraqis were smokin' hulks. The tanks were burning and, in the darkness, looked like a thriving oil refinery in Texas. One tank exploded as C rolled by, the *boom!* knocking down a couple of Bradley commanders. On another tank the Iraqis were halfway out: one Iraqi was burning and one who was charcoal was bowing to C as if saying, "You win," and as C rolled by, just inches away, it studied the Iraqi bodies. In night sights the Iraqis were green, the flames were green, the flames on the faces were— *cold,* were animate icicles, it seemed the Iraqis had died in a TV movie, *The War of the Pale Green People,* or (thought one boy) had gone to the cold seventh circle of Dante's hell or to Bosch's cold *Millennium.*

At 6:30, the sky became gray, and C saw the vast desert. It seemed to have been subjected to World War I. It was strewn with the Tawalkana: with twisted steel, shredded rubber, contorted bodies. To look at, the tanks had been there since 1918, and the bodies were ruins too: the feet at impossible angles, the hands (often clenched in a fist) often lying nearby, like the parts that a car mechanic had just removed. On the faces the eyes were shut, the mouths were open, as though the Iraqis had died saying, "Ooh! I don't like this!" the cheeks seemed to be of cracked plaster, such as on third-world walls, and a hurricane seemed to have hit the Iraqis' mustaches. All that C saw was charcoal black, and the smell of burnt rubber, burnt flesh, gasoline, was a nail in C's noses, ammonia-sharp. The fires were out, but the smoke rose until at a thousand feet it spread like a giant circus tent above the ex-Tawalkana.

There still were Iraqis alive. They must have been sleeping (must have been used to American bombs) for at dawn they came from the bunkers half-dressed and *oh!* they caught sight of C. Some turned and ran but C shot *tatatata!* at their feet, some ran to the bunkers again but the bulldozer buried them, and the rest surrendered. They seemed glad to do so. One said in English, "I live in the U.S.A.," and said he'd been visiting relatives when the Iraqis drafted him. One put one of his wrists on the other, saying in Arabic, *"Saudi,"* apparently meaning "Please handcuff me and send me to Saudi." One did a strange charade: he pretended to dig a hole, to put something in, and to cover it up, apparently meaning "I'm an Iraqi farmer." A lot of Iraqis grabbed C's hands, wrists and arms and kissed them, and C laughed and said, "I'm not into that."

C was gentle again. It told the Iraqis, "We won't hurt you," and took their rifles but not their money or Korans. It gave them MREs, and when the Iraqis signaled *no* and pointed to C's right hands, C gave them the MREs with C's right hands. It told the Iraqis, "Go west," meaning "Go to the POW camps," but out of pity it sometimes told them, "Go home." One boy in C who'd studied his *Soldier's Guide* said, *"Shammal,"* meaning "North," and pointed to Baghdad, and one boy squatted and, in the sand, drew a square house, square door, square windows, and at the side a wide-skirted wife and a child, then he told the Iraqi, "Go home." The boy (and the rest of C) wanted to go home too.

The Iraqis went west. At the POW camps, C learned, the Iraqis told all to the REMFs, the Rear-Echelon Mothers. Most admitted they'd sat on their fannies throughout the Battle of Al Qarnain but asked the Mothers, "What else could we do?" C had had night sights, said the Iraqis, and the Iraqis hadn't: C had seen *them*, they hadn't seen C. They'd tried to become invisible to C's fiendish sights: they'd turned off the motors, hand-turned the turrets, sat around fatalistically like in a clean, well-lighted place, and (aside from the desperadoes, who'd shot a dozen cannon rounds and a couple of hundred other rounds) seldom shot at C. In effect the Iraqis confirmed what Burns, C's careful captain, had said: that C's worst enemy was C's own itching fingers. At seven o'clock, indeed, as C ate its MREs, another impetuous boy to the south went *boom!* and, to the south, another two Bradleys exploded. A driver (who'd had his first child that day: her name was Larissa) was burned to a crisp, but he wasn't in C, thank God, and C hadn't done it.

At eight the fuelers pulled up and C started getting gas. C was completely uninjured, undead, but it didn't think to ascribe this to Captain Burns. "Hey, sergeant," someone said to the boy who'd radioed, *"Tank!"* and who Burns had told, "Permission denied." "Hey, sergeant, do you guys have pacifiers?"

"What do you mean?"

"The way Bullet Bob was treating you all! Like babies!"

The sergeant grunted.

"I'm glad you're alive!" the soldier said. "But that was fuckin' stupid of Bullet Bob!"

C was beyond being sleepy. Its brains were soggy wet sponges, *drip,* the dishwater dripping out, but the land of Nod was miles behind it somewhere in Saudi Arabia. A lot of C was engaged in the Battle of Birabuto: it hit the A and B buttons, stomped on the Tokotokos, sent missiles at the Rocketons and superballs at King Totomesu, all on the wan green screens of Nintendo toys. "I got 'em!" C cried excitedly. Its bones ached, its muscles faltered, its flesh was a moth-eaten overcoat that the dew and the damp passed through: it was *exhausted* but it was in rolling-rolling mode, the victim of Newton's First Law.

It got gasoline. It got ammunition. It listened to Walkmans like acidheads: in a trance, and the boy who'd been playing the Rolling Stones got obsessed with his *Paint It Black*. He sat on his tank now, playing, rewinding, playing it,

> *I see a red door, and*
> *I want to paint it black!*
> *No colors anymore,*
> *I want them to turn black!*

the boy thinking, *Yes, it's appropriate,*

> *I look inside myself*
> *And see my heart is black!*
> *I see my red door,*
> *And I have it painted black!*

the boy thinking, *Yes. A month in Iraq and I'll be black,* be staring like the Vietnam veteran he'd seen once in Kansas, empty-eyed, dead to events around him. Back in Vietnam the soldiers in C had put aces of spades on the enemy corpses, and the boy wondered, *Will I be doing that too?* Burns, Captain Burns, was against it, Burns had said, "Jesus Christ! We have families! We don't need that!" but the boy wondered if in one month he'd be so accustomed to killing that, if he killed an Iraqi, he'd then flip an ace of spades onto the Iraqi's tortured face. The boy couldn't picture it, but then neither could the Rolling Stones,

No more will my dreams
Seem to turn a deeper blue!
I could not foresee
This thing happenin' to you!

To the soldier in C?

I want to see it painted!
Painted painted painted!
Blaaack!

Another philosopher was Lieutenant Russell. At dawn he'd climbed off his tank, climbed onto an Iraqi one, and peered inside: the crew was burnt toast, the smell was molasses. Around him the sand was black, and the Iraqis who'd walked from the bunkers looked—*lost,* as if their world had just disappeared in one great atomic explosion. Russell had thought, *What a wreck!* and now, his gas and ammo aboard, he thought he should write about it to Tom, his ubiquitous son. "One man did it," he thought he'd write, "one man who thought of himself and not of anyone else and not—" And suddenly Russell had *déjà vu:* he saw that he, Tom's fond father, was just like Saddam Hussein.

He'd written in his diary every night. He'd written, "Good night, Tom," "God bless, Tom," but he'd indulged himself too, "I am your father, Tom," and "She," Tom's mother, "sure kisses ass. She never did that for me." He'd planned that if he survived in Iraq, he'd sue in Bexar County, in Texas, he'd get some of Tom's double helixes and say in a district court, "I want him on Saturdays," "I want him on Sundays," "I want him in June or July." Like Saddam Hussein, Russell had thought of *me me me,* but this morning he saw that unless he quit it, Tom wouldn't be like the grass in Saudi, the Russell Memorial Meadow, but like this wretched desert in Saddam's Iraq. Tom would become a battlefield, his father and "father" fighting for him, the two staking out a seventh, seventh and twelfth of him, the writs going boom! going boom! and Tom cringing in the crossfire, crying, and Russell thought, *That mustn't happen.* The battle had changed him, and Russell now saw that yes, the "father" was an impostor but Tom, dear Tom, didn't know it and Russell mustn't expose it. At eight o'clock, Russell, the combat soldier, surrendered to the rear-echelon man in Texas: he let go of Tom, forswore him, and now there was nothing, no woman, no child, in Russell's desert-dry life.

Nothing but C. At 9:30 Russell climbed onto *My Hillbilly Babe,* his tank, named for Tom's down-home mother, he turned the hydraulics on and tested the Cadillac, *left, right.* Russell couldn't see the sun, for far away the oil was on fire and the oily black clouds were a biblical plague. Ahead of Russell on Russell's antenna was one little ripple of color: his red, white and blue but *verboten* flag, and the colonel now radioed, "I want that *down.*" Dispirited, Russell untied it. "I may have to die for that flag today," he wanted to write to Tom, "and I should be able to fly it," but he didn't write it: for Tim, the zoomie in Texas, was now Tom's father, the world was old-mushroom-colored and Russell was simply a grunt in Iraq who, at 9:45, at someone's command of "We're moving out," was rolling, once again rolling, on to Kuwait.

Kuwait: The Battle

★

The clouds were from Exodus, *the wind brought the lo-custs,* there could be thousands, they swallowed the sky. The day was grave-digging gray but was day, not night, and Russell and C saw four thousand meters but the Iraqis did too: the armies were even, the field was level, the war was two-sided now. At 9:45 the colonel radioed to C, "Go two hundred meters left of Bravo," of Company B, and the XO, executive officer, said, "Roger," then said on C's channel, "Go two hundred meters left of Bulldog," of Company B. The other lieutenants said, "Roger," and at five mph all C went left—all C but Captain Burns, who *arrr!* roared off at ten, then twenty, mph, roared like a hot-rodder, *you got a Ford? well, I got an Abrams, you wanna drag?* and, to the XO's bewilderment, roared to the right not left.

Burns was now boiling mad. He felt that *he,* not the XO, had the authority to say to C, "Go two hundred meters left of Bulldog." Six hours ago at Al Qarnain he'd more or less lost control of C, he still hadn't recovered it and the XO had now usurped it. Burns didn't dislike the XO, the boy had an easy, palsy-walsy intimacy with C, a complement to Burns's I-am-the-honcho-here. One day in Saudi the XO had gotten letters to Any Soldier, the XO had opened them and read, "I'm thinking about you, XO," "I'm pray-ing for you, XO," and "Come home soon, XO," and the XO had wondered, *How did they know I'm the XO?* One boy had seen that it wasn't clairvoyance: the "X" meant kiss and the "O," as in tennis, meant love, and "Oh!" the boy had blurted a bit impre-cisely, "XO means Hugs and Kisses!" and from then on, the XO had been Hugs and Kisses. Someone would say, "Hello, Hugs and Kisses," and, chuckling, the XO would blow him a kiss, and the crew of the XO's tank, who till then had wanted to name it *Chicago* (the XO was from Chicago) or *Cannibal* (the XO was cannibalizing parts) or *Cerberus,* the dog from hell, had painted it HUGS AND KISSES. All of C liked the XO, the genial Lieutenant Light.

The trouble for Burns was, the XO wasn't cautious. His parents, when he was twelve, had come unstuck when he had leaned over, *over,* the world's highest suspension bridge to *snap!* to snapshoot the Royal Gorge, in Colorado, and Burns had crumbled on D-Day when the XO had jumped off *Hugs and Kisses* to use his rifle on the Iraqi trenches and yes, to *snap!* them too. "Now, don't get too bold," Burns had radioed him, well, *all* of C was too bold for Burns, who'd hate to have to pin silver stars on C's widows, C's orphans, but the XO was worst and Burns was venomous with him. "*Listen* to me," Burns had hissed on C's common radios. "Just fuckin' *listen,*" "Get a guy to *write* it," "Please fuckin' *tell* him, goddammit," "I need your fuckin' *help.*" A moment ago, when the XO had radioed, "Go two hundred meters left of Bulldog," and taken away Burns's scepter, Burns had reclaimed it by saying to Specialist Anderson, "Driver! Move out," and by shoving himself in front of C. "Driver!" he'd said. "How fast am I going?"

"Ten, sir."

"Go twenty! Go right," Burns had said, Burns who'd been catching some zzzs (no more than that: three zs) and who'd led C to twenty, not two hundred, meters from B, to bumps-a-daisy distance from B. "Okay," Burns was saying now. "Go straight," and C did, and the colonel got irritated.

"What did you *tell* him?" the colonel radioed the XO.

"Roger, I'll fix it," the XO said and he tuned to Burns. "Black six. Go two hundred meters left of Bulldog," the XO said, but the bald-headed lieutenant was not the commander of C.

"Get back on that fuckin' higher net," said Burns.

"Roger," the XO said. He tuned to the colonel's channel and said, "I'm back," but C was still fanny-to-fanny with B and the colonel still blamed the XO.

"You're ticking me *off*," the colonel said, well, practically rattled it, *rrrrr!* like a snake that the XO was stepping on. "Get your fuckin' company in the fuckin' right place."

"Roger," the XO said and he swiveled to Burns again. "Black six—"

"Get the *fuck* on that fuckin' higher net."

"Roger," the XO sighed. He was thinking, *We can't function this way,* was thinking, *We can't win the war this way,* but he tuned to his other master, the now apoplectic colonel.

"What did I fuckin' *tell* you?" the colonel began, but Burns had tuned to that channel too. Burns was groggy—well, everyone was, the colonel himself had said *north* not *east* and *line* not *column* ("I'll get it right," the colonel had stammered)—but Burns was too groggy to know he was groggy, and he believed what he radioed now.

"I don't know what my XO's doing," Burns told the colonel. "He fucked me. He lied to me. Where should I go?"

"Go two hundred meters left of Bravo."

"Driver! Go left," Burns said, and as C parted company with B, the XO cried, "Fuck this shit!" though not on the microphone that, in an uncommon act of non-nonchalance, he slammed on the cannon beside him. His crew was unhappy too. His gunner gave him an "Oh, brother" look, his loader said, "You never lied! You told him *exactly* what to do!" and his driver said, "Sir. He's fuckin' us."

"Whatever," the XO said, controlling himself. "Get into position," but as the driver went left, then straight, then, with the rest of C, toward Kuwait, the driver became a slow-boiling pot.

"He's fuckin' us. Sir, he's fuckin' us. I don't know why," the driver said, then he simmered awhile, then said, "The fucker! The goddam fucker! Someone oughta do somethin' *about* him!" He simmered some more, then suddenly boiled over, "Well, I'm gonna kick his *ass*! I'm gonna beat the *shit* outta him! The goddam *motherfucker!*"

"At ease," the XO said. The driver (whose wife was divorcing him) was silent but soon warmed up.

"He's fuckin' us. Sir, he's fuckin' us. You *know* that he is," the driver said, then he bubbled awhile, then said, "Someone oughta *frag* him," then *bubble!* his lid started rattling again, the steam coming out of his ears, then, "I'm gonna *frag* that fuckhead! I'm gonna *frag* him! He's fuckin' *dead!*"

"*Just shut up!*" the XO shouted. *We're falling apart,* the XO thought: in Kansas and Saudi and along the Wall, C had been soldiers, professionals, people who'd stood under mortar rounds saying, "Uh-oh. That looks close," but C had been rolling for seventy-seven hours and it wasn't responsible for its words, deeds, drowsy commands of "Fire." It once had been buddies, but now its enemies were its own: its captain, its looies, a PFC had smeared shit on a private, why, C was now *murderous* and had told the XO, "Burns's gonna have an accident, sir," the XO replying pointedly, "I hope that Burns doesn't." A day off and C, the XO knew, would be its old winsome self, but right now it needed a Valium, a sauna, a Bud, it needed an R&R in Cairo, sailboats along the Nile, flutes, it needed a breather, then back to Iraq. Above all, the XO thought, as C did this endless tunnel, the color of subways, all black and brown, the walls going by, *click clack*—above all, C needed sleep!

No way. "We go east," the colonel radioed, then go to Basra? Baghdad? Brobdingnag? the colonel didn't say and C tottered on. On the sand were a thousand duds, were Iraqi? American? Ruritanian? rounds, and C zigged and zagged through this silver-tipped-obstacle course. "I want everybody," the colonel radioed, "to concentrate. I know you're tired, but you got to concentrate. Now," he said at 11:25, "for your listening, uh, *viewing* pleasure, bringing you to the lovely emirate of Kuwait. Welcome," he said at 11:33, "to Kuwait," and C rolled into its El Dorado, the land it had left its wives, brides, girls and composure in Kansas for. Kuwait looked just like Iraq, which looked just like Saudi: sand, at the border

were no Kuwaitis, Iraqis, no walls, wires, CUSTOMS, أهلاً وسهلاً s,
flags, though one of C's tanks now had a Kuwaiti flag ("Or *something*,"
the colonel said: it was really a Lone Star flag) and the colonel said, "I
want that down." One of C's tanks had flames, and the colonel said,
"You got an engine fire," but the flames were a cardboard carton (it
had dropped onto the engine, nine hundred degrees) and a boy booted
the carton off. It started drizzling. At two o'clock, C at last saw an
Iraqi: a man in a truck, he just tootled along, the colonel said, "Fire,"
then, "Wait," then, "No. It's one of our people," for the man was an
inattentive lieutenant, a half-mile ahead of A, B, C, D. *We're tired.
We're feeling like shit. We're gonna get hurt,* the colonel thought.

It got worse. C went through a berm and lo! it saw its first
hills since crossing the Alps on New Year's Day. A thousand meters
ahead were masses of sand that, wonder of wonders, were tall as
human beings, were five, even ten, feet tall, for C was at an old
salt mine and the sand was the tailings, the saltless stuff. *Oh, fuck
it,* C thought, each one of those masses (to C they were *boogers*)
could hide an Iraqi tank, then *boo-boo-boom!* the Iraqis could
ambush the Good Guys, and C wasn't being paranoid, for as it
came closer it saw its *bête noire* at, well, call it Booger 33. A commander radioed, "T-55!" a tank made in Russia, another commander radioed, "T-55! At 1850 meters!" but Burns didn't
understand that C had arrived in Imminent Ambushland.

"I didn't understand a fuckin' word," said Burns.

"T-55!" the second commander enunciated. "1850! At one
o'clock!" but Burns still wasn't impulsive and, to be triply sure,
he radioed another commander.

"Confirm 1850," said Burns.

"I confirm 1820!" a fourth scared commander said, and Burns
concluded that yes, the Iraqis were waiting to ambush him but
friendly fire wouldn't help him, and Burns remained Captain Cir-
cumspect.

"Fire only," Burns said, "at *my* command. Do you *not*," he
insisted, he had sleep deprivation and he apparently meant "You
do not," "have *permission* yet."

But other Iraqi tanks were waiting for C. Another commander saw one at, call it, Booger 99 and cried, "T-55! Range 1930! At your eleven o'clock!"

"That's great," said Burns sarcastically, for he was still preoccupied with the Iraqis at Booger 33. "Prepare to engage. At *my* command. You may engage," he said carefully—*boom!* and two gunners fired and Burns said, "Target," meaning "You hit them." He then turned to Booger 99, and, to two other gunners, he gave the same slow, methodical order, they hit the Iraqis, and C went toward the 666 other boogers thinking, *The captain's insane.*

Now war, every war, is snafu (is *friction,* von Clausewitz called it) but what happened next, at 2:30, was not *situation normal,* it simply was *all fucked up.* To the left of C was more of the Big Red One: were 120 tanks and Bradleys, but somehow they slipped in back of C, and from his tank the general ordered them, "Move up." Not dawdling, the 120 all roared from the rear to the front, the right to the left—roared through the very center of C. See it as Sunday football: C, in green, was the offensive team, but on the same field, running, passing, kicking, double-reversing, tackling and *ugh!* getting tackled, saying, "Hey, I'm on *your* side!" were eight more offensive green teams, and the defensive team (the Iraqis) was in the same popular green. What's worse, the other teams couldn't talk to C. If, to return to Kuwait, if someone in C friendly-fired and if, in reaction, someone friendly-fired into C, Burns would have to tune to the colonel's channel and say, "Cease fire!" The colonel, on another channel, would say, "Cease fire!" the full colonel, on *another* channel, would say, "Cease fire!" then, on still other channels, the major general, another full colonel, another colonel, and a delirious captain would say, "Cease fire!" and, God and the gunners willing, the Battle of C would cease. The process would beat out a radio call to Jupiter, but C would surely become smokin' hulks, and C thought (as all around it, 120 tanks and Bradleys were like in a runback, *stop him! go!*)—C thought, *We're all gonna die.*

Burns was aghast. So far he'd been autocratic, but he was

despotic now. "Do *not* let your tubes point left," your cannons point left. "Do *not*," he ordered, his voice weighed a ton, it landed on top of C, *thud!*—"do not even *look* left." Burns, in his heart, was like a Wallenda, his sons were high on a wire, reeling, there wasn't a net and only his furious words could save them. Not all his gunners were God's noble creatures. Some, Burns felt, were loose cannons, one had once hit the bottle in Germany, thirty beers every night, one had once hit a *captain* in Korea, dropping to PFC, one had driven around in Iola, Kansas, and *bam,* with a baseball bat, had batted the mailboxes down. At the Battle of Al Qarnain the gunners had nearly friendly-fired in spite of Burns's "Cease fire"s, and Burns now became a Mogul, saying, "Move dead ahead! Come on! Get ahead of me! Get caught up! Can't you *see* you're behind? Don't sit like a turnip! Come on, goddammit! Look at me! Listen! Are you intentionally trying to shit on the name of the Fighting Aces? Let's go! Toe the line! Pull your heads out! Stay with it, goddammit! You've done a *miserable* job!"

"Six," a commander radioed. To the left, in the boogers, he saw some of the Big Red One and said, "I got two Bradleys."

"That's great!" said Burns sarcastically. "Why is your weapon on 'em?"

"I was just looking for Soviet tanks."

"Get it the hell off 'em!"

"Roger."

The day was gray. The drizzle on C was like steam on C's glasses. On one tank in C, the commander looked to his left, looked to where the two Bradleys were, and saw—well, he *thought* that he saw an Iraqi tank.

The time was 2:45, the tank in C was *Crusading for Christ,* and the commander was Sergeant James, the boy who felt God would guide him. A month ago in Saudi he'd called up his wife in Kansas, who'd told him, "Let's have a fast day. A day every week," and James had answered, "How about Wednesday?" From then on, James (and nobody else in C) had known if a day was a Monday, Tuesday, Wednesday, Thursday, Friday, Saturday or Sunday, he'd checked his calendar watch every day and, by coincidence, today was a Wednesday fast day. Since midnight, James hadn't had any MREs, any Al-Ghadir, any sleep, and his eyes were warm butterballs when, at 2:45, he looked toward the Bradleys and saw— well, he wasn't sure. He asked his gunner, "Is that an Iraqi tank?" or rather he asked him, "Is that a tank?"

His gunner was Specialist Penn, the pockmarked boy, the one the black girl had told, "I'm pregnant," the one James had told, "Well, you can be saved right *here,*" the one the first sergeant had told, "You just had a boy," and the one James was asking, "Is that a tank?" Penn answered, "Where?"

"Right there," James said, and, his hands on his Cadillac, he turned the cannon, turret and Penn hard left. Near them another commander thought, *What is James doing?* for to the left he saw only boogers and the two Bradleys.

Penn bent forward. He looked in his sight: his *night* sight, for the day was almost opaque and Penn was watching a pale green and dark green world. On the sight hung a silver cross, and on the wall above it in India ink was KENDRELL, his baby's name, and KENDRICK, the name of his wife's other son. "I see it," Penn said to James.

"It's a tank?"

"Yeah."

"What range?"

"690."

James tried to tell this to Burns. But another commander was on C's radios, saying, "We have another T-55," a T-55 far ahead of C, and Burns was replying, "We're dorked right now. I can't *begin* to have confidence it's not a friendly," and James couldn't cut in. Instead, he stood up in *Crusading for Christ* and gestured like a college cheerleader: he pointed left left *left,* but the black lieutenant misunderstood and told his driver, "Go left." Now, James knew that God took care of C. But recently God had referred him to I Samuel 17, where David says to Goliath, "I come in the name of the Lord of Hosts," but carries a weapon, too, and James had noted that C had cannons to do God's momentous work. To his tired eyes, the Iraqi tank moved, the turret turned, the cannon pointed at one of C's vulnerable grills and James cried immediately, *"Fire!"*

Penn fired. The cannon went backward, *boom!* it yanked at the loader's hand, and the round went *whoosh!* by the black lieutenant. The round was red-hot, it warmed the lieutenant's cheeks and hit the Iraqi tank, whatever, there was a bonfire, *boom!* and the Iraqi commander, whoever, tried to climb out but, the flames like an aura around him, red, orange and yellow, fell to his side still afire. A split second later (or some thought, earlier) a round from out of the Big Red One went to C. It missed and the black lieutenant went on C's radios.

"White!" the lieutenant cried, *white* was his four collected tanks. "Don't *fire* till you got *permission!*" then onto C's radios came Burns.

"White! White! White!" said Burns. His words were stones, they fell with an awful finality. "Cease! Fuckin'! Fire!"

The colonel was watching too. He'd seen the two Bradleys, one went behind a booger, then *boom!* he'd seen an orange bonfire where the Bradley should be, and he'd seen the retaliation round on C. "Cease fire!" the colonel radioed to Burns. "You may have shot a Bradley!" and someone in Operations went on C's channel, went over Burns's head, went, "Charlie Company! Cease fire! Cease fire!"

"Who shot? Who shot? White two," Burns asked. "Did you open fire?"

"Roger," said Sergeant James.

And crump. Something in Burns went limp, Burns was a man

who'd been de-boned. He too was C's shepherd, the Congress had commissioned him, the be-all, begin-all, and end-all of Burns's existence was *C must survive.* Last year in Kansas he'd lain awake, his pale green digital clock going 1:00, 2:00, 3:00, the rain on his roof going *pit* and *pat,* his wife and his cat in bed with him, he'd lain there thinking of C, of C, *How can I get them through this?* his wife getting up for orange juice, saying, "You want some?" "No." The lives of his sixty-four—*sons,* would be his responsibility, no man would choose to bear it, in Saudi he'd told the first sergeant, "I don't want to *do* it, Top," he'd even pretended to cry, saying, "Top, I want to go *home,*" the sergeant replying, "A *lot* of guys want to go home, sir," and now Burns felt that he'd failed, he'd flopped. To his front was his doomsday scenario, was *boom!* were bonfires from hell as, in back of the boogers, much of the Big Red One was battling with American tanks? American Bradleys? his soldiers in C? "Everybody stop!" Burns cried, and, ignoring his mission to shoot at Iraqis, he sought to get his protégés out of the sights of the Big Red One. "Back it up! Back it up! Back!" Burns cried.

The colonel, meanwhile, had tuned to the full colonel's channel and said, "Devil six!" The tough little colonel, too, was limp, his breath, blood, spirit seemed to have drained from him, he'd actually felt them go. Six years ago at Fort Leavenworth, Kansas, he'd earned his second master's degree, his thesis had been the Battle of the Bulge—the battle, until today, with the most tanks in American history. A general had told him, "The confusion was—well, I can't describe it," and the colonel had concluded, "The engagements were confused and confusing," and "Commanders must tolerate confusion." His thesis ran two hundred pages, but for his troops he'd often cut it to two pithy words. He'd told them, "Shit happens" ("Or as Clausewitz said, *'Die scheisse passiert'* ") but today he was *drowning* in shit: in drizzle, in black clouds of oil, in darkness in midafternoon, the colonel couldn't tell who was shooting whom and he couldn't tolerate it. "Devil six!" he radioed now. "My guys," he said, hoping his words would wend their way to the rest of the Big Red One—"my guys fired on a friendly unit. They fired on us, and we returned fire. I think it's a Bradley."

One boy in C who wasn't distraught was the XO, executive officer. A moment ago when James fired, the XO had thought, *What's he doing?* he'd then heard the *boom!* he'd rolled forward and lo! in back of a booger was a blazing—*what?* It looked to the XO like an Iraqi tank, and he was more certain when the commander, a devil, a human torch, fell to his side certifiably dead. At Al Qarnain, the Iraqis alone were dead and the XO still felt that someone who's dead must accordingly be an Iraqi. On the radio the colonel was saying, "The Bradley," "The Bradley," but the XO broke in. "Negative!" the XO said confidently. "It's not a Bradley! It's a T-55!"

Goddammit, Burns thought, for a Bradley looked more like a Buick than like an Iraqi tank and the colonel had called it a Bradley. *The XO's lying,* Burns thought, for Burns didn't consider that in this confusion the XO was prone to honest error. "No!" Burns wanted to yell at the XO. "You can see it's a *Bradley*!" but Burns was still yelling at C, "Back it up! Back it up! I'm right here! Hand up in the air!" two arms above him like Ike, like touchdown for Army. Burns felt like an air controller when one, then another, plane is crashing, exploding and burning, for in back of the boogers the Iraqis or Americans were turning to red tornadoes. "Look at me! Get oriented on me! Back up!" Burns yelled, and C was soon out of the boogers and out of harm's wanton way.

"Black six," James radioed to Burns.

"White two! Clear the net!" said Burns, and James stayed silent. "Okay," said Burns. "Who shot?"

"White two," James said.

"What did you shoot at?" said Burns. His voice was now cool, no, *cold,* each word was a pellet from an ice machine, it scratched like a cat's claw on James's face. Deep down, Burns was enraged, for James had started the free-for-all, the ten tornadoes, the boys who were soot, osso buco, were, he assumed, being shoveled up, but Burns's anger didn't spill out, it *leaked* out of Burns's pores, from under his fingernails, toenails, from out of the slit between his lips. "What did you shoot at?"

"I shot a T-72 tank," said James, and Burns thought, *Goddammit,* the XO called it a T-55 and James a T-72, they didn't know *what* they were shooting. "A tank," James continued, "that we was bypassin' that was about to get a grill-door shot."

"What made you *think,*" said Burns, his voice was now frostbite in James's ear, his *think* meant think when you're wrong wrong wrong—"it was going to get a grill-door shot?"

"We was bypassin' it," James repeated. "It was to our left, and we was almost passin' it."

"Everybody cease fire," said Burns, though no one in C was firing now, and Burns's last pellets to James were forty below. "You popped a fuckin' Bradley," said Burns.

"It wasn't a Bradley!" James cried.

"Did you not," said Burns, a DA who's twisting a Bowie knife into a desperate witness—"did you not completely understand you could only engage with my authorization?" He waited a moment, then said, "That's the *infantry* there," but James didn't answer him. Aghast, James had twisted his "key" and was talking to Penn, his now unstrung gunner.

"Did *you* see a T-55?" James said.

"No!" said Penn, who'd seen nothing except in his night sight a pale green glow. "You told me to shoot it!"

Dear God! Dear 72,000 angels! James reached behind him, James grabbed his Bible, God or coincidence opened it to John 14, his eyes were those of a man who's trapped in a fire, they darted to and fro and, over and over, saw Jesus's words, "Let not your heart be troubled," "Let not your heart be," "Let not your heart," and Burns, having ripped up James, now radioed the XO, the boy who'd deceitfully told the colonel, "It's a T-55."

"Go," Burns said to the XO, "to green," meaning the XO should turn on his scrambler so C couldn't listen in. The XO did, and Burns at last vented himself, took off his skin, nails, nostrils, lips, let out his rage like lava out of Mauna Loa. "You're *fuckin'* me, XO," Burns erupted. "You said it's a *T-55* and it's plainly a *Bradley*!"

"No, it's a T-55!" the XO protested.

"You're lying to *me*! You're lying to the *colonel*! Get your head out of your *ass*! The guy shot a *Bradley*!"

"No, I could see it!"

"I don't even *care*! You don't tell the *colonel* until you tell *me*! I am the goddam *commander,* and—"

Let not your heart. On *Crusading for Christ,* the Bible didn't comfort Sergeant James, he read it, reread it, the verse was in pale pink like dawn, he'd highlighted it in Kansas but still his heart ached. He knew that God had told him, "Go to Iraq," had told him, "Be pastor to C," and had just told him, *"Fire!"* and if God's words led to death in Iraq and grief in America, *your wives shall be widows,* the Bible said, *and your children fatherless,* what sort of God could He be? Who had James praised in Virginia when at age three he'd sat in a tie and red blazer saying, "Praise God," and who was James serving now? His faith in God wobbled, went like a rumble inside him, and in despair he resigned from *Crusading for Christ.* He radioed the first sergeant, saying, "Give me the hummer, give me the hummer, take this tank away from me."

Penn, James's gunner, felt like James, but he also told himself, *No,* a Bradley would have been warm and, in the night sight, dark, and Penn was sure he'd shot something pale. The loader thought, *What'll happen to us?* the driver (who couldn't see anything) thought, *What's happening?* a lot of C thought, *The war's crazy,* and nearby in Company D the Indian radioed, "Guys, look left. What's burnin' there is a Bradley. Someone lit up a Bradley," the Indian sounding as sad as Chief Joseph, "I'll fight no more, forever," the Indian sighing, "He fired without authorization." On hearing this, Lieutenant Russell, who still was attached to D, said, "Oh, man, I'd rather die," and his Samoan gunner, who'd still never shot an Iraqi, anyone, thought, *Amene,* meaning *Amen.*

One boy at C like nobody else was Specialist Young, the Mouse-married man. Young was outdoors on the desert and he was pacing east, then west, like a boy doing double time at the Tomb of the Unknown Soldier. Young was in mad-dog mode. Ten minutes earlier he'd looked to the left, seen the two Bradleys and, half-hidden by a booger, seen an Iraqi tank, a T-55, to Young the tank was a one-ton bomb, the turret was turning, the cannon was zeroing in on Young's grill, his Achilles' heel, and Young had thought, *Shit!* He'd had a machine gun, it rode on a rail, he'd rolled it around, *around,* it wasn't aimed right, the safety was on, "Be careful" was Burns's iron rule. *"Go left!"* the commander had shouted, the gunner had *slooowly* turned, the Iraqis had laid their cannon on Young when *boom!* then *boom!* the Iraqis had exploded and Young was alive thanks to Sergeant James. "Who shot? Who shot?" said Burns, said Captain Fire-When-I'm-Ready, Captain Who-Cares-About-Young, and Young had thought, *Fuck him!* then Burns had told James empty-headedly, "You popped a Bradley," and Young had torn his helmet off and shouted, *shouted,* he'd had the voice of the Xtabay, no longer was he Johnny One-Note, "I need to get out of this fuckin' tank!"

"Is something wrong?" the commander had said.

"No no, I just need *out!*" Young had shouted. He'd jumped to the desert and, like a madman, was now marching east, then west, sending up a spray of sand like a desert storm, thinking, *I was almost waxed!* was almost killed, yes, *him,* the natural soldier, certain survivor, *him,* the Good Soldier Young. His helmet was off and Young couldn't hear what C now proclaimed to Burns: the "Bradley" was an Iraqi menace, a T-55. One boy told Burns, "I can see the *gun,*" and the colonel himself said, "We checked. No one shot a Bradley." The round from the Big Red One had really been from the T-55, the Iraqis had fired at C and had aimed at Young when James, half asleep, had destroyed them. The colonel had radioed to Burns, "You may have shot a Bradley," and Burns had interpreted this as "A Bradley's been shot. And *you* may have shot it," and Burns had concluded (oh God, the *confusion*) that James had disgracefully done it. What else? Oh, the bonfires, the ten red tornadoes—those were Iraqi tanks, more T-55s, being hit by the Big Red One.

Burns didn't say, "I was wrong." Those words weren't in Burns's language, *I must be perfect,* he thought, *or the troops won't trust me,* and Burns said to C sarcastically, "We survived that one. It was, in fact, a T-55," then he drove to *Crusading for Christ* and said, "Sergeant James."

"*Sir,*" James cried, really cried, the tears were running down James's cheeks. "That was a T-55!"

"I understand that," said Burns.

"I'm *sure* it's a T-55! I saw the turret traverse!"

"I understand that."

"I know I shouldn't've shot it! But sir—"

"You did the right thing," said Burns. He climbed onto James's tank and said, "But understand how I see it. I'm bound by the Tanker's Bible," *The Gunnery Manual for Tankers,* Field Manual 17-12-1. "It says in Chapter Seven that *I* will control the company's fires."

"Well, maybe," said James—"maybe next time I won't fire!"

"No. You may have to. You may have saved someone's life."

"Sir?"

"You may have saved someone's life," said Burns, then he climbed off and drove off as James thought, *What? have I saved more than C's souls?* and as Young, the madman, the east-and-west marcher, came up to James's tank. "Thank you for shooting it!" Young said.

"I wasn't gonna let it shoot *us,*" said Penn.

"I don't know why I done it," James murmured.

"I'll back you up," said Young, "if Burns—"

"He said everythin's forgiven," said Penn.

"Oh, great," said Young, then more of C walked up. Each person in C believed the Iraqis had aimed at *him* and James had saved *him,* and each person said, "Thank you, sergeant!"

James was still stunned. "It was like God had me to do it," James said, and as C went to its tanks, climbed on, and *arrr!* started rolling again, he asked himself, *Why?* Why hadn't God with terrible lightning hit the Iraqi tank Himself, why had He called on James to do it? Why, long ago, had God called on Noah, Moses —*David,* why had He put the slingshot in David's hands when He could wield it Himself? And slowly James saw that God didn't sit in the clouds, that God did His work through man, through *him,* that God had surged in James's throat when James had cried, "Fire!" that James had been God's own trumpet. James felt the spirit of God (not just the awareness of God) inside him and James started crying for joy. He stood up in James's Ark, in *Crusading for Christ,* his tears wet his helmet strap, and as C went east he sang in a shivering voice,

> *When I think of*
> *The goodness of Jesus*
> *And all*
> *He has done for me,*

his arm above him, his arm swaying left, right, left, like a palm, like when Jesus went into Jerusalem, the black lieutenant thinking, *What is he signaling me? Go left?* and telling his driver, "Go left,"

> *My soul cries out,*
> *Hallelujah!*
> *I thank God*
> *For saving me!*

No longer was James subdued, James had surrendered to God, and God, like blood, was pulsing inside him, was in his arms, his fingers, his *voice*, which soared at God's every beat,

> *My my my soul cries out,*
> HALLELUJAH!
> *I thank God*
> *For sa, for saving me!*

It was 3:15. Except for James, C was drained dry. On its radios the colonel said, "Cowboy, I mean Bulldog, is moving out," and C went east too. The clouds were ponchos: wet, wide and drably black, the ponchos shut out the sun and the edges dragged on the desert, becoming fog, had the sun burned out? had Pluto eclipsed it? the gloom was like in El Greco and C put its lights on. The boogers got bigger, the Iraqi army (hell, the Iraqi *navy*) could be in back of those pyramids waiting for C, the boogers got closer together till A, B, C, D and the A, B, C, D of another colonel were in Indian file, the A's, B's, C's and D's mingling, the 140 tanks and Bradleys moving like at a Last Chance for Gas, one mph. Night descended. The world was blackberry jam, at intervals there was a *boom!* an enigmatic explosion, and at ten o'clock the colonel radioed the full colonel, "We gotta stop."

"Negative," the full colonel said. On his map was an empty desert, though in ⅟₃₂-inch type, in flea-circus type, in type so diminutive that a one-inch square could accommodate the Gettysburg Address, the full colonel saw the words NUMEROUS QUARRIES.

"No, we're dorked up," the colonel protested. "We're going to get somebody killed. We're—"

"Okay," the full colonel said, and the A's, B's, C's and D's stopped. In their night sights, they saw the Iraqis ("What's *that?*" "Someone. Unless it's an Iraqi counterattack") and C only slept from twelve to two or from two to four, when *you've-got-to-get-up,* it rose once more and had MREs. As usual, C was chipper, but its eyes implied that it had been slipped some frogs, toads, and *fugu* fish and was now Haitian zombies. At seven the night abated and C saw fog: the world was in gauze but was dangerous again, for 960 meters ahead was the ghost of Heathcliff? the hound of the Baskervilles? what?

"I identify a T-55!" a commander radioed.

"One hundred percent identify?" said Burns.

"No," the commander said. "Not one hundred percent." The fog, like a special effect, then eddied, the ghost, the hound, or the Iraqis coalesced, and the commander radioed, "Yes! It's a T-55! A hundred percent!"

Its cannon was pointed at C and precisely at Specialist Walters, the boy who'd received a "Dear John" on his answering machine in Kansas but who'd won the lady at Bushwacker Bar. She'd recently written to Walters, "Pumpkin! I miss you! Keep yourself safe! Come back to me! I love you!" and Walters, eschewing all !!!s, had written from Saudi, "It's boring," "We're waiting," and "We're sitting around," but Walters wasn't bored today. He was a driver: last year of a cart that collected balls on a golf driving range at Fort Riley and now of a tank an Iraqi, wrapped in the fog, was apparently aiming a cannon at. On his Walkman was Jimi Hendrix, was *Purple Haze,*

> *Purple haze*
> *All through my brain!*
> *Livin' things*
> *Don' seem the same!*

On his earphones the gunner was saying, "Let's shoot it!" but Burns (hey, who was this man? the United Nations?) was saying, "Stand by,"

> *Actin' funny but*
> *I don' know why!*
> *'Scuse me while*
> *I kiss the sky!*

"*Damn!*" said Walters's frightened commander and Walters was frightened too. "Why won't he let us *shoot* it?"

> *Purple haze*
> *All aroun'!*
> *Don't know if*
> *I'm up or down!*

Not far away, Burns didn't think that the foggy ghost was American. He saw its Iraqi contour, Iraqi cannon, even an Iraqi (the gunner, he hoped) sitting on top and smoking, and Burns was sure the tank was Iraqi. But Burns, who at Al Qarnain had squashed an Iraqi and said, "I feel like shit," Burns cared for C but cared for Iraqis, too, and he didn't want to kill them wantonly. He felt the Iraqis' cannon was six inches higher than it would be if it truly was pointed at Specialist Walters. He knew that the Tanker's Bible, *The Gunnery Manual for Tankers,* didn't discourse on How to Capture a Tank, its doctrine was just demolish it, but Burns now radioed the lieutenant from West Point and said, "Go get it," meaning "Go capture it."

Walters went stiff. He lay on his Barcalounger stone still. On his Walkman was

> *Help me! Help me!*
> *Oh, no, no! Damn!*

but Walters, age twenty-one, also felt, *Burns is right,* felt, *If we don't have to kill 'em, we shouldn't.* No one had greater love than that: to die perhaps for Iraqi motherfuckers, and Walters lay stiff as a soldier who'd died, yes, stiff as that soldier's sarcophagus lid, as *arrr!*

the lieutenant's tank set out. The smoker saw it, apparently, for Walters saw him jump into his tank, but Burns stayed silent and Walters remained the Stone Soldier. And then Walters saw the Iraqi again. He was climbing out, and in his hand, held high, as though to catch pennies from heaven, was a little white plastic pail. It meant *We surrender,* and Walters went limp.

C captured six Iraqis. Walters and C were happy about it, for one minute later the general radioed, the full colonel radioed, the colonel radioed, and Burns then radioed to C, "Cease fire. Peace," Burns said, as somber as he might have been at Appomattox— "peace is breakin' out," and Walters thought, *Gee. I'd be feelin' bad if I'd killed an Iraqi a minute ago.*

But peace wasn't breakin' out. In Washington the President said so, but the Iraqis behind the boogers didn't hear him. "I want to remind you," a voice on C's radios said, "that though you're under cease fire you can still get killed. You can fire if fired upon," and C answered, "Roger!" At eight o'clock an Iraqi lieutenant walked up to C, his thumb and a finger carried a pistol, he gave it to C and said, "Saddam fucked us," and C answered, "Yeah. He fucked us, too," but a lot of Iraqis stayed in their trenches, bunkers, *tanks,* and Burns, even Burns, that prince of peace, told C, "You may still carry rounds." C got its second casualty now. A sergeant known as Transformer (*click!* he could change in a flash from a lamb to a lion) was in a Bradley and hit a rut, and fifty cannon rounds fell on Transformer's foot. "My foot! I done fucked it up!" he cried, and a red-crossed vehicle carried him off.

The rest of C, *arrr,* left the boogers but not the Iraqi presence. It stopped on the open desert, but at four hundred meters it saw an Iraqi bunker, and the black captain of A, an all-state basketball player from Alabama (in lay-ups he'd pass the ball behind him into his other hand)—the captain told A, "Now, stay on your *p*'s and *q*'s," and went in a Bradley to the Iraqi bunker. "Come out," the captain, whose name was Womack, cried.

"No," an Iraqi said in English. "We want to go home."

"No, you got to come out," the captain said, for by order of the President he couldn't say "Fire!" and blow the Iraqis into the Caspian Sea. *This isn't realistic,* the captain thought, then the colonel drove up.

"No, you got to come out," the colonel said.

"No, we're afraid you'll hurt us."

"No, we won't hurt you."

"No."

The colonel got livid. He was like C at Al Qarnain: in the midst of Iraqis, armed Iraqis, he wasn't allowed to shoot at, and *"Bullshit!"* he cried in spite of the President's orders. "Come out! Or we come in shooting!" and the Iraqi and two dozen others came out. *This cease fire,* the colonel thought, *will kill us,* and, furious, his scar turning ultraviolet, a man needed goggles to view it, he yelled at an American lieutenant, "You! Did you shave today?"

"No sir."

"Goddammit! Then do it!" the colonel yelled, really *yelled,* his scar was a red-lipped, wide-lipped mouth and his index finger a claw, jabbing at the lieutenant's face. "The war isn't over!" the colonel yelled, then *arrr!* he drove away.

He wasn't happy. He wanted this war to end, really *end.* He was part Indian: Choctaw, and he'd often boasted, "We're one of the Seven Civilized Tribes," and he'd had enough of—what? the Iraqi War? At age eight in Alabama he'd found a cave, his father (a sergeant) had told him, "No, stay away," but he'd told the cub scouts about it, "It's neat!" "How neat?" "You can see things!" "What can you see?" "I don't know. Animals!" "We wanna see it," and he'd led the cub scouts inside it. "It's neat," the cubs had agreed, but the racket had rattled the dirt around them, and the dirt *crump!* collapsed. In dirt to his chest, his head out like Ugolino's, the not-yet-colonel cried, *"Help,"* then, like a boy who's gone overboard, flapping, flapping, his arms like a seal's flippers, he swam to the surface and dug out the others, one of them white-faced, blue-lipped, dead. "You went against God," the Catholic priest later told him. "You'll burn in hell forever," and for years the colonel had believed it. *I'm like the Angel of Death,* the colonel thought now.

He went into the Operations tent. It was, of course, without windows, was dark as an underground room, but a couple of dull fluorescent lights lit it. He sat down alone at a table, pop-topped a Diet Pepsi (its label in Arabic) and, while sipping, thought of the people who'd died in Iraq. Two were from A, B, C, D: the boy who'd picked up the Easter egg and the one who'd watched, and the colonel now blamed himself, *I should have— I should have— Well, what?* just as he'd blamed himself when Sean, age seven, died in the Alabama cave. He thought of the twenty-one boys who'd died in the Big Red One. In his dreams, they were burning, he smelled their flesh, and he'd even woken up yelling, "We're under attack!" and he thought of the four hundred dead in the Tawalkana. A lot had been buried alive at Al Qarnain, and the colonel knew that the soldier who'd done it—the dozer driver, a Mormon—was now having nightmares too, the Iraqis staring, *staring,* the dirt curling over them like surf, the Iraqis floundering, *whoosh!* they were gone, their tombstones were obstinate arms, were arms that pointed to God, *Dear God! You see what America did!* One day the Mormon boy had confessed to the colonel, "I'm hurtin', sir."

"What happened?"

"Well, look what I did."

"You did the right thing," the colonel had said—had said quite uncomfortably, for *he* was the man who'd said in Kansas, "Don't fight fair," "Sneak up on 'em," "Kick their nuts," "Gouge their eyes," and "Bury them." He'd told the Mormon boy, "You saved American lives."

"I feel I'll go to hell for this."

"You won't go to hell," the colonel had promised, but he'd also flashed on Father Murphy in Alabama, "You'll burn forever," and he'd felt rotten about the Mormon. How long would this war go on? How many more Iraqis would the Mormon bury alive?

The colonel, at Operations, sipped from the Arabic-curlicued can. At nine o'clock some captains arrived, they went to the coffee machine, and with Styrofoam cups, the coffee seesawing inside, they sat at the colonel's table, and the Personnel captain went first. He said, "All the elements—"

"*Elements?*" the colonel growled. "Barium? Thorium? Fuckin' uranium? We have *units.*"

"Yes sir," the Personnel captain said. He thought, *The colonel's moody today,* and he said there were two dead, four wounded, boys in the colonel's units.

"I want their addresses," the colonel said joylessly. "I don't want to write these letters but I'm going to do it." He then lit a Carlton and called on the Intelligence captain.

"Yes *sir,*" the Intelligence captain said. He said that forty miles north, the Republican Guards—the Medina and Hammurabi Divisions—were massing along the Euphrates. "We may go north," the Intelligence captain said.

The colonel muttered, "Do we have maps?"

"We have *parts* of maps."

The colonel threw down his Bic. "Well, who cares? We don't need no stinkin' maps," he growled, then he dragged on his Carlton. Even without it, the air reeked from the Kuwaiti fires.

"It's hydrogen sulfide," the captain explained.

"What'll hydrogen sulfide do to you?"

"It'll make you nauseous."

"I'm *already* nauseous," the colonel said. A former history teacher, owner of two master's degrees, his own gift to history would be the four hundred corpses at Al Qarnain, *Yes,* he thought, *they'll be my magnum opus.* "What we did there," he told his captains now, his tone almost saying, *"J'accuse,"* "was horrendous. We killed lots of people. We killed the sons, brothers and lovers of other people, and I'm not proud of it. None of us enjoys taking human life, as far as I can tell. Well," the colonel considered, "maybe Bushyhead enjoys it," but the Cherokee put his hand on his head like for an Excedrin headache. He shook his head sadly, meaning *no,* and the colonel recanted, "but I don't think even ol' Bushy enjoys it. I am not," the colonel continued, "a greatly religious man, but I think I'm a spiritual man and I'd like to offer this prayer. May God," the colonel began, and the captains bowed their heads—"may God grant us the good fortune to have been done with this, and may God grant us the good fortune not to do it again."

The captains said, "Amen," and Burns of C nodded solemnly.

"All right," the colonel said and he moved to a more urgent matter. "We may have forty-eight hours before we're back in combat. All right, we're outta here."

He stood up and Burns did too. Nearby was a metal coat rack, and Burns took his helmet from it, then, putting it on, he went through the tent flap: the air was cold, the wind was a lion lying in wait, in the distance were forty skyscraping fires like on a giant's birthday cake, and Burns went by hummer to C. By now the colonel had radioed to C, "On order, we will attack the Medina and Hammurabi," the Iraqis who, to C's north, were still shooting at Americans, and C was on top of its tanks still using up fat, bone marrow, bones and brains, getting ready to go. C was still bugged at Burns, was calling him Gus, Bullet Bob, the Four M'er, saying, "If we go, I'm not askin' for permission to fire, yeah, *fuck* permission to fire," and Burns now sensed that he shouldn't go north till he'd had a heart-to-heart with C.

He thought about what he'd say. At the Battles of Al Qarnain and the Boogers, he'd put the tightest grip, the fullest nelson, on C, and he wondered, *Well, should I have loosened up?* Could he have relaxed and yet killed the Iraqis and *yet* preserved all of C? Could he have applied a seven-eighths nelson, saying, "You need a *lieu-tenant's* permission," could he have prudently said that to C? His lieutenants were competent men, and *Maybe,* Burns thought, *I should have eased up. Maybe,* Burns thought, *I was wrong,* and on a white envelope he put three dots and

- *What I Know Happened*
- *What I Think Happened*
- *My Temper*

and, in his hummer, went to C's soldier-swarming tanks.

He got out. On his hood he put maps, and, as the boys collected around him, he spoke of what happened at Al Qarnain. He then said, "The next thing here is My Temper. I know why I lose it," he said, though he felt uncomfortable saying it, "and I don't want you to think I don't like you, or think you're beneath me, or think you're not a Great American. The thing is, I've got to take control before my guy shoots somebody else or somebody else shoots *him.* Uh," Burns said as C listened silently, "I don't know what else to say on My Temper. Let's talk about Control," Burns said, and his awkward apology ended. "You needed authorization," said Burns, "because the sit," situation, "was so fuckin' flaky that nobody knew where the *good* guys were or the *bad* guys were. You remember—"

Burns never said, "I was wrong." Burns constitutionally *couldn't* say, "I was wrong." He still hadn't told the scrappy lieutenant, the boy who'd saved him at Al Qarnain, "I was wrong," and still hadn't told the XO, the boy who'd said at the boogers, "It's not a Bradley," "I'm sorry, XO, I was wrong." This morning, the XO had hovered by Burns, rehearsing, silently saying, "Sir, could I talk with you?" and when Burns had looked up, the XO had blurted, "Sir, could I talk with you? I'm human and I've made mistakes, but I—" "I'm busy," Burns had grunted, and the XO had thought, *We can't function this way,* as Burns drove off to defend himself to C.

"How many men," Burns was saying now, "did this task

force," did A, B, C, D, "lose to enemy fire? *Nada*," said Burns, meaning "None," and Burns's arm drew an o in the air. "How many men," he continued, "did this task force lose to friendly fire? *Nada*," said Burns, and Burns drew another o. "How many task forces didn't lose a man to enemy or friendly fire? As far as we know, we're the only one. *Thank* you," said Burns, then he grabbed the hand of the closest boy and shook it. The boy thought, *Oh, what a jerk,* he thought of a pol he'd once seen in Seattle, pumping and pumping people's hands, and Burns may have sensed it, for Burns tried to joke about it. "You won't believe this," Burns said, "but my new nickname is Iceman, because I'm so calm and so cool on the command net," the colonel's channel. "Tell that to any *soldier,*" said Burns, and C laughed uneasily, "and he won't fuckin' *believe* it." C laughed a little louder and Burns said, "It's like—"

"They couldn't hear you holler to XO!" someone shouted, and C now roared.

"Goddammit, XO, answer me!" someone shouted, and C roared again.

"Heed what I say, XO!" someone shouted, and C roared and roared.

Burns smiled thinly. He rolled up his maps, got into his hummer, and left, and C got onto its tanks, still snickering at or in spite of Burns, still thinking, *He tried to bullshit us,* still hating the man who'd preserved it, so far, throughout the Iraqi War.

The next day the Hammurabi and an American unit had a battle royal (hundreds of Hammurabis died) and C went to Redcon Three, to Ready Condition Number Three, to Ready for the Hammurabi. Planes full of MREs, water and mail landed on a Kuwaiti road, and C went like bees to, you guessed it, the mail, its first since in Saudi. Since then, C hadn't heard from a woman except, one enchanted morning, from one on C's radios, who'd said, "This is

Juliet four," "Uh, Juliet four. Is this the net you want to be on?"
"Negative. Thank you. Out," but now C had mail from its wives,
brides, girls, it had mail on pink paper, sweet-smelling mail, mail
like "I miss you," "I love you," "Come home." Medine, the boy
who'd once grabbed his Beretta, thinking, *I'll kill Captain Burns,* got
peach-colored mail from England, his English fiancée, and Penn,
who'd fired at the blip that *hallelujah!* wasn't a Bradley, got a photo
of Kendrell, his premature son, his very black premature son. One
boy got mail from a college, saying, "PEACE RALLY. NOON," and
Captain Burns, in his function as Any Soldier, got mail saying,

> *Roses are red,*
> *Violets are blue,*
> *I hate Saddam,*
> *Will you torture him too?*

Some of C's mail was disappointing. Gilliam, the *thunder* gunner,
got a Dear Greg,

> *It's not what it use to be. I don't feel the same as I did. I'm*
> *unsure! I need help, I mean mental help! I'm very confused,*

and Gilliam said, "What does this mean?" and C said, "She's dumpin'
you, man." Gebert, who'd married the War Resisters, got the same
mail as in Saudi: none, the girl with the other half of "THE LORD
WATCH OVER THEE AND ME" was tongue-tied, tight-lipped, or otherwise occupied, and Gebert just kicked the sand saying, "Shit."

By now C had slept, yes, C had made delta waves, had recovered its mental faculties, and it now wrote to Kansas. The boy
who'd written, "Say hi to Irene," meaning "I'm in Iraq," today
wrote, "Say hi to Kevin," meaning "I'm in Kuwait," and Young,
who'd written to Mouse, his bare-bottomed wife, "We are doing
things fucking wrong," who'd thought, *No, that isn't for Mouse,*
who'd then torn the letter up—Young thought, *I'll write her. But
what will I say?* and sat on his tank today, pondering. A few miles

away, the oil wells were torches, the furnaces hummed in Young's ears: white noise, and Young opened an MRE. He took out the candy, then, as if it were some choice morsel, nibbled it, slid it along his incisors, licked it slowly, sensuously—yes, Young was a Frenchman who was French-kissing his Bar, Chocolate, Mars, was almost seducing it and was thinking, *What will I write to Mouse?*

He thought of the Battle of Al Qarnain. He thought of the gunner who'd asked him, "You wanna play gunner?" of Young who'd said, "Yeah!" and, one minute later, of the Iraqi he'd seen running into a BMP. "I have a Bimp!" Young had cried.

"What range?"

"I got 1790!"

"Shoot it!"

"On the way!" Young had cried, and *boom!* the BMP and ten Iraqis had gone to paradise. *"Hoo,"* Young had cried, "I got one," and he'd tied a knot in his camouflage cord—tied *one,* not ten, for ten knots seemed cold-blooded even to Young. Once, Young had felt that war was fun: the army, the mercenaries he'd been in in Mexico, the knight-in-armor people in Texas, the sense of being alive, *alive,* that he couldn't conjure up in Kansas. But now Young thought of the Iraqis who'd died, *They died for Saddam,* thought of their war for Kuwait, *For sand,* and thought of the boys in C, *We're grown-ups. And we're killing grown-ups. Why?* and Young knew he couldn't write to Mouse, "I killed ten Iraqis, dear."

He thought of the Battle of the Boogers. He thought of the T-55, the Iraqis who'd aimed at his grill, his Achilles' heel, of Young who'd thought, *Shit!* who'd walked east, west, and sent up a second desert storm, who'd thought, *I was almost waxed! almost killed! no, I'm not immortal!* And now, the horizon afire, he thought of the Medina, Hammurabi, thought, *I may die tomorrow,* but Young knew he couldn't write to Mouse, "I may die." Before showing up in Saudi, Young had worn a rubber stopper, his voice had dripped through it, *drip,* like drops from a rusted faucet, but in Saudi and north of Saudi his throat had widened and it could *roar* in this letter to Mouse. But roar what?

He reached into a pocket and pulled out a plastic bag. Inside it was marijuana that, in Kansas, he'd stashed in his tank behind —far behind—his forty cannon rounds. The stuff was his last quarter-ounce, for in Saudi his three other quarter-ounces, *whoo!* had blown to the Gulf, to the giddy fish in the Gulf, but today wasn't windy and Young rolled a J and *ahh!* took a toke, success! He felt he'd just put the American flag on Mount Everest. Above him the clouds had solid-silver linings that, if Young hit them, would surely go *ping!* like chimes, and Young felt alive although, no, *because,* he also felt, *Yes, I can die.* Oh sure, he might survive the Medina, the Hammurabi, but still he was doomed: he had fifty more years, and if he didn't wallow in them before 2040 he'd never wallow at all. In his head he heard the *Rhine Journey* from *Siegfried,* and he pulled out his Bic pen and pad.

He'd often done this. He'd done it sixteen times in Kuwait, but his letters to Mouse had gone into fires full of wrappers of MREs, and he was ecstatic when, with no effort, a letter jelled in the part of his head that listened to Wagner and sped like tingles down his arm and into his Bic. The words weren't "I might die" but

> *Love,*
>
> > *The past week, one question kept nagging me. I can't figure out what I did to deserve you. I'm normally not that lucky. . . .*
> >
> > *I guess some people like me don't realize what they've got until it's not there. . . .*
> >
> > *The only thing that kept me sane was knowing you'd probably leave if I came home crazy. . . .*
> >
> > *No one will ever love you more than I do. Wait and see!!!*

then Young signed it *"Tiger"* and wrote a P.S.,

> *P.S. I'm sharpening my claws!!!*

then, inking his fingertips, he made a paw print, jumped to the
desert, abandoned the J, hell, the camels could have it, and put
the passionate letter in the first sergeant's hummer, the "post office" here in Kuwait.

By now the contingency plan was at A, B, C, D. It said
SECRET, then said the Iraqis (the Adnan, Medina and Hammurabi)
had six hundred tanks, were at the Euphrates, and were defending
it, then said that on D-Day all A, B, C, D would attack. One
morning the colonel radioed, "We move in three hours," but later
radioed, "No," today wouldn't be D-Day. Maybe tomorrow.

The colonel was still unhappy. He'd now seen the Highway
of Death, the miles of Iraqi vehicles, upside down, inside out, on
top of each other like dogs, like people who'd died at cries of
"Fire!" the vehicles carbon-paper-colored, casualties of American
bombs. In the seats (and, like clowns, climbing out of the windows)
were the Iraqis, all dead: some gooey, as though made of glue,
some molten, as though of old candle droppings, some just Hal-
loween skeletons. The one indestructible thing was Iraqi zippers,
silver zippers, they glittered on the Iraqis' ribs like Iraqis' souls,
they were immortal entities and, at this stomach-spinning sight,
the colonel had felt like Attila. A lot of his recent mail had said,
"Go to Baghdad," even some soldiers in C had said, "We should
go to Baghdad," the President might say, "Go," any day, but the
colonel felt wretched about it.

His first master's degree was from North Carolina. His thesis
was partly on the British troops who had marched on Baghdad in
1916, lost, surrendered, and died of typhoid in Turkish camps, and
he didn't want his A, B, C, D to follow the British steps. To put
pontoons across the Euphrates and Tigris. To cross those rivers,
wider than the Rhine, under Iraqi artillery fire. To go three hundred miles to Baghdad, bigger than Berlin, then go from house to

house as Iraqis dropped mortar rounds instead of confetti out of their windows, thirty floors up. "Saddam's alive," said the colonel's mail. "We should get him," but Saddam, the colonel knew, could run to the Zagros Mountains, and A, B, C, D then would follow him to that cold, snow-covered realm. In time, much of A, B, C, D and hundreds of other companies would be dead, wounded, missing (or be in control of Iraq, fighting off Iranians and Syrians) and the colonel's mail would say, "You shouldn't have gone." *Dear God! Let this war end,* the colonel thought, as in pencil he mapped the attack on the Adnan, Medina and Hammurabi.

He spoke to C plainly. One morning, he stood on the desert surrounded by C and said, "Guys. There's nothing glorious about what we did. We—" *Kkkkk!* A radio interrupted him, and the colonel snapped, "Will you turn that *down?* and I hope you understand that. I don't know," he continued, "what you guys want out of war, but I've had all I fuckin' want, it's all the war I need. No way they could make me happy, except," he said, and he pointed an unlit cigarette west at America, "by takin' my ass outta here. I won't be sorry at all, I could walk off this fuckin' thing right now." He also told this to his captains and, one day, to his full-colonel boss, as they huddled at Operations. "My heart aches," the colonel told him.

"No one," the full colonel said, "likes doing this." He then left, but a captain who'd overheard the two sat down with the heavy-hearted colonel.

"Sir," the captain began. "Before I'm a soldier, I'm a Christian and a man of God, and when I see someone whose heart aches, I share God's word with him." The captain, a Korean immigrant, pulled out a Bible, opened it to Luke 12:34, and read,

Where your treasure is, there will your heart be.

"That's heaven," the captain explained.

To the colonel, the words were utterly—*useless,* were painfully so, and he started crying. His tears wet his scar, they trickled like blood, he wiped them away and said, "I feel like the Angel of Death. Like all I do is kill and kill. I love my soldiers," the colonel said and he started crying again, "but I feel sorry for the Iraqis. They're human too." He didn't wipe the tears away but said, "I don't look so tough now, do I?"

"We don't think you're tough, sir. We know you're compassionate, sir," the captain said. "But what you did," and he meant the Iraqis that A, B, C, D had shot, burnt, buried alive, *especially* buried alive, "saved lives," then he opened the Bible to Psalm 57 and read,

> *They have digged a pit before me, into the midst whereof they are fallen themselves. Selah.*

"What happened to the Iraqis, sir," the captain said, "was unfortunate, but you couldn't help it."

The colonel kept crying. He said, "No, I'm more than this. If all I am is the Angel of Death, then I need to— I need to—" The colonel stood up. "You've got to excuse me," he said, and he hurried out to the empty desert. He thought of the desert in Arizona, a cabin, a cup of coffee, the sun coming up, going down, his wife and him watching, and he resolved to resign from the army as soon as (and if) he returned from Basra or Baghdad.

And one day his orders came, and A, B, C, D went north to Iraq. And later—the first day of spring, ironically—new orders came, and A, B, C, D went east to the Gulf, to Iraq's giant naval base. For thirty minutes C waited. It didn't see the Gulf, ships, Iraqis, it just saw—*pipes,* then more orders came, and Burns, Captain Burns, said, "We're going back," and C started rolling south, *arrr.* It rolled to Kuwait, to the boogers, to Al Qarnain, it rolled to Ten Kilo, Six Kilo, Four, the trenches it had hosed and dozed on Shadrach, Meshach, Abednego Day, it rolled, it rolled, and *Hey,* C concluded. *The war's over. We're goin' home.*

7

The U.S.A.

One day C rolled through the Wall. The colonel had often told it, "The fat lady hasn't sung," and C had asked, "Is she on the stage?" and the colonel had said, "Yes, she is," but now the fat lady, dieting, was wriggling into her Walkmans and hitting each note from A to Z for Zappa. The commander who'd listened to GO TO WAR now listened to GONE TO WAR, a tape of I'm-comin'-home music like *Hippie Chick,* by Soho, another commander listened to *Always,* by Atlantic Star,

> *Girl, you're to me*
> *All a woman should be!*

and one driver listened to 2 Live Crew, *As Nasty as They Wanna Be,*

> *Listen up, y'all,*
> *Cause this is it!*
> *Forget that ol' dance*
> *And suck my dick!*

the driver's hands on his handlebar, his fingertips tap-tap-tapping it. C got to the Wall of Iraq, *correction,* of Saudi, and saw the colonel: he stood at the gap, held a Styrofoam cup, had *mmm,* had coffee, and smiled like someone in Paris as tanks full of Yanks went by. "Hot damn!" the colonel yelled. "We're outta here!" but C, going *arrr,* didn't hear him and, just seeing dust, dust, *dust,* didn't recognize the Wall, and C didn't know this was Saudi until, in the evening, it stopped and the first sergeant told it, "Don't litter." Then C, the rascals who had been throwing out MRE wrappers and MRE cartons as if it had never heard of $500 fines, minded its manners, dug its sandpits, burned its litter, and said, "Hey, we're back in Saudi."

C didn't pee on Saudi sand. It got empty bottles of Al-Ghadir, cut off the bottoms, stacked up the bottles, and peed in these humble urinals. It used wooden toilets in Saudi and yes! even spoke to the Saudis, saying, "You been to Cairo?" "Yes," "To the pyramids?" "Yes." It also played cards, played spades, with the Saudis, who won and explained to C, "You watch TV. We play cards," and one day it put its tanks on the Saudis' trucks and it joined the Barnum & Bailey parade down Suicide Drive. En route, C called to a cop in a black beret with a Saudi shield, "I give you this," an American helmet, "for that," the Saudi beret, but the Saudi just laughed, held up a finger—an index finger—and answered, "One," meaning "Guys, I've got only one," and C laughed too. No longer did C think of Saudis as *ma-hakana-hakana* mothers, for C wasn't killing the Arabs and didn't hate them.

C rolled to the Gulf. The day was hot, a hundred degrees, and as C binged on Al-Ghadir, it climbed out and rolled out its sleeping bags in a six-story structure, the Towers. C wasn't safe yet, for the Iraqis were killing the Kurds and C's mail said, "We should help the Kurds," and at the Towers the consequent rumors were "We're going to Iraq," "We're going to Turkey," "We're staying in Saudi all year." Four months ago, the rumor was that the SS *Jolly Rubino* was crawling with Taiwan rats, and though the rumor was false, the prank of some people at Public Affairs ("Someone got bitten by Taiwan rats. In the latrine. On the ass"), a lot of C had believed it, and C now believed its alleged departure dates to Kansas. Today. Tomorrow. Not until Christmas.

Still, C gave thanks to God. At the Towers the chaplain held services, playing his 33⅓s, pouring his Angelica wine, saying, "I've got the only wine here, guys," lamenting the war, "What darkness! What darkness! What horror!" asking, "Who's read Psalm 91?" and when someone in C said, "Every damn day," then hemming, "There *were* some damn days, weren't there?" He was awkward, this chaplain, his arms were windmills, he stammered ("c-cancerous c-crud") and he certainly wasn't in C, and some of C, yes, and the black lieutenant, went to the closest thing in Saudi to the Church of Deliverance, the stampin' and stompin' spot in Kansas. The lieutenant, who all through the war hadn't said, "God, I love you," "God, please help me," or "God, I'll go to church on Sunday," thought, *I should thank Him, I owe Him that,* and one night went to the "church" in the Towers garage.

The place was gray but the preacher was Sergeant James. The pastor de facto stood at a concrete pillar and said, "Why did God send us to Iraq? *God,*" James continued (and James almost *glowed,* the spirit of God suffused him)—"*God* could have use' the earth-quake! *God* could have use' the tornad'! If *God* had numerous things, why did God use *us?* So we could see the power of *God!*" then C sang *Amazing Grace.* The black lieutenant told James, "I don't know the words," but James said, "Sing! And they'll come!" and the willing lieutenant sang,

> *Amazin' grace,*
> *How sweet thou art*
> *To save a wretch*
> *Like meee,*

> *I once was lost,*
> *La la la laaa,*
> *Was blind but*
> *Now I seee.*

At first the lieutenant parted his palms like a fisherman saying, "It was just three inches long," then he put them together, then at last clapped them like at a square dance, saying, "Thank you, Jesus!"

Night after night, the lieutenant went to James's church. The boy who'd said *fuck, fucker, fuckin'* and *motherfucker* as though they were *ay*s in Pig Latin or *op*s in Oppish was not *eff*-effusive now, the boy whose theme was the *Dogs of War,* the God Spelled Backwards of War, was *la-la-la*-in' along to *God Can Do Anything but Fail.* And one day the boy who'd been told to clean up the Highway of Death and who'd said, "I'll do it. I'll be an intestine-covered motherfucker, I'll be a throwin'-up motherfucker, but I'll be a goin'-home motherfucker," the black lieutenant and C woke at six in the morning, got on the buses, went fifty prudent mph, got to the airport, and—and waited and waited. At noon a general came by and asked the colonel, "Can I do something for you?"

"Yes sir. Get us an airplane."

"I'm working on it."

"I hope so," the colonel said.

At midnight C got its airplane, got on, and at two in the morning, a star-spangled night, it rolled down the runway, then, saying *ahhh!* emitting a seismic sigh, it rose off Saudi Arabia. The land with no lights disappeared, and C watched *Havana, My Blue Heaven,* and *Kindergarten Cop* while flying to Brussels, then Bangor, Maine. It was one in the afternoon in Bangor, but as C got off and made telephone calls ("Mom, I'm in Bangor") it heard an ear-shattering band ("Mom, I can't hear you") and saw the two hundred people who'd come to greet it. Among them were girls! were girls! such as C hadn't ogled (except for the BMOs, the Black Moving Objects, and an American woman who'd sat in a tent with a coffer of ten-dollar bills: the paymaster-mistress for C) for 128 weird days, and to C all these sudden girls were Misses Americas. One who was wearing spandex had a boyfriend in C. Months ago, C had seen her photo and said, "She's ugly. She'd lose some weight if she cut off her head," but now C was gaga about her, "She's cute!"

By now, C wasn't worried that it might return like the C in Vietnam to cries of "You're murderers." At two in the afternoon, it rolled down the runway, and at four it landed in Kansas, the airport that it had left from on New Year's Eve. It walked to the coconut-doughnut hangar: there were no dollies now, but more people stood at the fences, cheering. One, who was silent, whose hair was long, and whose hat was dripping with medals, ribbons, and an embroidered VIETNAM, was clutching the fence as if without it he'd suddenly blow off to Oz, and he was staring at C with the One-Thousand-Meter Stare. Seeing him, the colonel went up, put his hands on his, and gently said, "Welcome home, man," the Vietnam veteran nodded, then C got on buses, rolled to Fort Riley, and, at five in the afternoon, got out and walked in single file but at double time to the other coconut-doughnut hangar from New Year's Eve.

C walked inside. And *yiiiii!* the sound of a thousand people, all sharing the screaming meemies, assailed it. In place of the HURRY HOMES were hundreds of WELCOME HOMEs and a TOTO! WE'RE NOT IN SAUDI! and so much red, white and blue on balloons, banners and flags that the hangar could be the scene of a Democratic or Republican convention. The delegates were C's girls: were C's wives, brides, tootsie-wootsies, as well as C's children, mothers, fathers, grand-thises, grand-thats, mostly in red, white and blue: in shirts with circle-shaped, heart-shaped, flag-shaped flags, in sashes with 3-by-30-inch flags, in Levi's with flags where the flag shouldn't be, in wig-wag rags like on a vast cover of *The Saturday Evening Post.* "*Yiiiii!*" all these people cried as C walked in, a "*Yiiiii*" as loud as the sounds at Al Qarnain. An ear-smashing band (on cymbals: a sunglassed sergeant, a good-looking girl) did Sousa's *Three Cheers for the Red, White and Blue,* and on rock-concert speakers a colonel cried, "Welcome home, heroes!"

C couldn't see who was who. Its wives, brides, etcetera couldn't see who was who in C, for C wore camouflage clothes and, at eye level, camouflage-covered helmets, its chests had red-lensed or blue-lensed flashlights and Beretta holsters, though not Berettas, and its pockets had American flags from Bangor and all of C looked alike. As ordered, C kept walking. It strode to the center of the hangar and fell in in back of Captain Burns, then C heard a *"Yiiiii!"* and Burns's wife, who had red-and-white stripes and white-on-blue stars on her shoulders, broke like a fuzzy-wuzzy into C's square, rushed up to Burns, hugged him, kissed him, and told him, "A sight for sore eyes!" and Burns, now *smiling,* the sourpuss was *smiling,* whispered to Tammy, "I missed you!"

C's other girls still couldn't tell who was who. No matter: they also went *"Yiiiii,"* all except one who was crying and was the bride of Specialist Young, was Mouse. One hour earlier, she'd been euphoric, her breasts had bounced as she said to C's wives, "You look pretty!" "You look patriotic!" "Yes, I asked Michael to marry me!"

"What!" said Tammy, Burns's wife.

"Yes, I got on my knees and I took his hand and I looked in his face and I *said,*" Mouse had said, and she'd gone up an octave like Betty Boop—"I said, 'Will you marry me?' And Michael said yes!"

"Ohhh!" said Tammy, her hand on her red-and-white-striped heart.

"Yes! It was quite romantic!" said Mouse, and as C walked in, she'd stood in her spandex pants and her spattered shirt, an American flag as Jackson Pollock (or someone with spray paint) might paint it, she'd stood close enough to kiss everyone, crying, *"Yay!"* not *"Yii!"* But now Mouse was *really* crying, saying, "He wasn't with them!"

"He's there, don't worry," someone's kind mother said.

"I watched them! I didn't see him!" Mouse cried, wiping her eyes with the hand that didn't hold the American flag.

"He's there, calm down," the kind mother said.

And *kkkkk!* The speakers squawked, and as C's restless eyes went left, right, left, the colonel who'd said, "Welcome home," said, "We are proud of you beyond words." His words rose into the I-beams, then echoed around this Hall of the Mountain King, "You are *ooooo,* and you are the *ooooo.*" C didn't know it, but the next speakers—*singers*—would be C's wives, brides and sweeties, who by prior arrangement would sing,

> *I'll gladly stand up!*

and would then stand up,

> *And defend her today!*

and would light their cigarette lighters,

> *Cause there ain't*
> *No doubt*
> *I love this land!*
> *God bless the U.S.A.!*

Accompanying this in Indian language would be a Kiowa mother, "God," and her hand would spiral up, "bless," her hands in a prayer, "the U.S.A.," her hand would point north, east, south and west—well, that was the *plan,* but C was impatient and C's girls chanted, "We want the men!" and the colonel just said, "God bless you. Go find your families."

And *yiiiii!* The cry of the Kiowas echoed in Fort Riley, Kansas. The hangar rose one or two feet, it cracked off the concrete floor, and, as the sunlight slid in, it floated above like the Mother Ship, and underneath it the Bacchae who were C's girls cried, "*Yiiiii!*" and descended on C. Oh, what a frenzy there was! The girls could be storming the Alamo, could be Germans in World War I or II, a human wave in Korea, their kisses could be a VC barrage. From nowhere came, *yiiiii!* came Mearrie, Penn's corn-braided bride, but not the new baby, *yii*-ing at Grandma's, and out of yesteryear, *yiiiii!* came Caroline, Gebert's bride, still wearing a rose-covered gown and the bright right half of "THE LORD WATCH OVER THEE AND ME." All year she'd written to Gebert, but her "I love you"'s had gone to an army hospital in Saudi: a MASH, neither Gebert nor God knowing why. From yesteryear, too, came Jennifer, the doughnut dolly, the girl who'd once said to Russell, "You were looking at me" ("No, *you* were looking at *me*") and *yiiiii!* who went through the riot to Russell, hugged him, kissed him, and told him, "We've got to stop meeting like this!" She was the best-looking girl in the hangar, hell, in Kansas, and Russell shone like the sun.

In seconds C had been overrun. Its captain and Tammy were *laughing,* were saying *haha,* and to the music of *Soldier Boy* the colonel and Dana, his all-yellow-wearing wife, were fox-trotting and, on the colonel's hip, his gas-mask bag was bouncing along. James and Teri were saying, "Praise God," but Mouse was high in the stands, still crying, one hand wiping the wetness off, and, in the other, her American flag dangling upside down. "I'll never find him!" Mouse cried. "Oh, that looks like *him*! That's *him*!" she cried, and she leapt from the bleachers, *yiiiii!* as if to tear goalposts down, she ran to Young, *yiiiii!* and hugged him, her body shaking, the red and white stripes on her shoulder waving, her tears dropping onto Young's first-aid kit, and Young, who *yiiiii!* who once couldn't say $_c a^0$ or $^c a_0$, now hugged her and hugged her and told her, *"Hi!"* in all four tones of Chinese, for (thanks be to Burns, that thankless man) no one in C had died overseas but one boy had *yiiiii!* come alive.

C got into Fords, etcetera, and at six o'clock rolled from the tunnel that, like the crew of a handcar, *down, up, down,* it had been pumping along in, and it rolled home. By Dodge, Young and his Mouse went to Jefferson Street, then walked to the Youngs' apartment, where Young found a sort of Shinto shrine and Young's photo, Young's name tag, Young's buttons, a rose, a candle, an American flag, and a plaque with *A GI Family's Prayer,*

> *It's going to church*
> *To kneel and pray,*
> *And really meaning*
> *The things you say—*

all this creating an altar where, on a pillow depicting an American flag, Mouse had been praying for Young every day. And today as Young took his camouflage off and *ahhh!* slid into a hot, hot bathtub like into a Jacuzzi, Mouse didn't do as C had predicted, didn't drop an electric appliance in or dispatch him like Clytemnestra, no, she just giggled, "I'll get you one," and brought him a Michelob. At other homes C had Buds and Domino pizzas ("What kind?" said Penny. "Whatever!" said Penny's husband. "How about a Super Supreme?" said Penny. "Sounds good!" said Penny's husband) and Burns and Tammy had Dewar's Scotch, but most of C went to its barracks to get out its wrinkled civvies for Bushwacker Bar.

No need to. Bushwacker—that is, the *heyyy*-saying girls—was in the barracks already, and as C rolled in, its olive-green bags on its shoulders like sailors, the girls ran to C voluntarily. One, who had knotted her blouse to reveal her stomach, started to make up C's beds, smoothing the sheets, plumping the pillows, patting them, even saying to C, "Hey, get off my bed." Another, who was in shorts, asked, "Why are you eating *meat*?" as C ate some Colonel Sanders. "I wouldn't eat *you*," she explained to C, "cut off your *arm*, chow down on *it*. Why do you cut up a chicken and eat it?"

"What are you? A Californian?" said someone in C.

No longer did the girls play the waiting game. One, who'd opened her denim jacket to disclose her bursting black bra, said, "I've been home for five fuckin' months, and I need someone to fuck me," and one girl in very short shorts, a high school senior, seventeen, brought a boy's bag to his room, dropped it *(plop!* and the sand drizzled off it) and literally jumped him, her legs like a web belt around him, her weight pulling him to his bed, her hands undoing her shorts, and her partner panting, "I can't believe I'm home!"

That boy was Sergeant Spence, the one who'd seen an Iraqi and thought, *I'll kill him. The girls will look up to me,* but who now understood that the girls considered him ten feet tall. The girls even wooed the homeliest boy in C, the one whose face was an anvil, *clang!* the face on an Indian nickel, and they ganged up on the best-looking boy, who was Specialist Gilliam, the one who'd shot at Iraqis to the tempo of *Thunderstruck.* Four, count 'em, four of Gilliam's girlfriends went to Gilliam's bed, one girl making it lovingly, one stomping on it like an Apache, saying, "*I'll* show you how I'll make your fuckin' bed!" one dousing him with a Bud, and one jumping *into* the bed and saying, "Oh, Greggy, you're cute!" till Gilliam whispered to C, "You see this fuckin' fiasco?" and tiptoed out for a whopper at Burger King.

The rest of C said, "I want to get outta here. Are we allowed to?" "Yeah!" and in jeans and T-shirts (HARD ROCK CAFE BAGH-DAD—CLOSED) it didn't drive to Bushwacker Bar but to a Bud-weiser garden, Last Chance. And oh! what a wonderful time C had! It drank, it drank, it *yo heave ho!* it lifted the girls who at seventeen didn't have an ID and lowered them into Last Chance, it treated the ID-less girls to Buds, it, *yum!* it bit pretzels and pretty girls' necks, and at the top of its lungs it made happy-hour conversation, "If I give my piece of gum to *you,* and you give that piece of gum to *her,* and she gives that piece of gum to *me,* is it my piece of gum or her piece of gum?"

"It's hers."

"No, it's yours. . . ."

C didn't talk about war. Well, C did just once, when Specialist Anderson, Burns's driver, went to the men's room and a civilian asked him, "Were you there?"

"Yes."

"Did you kill anybody?"

"Yes."

"How did you kill him?"

"Ran him over," said Anderson, then he zipped up and left that uncomfortable room, and to the music of *She Goes Down,* by Mötley Crüe, he danced with the sister of Specialist Walters. The drummer went *boom!* went *boom!* the mirror-moon glittered like fairy dust, the girl wrapped herself around Anderson, *whoo!* she clung like a wet suit to Anderson, *WHOO!* and Anderson soon forgot that he'd been in Saudi that very day.

T he next day, C slept late. It stirred at eleven o'clock, when Anderson showered and C asked, "Did you get lucky?"

"No, I never laid a hand on her!"

"Oh, you didn't use your hands?"

At two, Sergeant Spence, who'd yesterday said, "I can't believe I'm home," was asleep when the girl in the short shorts returned. Just after their tryst, they'd gone to Last Chance ("What was your thought when you saw me?" "Oh, there's a nice girl, I want to have dinner with her," "No, what did you *really* want?" "I want to fuck her!" *"Giggle"*) but the girl was a high school senior, had had to study, and had left. It was now afternoon, and the girl went to Spence's room and said, "How come you're asleep?"

"Huh? I got zero hours last night."

"How come? You party all night?"

"No, I—well, I met this girl—"

"You *what*?"

"And, uh—I stayed with her."

"You *what*?"

"I'm sorry if I've hurt you."

"Well! It's a little late!" the girl yelled, slapping her father's car keys on the palm of her other hand, *slap!* "I was the one who wrote you in Saudi! and met you at the hangar! and came with you to the barracks! and I don't think it's right if you fuck another *girl!*"

"I'll be at your graduation."

"*Fuck you!*" the girl cried, storming out of the barracks, and Spence thought, *Well, I can believe it, I'm home.* The war had been like the Red Sea (or, more precisely, the dry land) and C had now crossed it and *whoo!* the past and the future had splashed together, the war had just—*disappeared,* and C was what it had been last year, some soldiers in Kansas, U.S.A.

The first sergeant said, "Fall in." C did and the first sergeant said, "You all growed men. If you drink, don't drive. If you go to jail, I'm not gonna bail you out. If," *blah, blah,* then the first sergeant said, "Dismissed," and C's day ended. Today was a Friday, Thank God Day, and C went to Bushwacker Bar and the Klub Kamille and gave dollar bills to the Wild One, for Mouse was demurely playing pool. Specialist Anderson, who'd run the Iraqi over, called on Kallie, the hand-kissed girl, who had turned three today and had been saying, "I love him. We're having a wedding." "Hi, sweetie," Anderson said. "Do you want to squosh me?" "Yes!" Kallie said and hugged him, and Sergeant James went tonight to the Church of Deliverance. In the past he'd awaited the Call, the Call, but in Saudi he'd heard it (or learned that he'd *always* heard it) and tonight he stood up in his pew and said, "Praise the Lord."

"Praise the Lord," the congregation murmured.

"I jus' want to let you know," said James, who wore an aloha shirt tonight, "that before we went into battle, that God had been ministerin' to me. God was mentionin', 'Read the Word,' and I said, 'Lord, I don't want to read right now.' And He kept mentionin', 'Read the Word,' and I did and God took me back to David. He was showin' me that when you go into battle, you go in the name of the Lord of Hosts."

"Yeah," the congregation said.

"And when I went into battle, I knew I was goin' in the name of," and James's voice dropped dramatically, "of *Jesus,* Jesus of Hosts," and James's voice soared, James was now Martin Luther

King, James had a dream come true, "and *that's* what made the big difference! It wasn't *man* that brought us through! It was the goodness of *God*!"

"Yeah!!!"

"It was the prayers of the *righteous*!"

"Yeah!!!"

"*It was because of God!!!*" shouted James, his hand high above him. "I can come back tomorrow to share another *part*! and I can come back the next time to share a little bit *more*!" and the congregation (part black, part white) applauded its novice preacher for, count 'em, for twenty seconds.

The rest of C forgot about war. The war had been ugly, inglorious, and C just dismissed it until, tonight, it *clump!* it heard sounds and saw the Ghost of Iraqi Past, saw PFC Kostic, the boy who'd stepped on the Iraqi mine (or American egg) and *clump!* who now limped into C's barracks. Kostic wore a blue sweat suit. He had two crutches and, on his right foot, a cumbersome boot, a couple of toes sticking out like fungus on fallen logs, and C was embarrassed (and embarrassed to be embarrassed) by Kostic's anachronistic wound. Why, C was in Kansas, alive! It didn't want to think about war! It looked up as Kostic came clomping in, and it was relentlessly cheerful. "Hey," someone shouted. "How many toes you got?"

Kostic said nothing.

"It's on the wrong foot!"

"No, it's the right one."

"So how's the leg?"

"The foot."

"When'll it be healed?"

"Well, probably never."

"Hey, Kostic! Jus' cause you had one bad mornin' don't mean—"

At last Kostic smiled. "Bend over," he said to the boy who'd said this, and he pretended to kick him. "The doc said to elevate it," said Kostic, and C laughed at Kostic's joke.

"Have you received a purple heart?" said Captain Burns.

"That's funny," said Kostic. "I was sittin' in an ambulance. And this colonel came, and I was loaded on morphine, and I really wasn't listenin'."

"But you did get your purple heart?"

"Yeah."

"Good," Burns said. What's done was done, and Burns could do nothing for Kostic (or for Transformer, who'd broken his own right foot) but to assure him an ounce of brass and a cameo of George Washington. Burns had a silver star himself, for saying to C, "Don't fire," "Don't fire," and for C's not killing itself. One other boy in C, on Burns's recommendation, had a silver star: that boy was Sergeant James, for boldly disobeying all of Burns's "Don't fire"s. War, C had learned, wasn't glorious. War was dumb.

One month later the barracks was empty, for C had scattered across America, even Europe, calling on loved ones. The black lieutenant and Esse, his wife, went to Ohio, but the lieutenant avoided the *Taps,* etcetera, at the Memorial Day parade. Specialist Walters, the boy who'd thought, *I'd be feelin' bad if I'd killed an Iraqi,* went to Arizona, the new home of Stephanie, his crippled girlfriend, who Walters discovered had sued and won $7,000,000. Walters, too, evaded parades, and Sergeant Medine, the boy who'd thought, *I'll kill Captain Burns,* put the Atlantic between him and Memorial Day. Medine took a plane to England and a train to the border of Scotland, and from a car he spotted his pen pal crossing the Derwent River Bridge. "Hi!" said Medine, and "Hello!" said Carol, they stopped at the Wild Duck, they ordered two turkey-and-mushroom pies, he had tap beer and she had tap wine, he had green eyes and she had blue, she had clear nails and Medine said, "There's something missing. There should be a ring on that finger."

"Yes, definitely," said Carol.

"How about April?"

"Yes."

Medine and Carol didn't talk about war, but Specialist Gebert, the boy whose mail had been mashed, did a virtual after-action report for Caroline's father in Texas. The man had resisted the Vietnam War and still was a War Resister, but (as Gebert now learned) he'd also believed that Saddam Hussein was like Hitler, that Saddam wanted Kuwait, then Saudi, Syria and Israel, and that Gebert made peace, not war, by confronting him. At church one day, Caroline's father had said, "We need to go to Baghdad" ("Why, Bill! Of all people!") and when Gebert came to Texas, Caroline's father got a map of Kuwait and asked him, "Were you in VII Corps?" "Were you near the British?" "The French?" "Did you go to Iraq?" "Kuwait?" Graciously, Gebert answered him, but Caroline's father didn't ask, "Did you kill an Iraqi?" for Caroline had warned him that Gebert would rather forget it.

Another tourist in Texas was Lieutenant Russell. On New Year's Eve, the day he'd met Jennifer, Russell had told her, "We'll have to go there someday," and now they were in Russell's Tempo, the hills of Texas (the hills! the highest things he had seen this year were the boogers!) gazing upon them, Fajita, the golden labrador they'd found in Oklahoma, going *woof,* and Russell and Jennifer nibbling chips from the Casa Olé, in Killeen. The two didn't butt in on Tom, Russell's son, or bring him his little diary (they didn't even have it: in Saudi, the Samoan had thrown it away) but for Russell the grass was green again, for Jennifer, a practical nurse, police volunteer, army reservist, civil defender, doughnut dolly, tornado spotter, et cetera, was a heaven-made mate, an American patriot.

They both loved country music. In the Tempo they sang along with Randy Travis, but Russell faltered at Travis's *Point of Light,*

A ray of hope
In the darkest night,

and Russell asked her, "What's that?"

"The President asked him to write it," Jennifer said. "It's about the war," and Travis said that Russell and everyone else in Iraq were heroes.

"I don't understand," Russell said. "We didn't do anything, we did our *job*. Why write a song about us?"

Jennifer smiled, but C, now strewn from California to Maine, felt exactly as Russell did, felt, *That's what we soldiers do. We win wars*, and when someone made a fuss about it, C didn't understand. One boy was asked in Illinois, "Did you kill anyone?" and answered uneasily, "I was involved," and one boy was asked in Ohio and said, "It's not like TV." One had a birthday party in California (he'd just turned twenty-one) and as he sat eating cake, someone asked, "Did you see dead bodies?"

That's morbid, the party boy thought, but he answered, "Yeah."

"Was it neat?"

Well, damn, the boy thought. *Some poor dead sonofabitch?*

"Did you kill anyone?"

The boy put his cake down. He'd killed some Iraqis, sure, but that didn't imply that he'd liked it. "Yeah!" he stood up and said. "I bit some guy's jugular vein! With my teeth!"

At times C met someone unhappy with C. Its critics (the colonel had called them the Izod-polo-shirt crowd) said, "You didn't accomplish anything. Saddam is still in Iraq. He's hurting the Kurds, he's making atomic bombs or anyhow trying to, he's making the UN inspectors sit in their buses eating their MREs in a parking lot on Rasafi Street," and the colonel, for his part, jabbed at their alligators and said, "Our job was to do what you told us to do. Well, we did it!" In Texas, someone in C met a girl still stuck in the '60s, the "Hey, hey, LBJ" days, who asked him, "How many children did you kill?" and the boy, who'd once seen a child who'd been shot in the head by Iraqis, just walked away. But in Kansas a man in a bar said to Sergeant Spence, "It was bullshit. You shouldn't have gone," and Spence answered, "Motherfucker! I'll kick your ass!" and, throwing the man against the wall, said, "I didn't want to go! They just sent me! That's my *job!*"

The bartender broke them up.

In time C itself broke up. Spence went to Korea and Gebert to Germany. James went to Germany too, and, as a minister for the Church of Deliverance, he preached at its German chapter, decrying the sort of music cherished by C like *Like a Prayer,* by Madonna, saying, "Now, 'Donna says that she's bringin' souls to Christ, but Christ said, 'If I be lifted up, *I* draw all men,' so 'Donna," James thundered, raising his arm, "should lift up *Jesus* and He'll do the drawin'!" The first sergeant, Harn, was in Texas in sergeant major school, and the lieutenants were captains now: Russell in Korea, McRae, the black one, in Texas, his answering machine announcing, "This is Future General of the Army Bennie McRae," Jones, from West Point, in Kansas, and Homer, the scrappy lieutenant, in Panama and in Military Intelligence. Many captains were majors now, and Burns was in Macedonia observing the UN army, Womack of Company A in Georgia, Toro of Company B in Kentucky, and Bushyhead, the Chief Big-Bear, in the American embassy in (*Join the army! See the world!*)—in Vienna. The colonel, who'd said in Kuwait one day, "I wonder if I'm cut out to be a soldier," didn't resign, for he felt obliged to teach everyone what he'd learned in Iraq, and, as a full colonel, he was director of the School of Advanced Military Studies at Fort Leavenworth, Kansas, or, as his students called it, the Jedi Knights. "I'm Yoda," explained Colonel Fontenot.

A lot of C didn't reenlist, or, to be blunt, wasn't asked to, because of bad checks, harassment of women soldiers, awols, or

DUIs. The XO, Lieutenant Light, who Burns had once told, "If I screw up I'll still blame you. Or the troops won't trust me," resigned, but he got A's in accounting at Northern Illinois. The Laotian, whose name was Lim, applied to Nebraska, but Gilliam dropped out of Tennessee to become a Terminex exterminator. Some of C made money, some didn't. Grandpa, whose name was Levesque, made $80,000 a year doing just what he'd done in Saudi: working on tanks in Saudi, and Jones, *stop the press,* resigned, becoming a telecommunications executive in Chicago. Anderson, a steel salesman, bought a home on a golf course in Tennessee, but Penn was a clerk at a Quik Trip in Kansas, Walters a clerk at a Walmart in Ohio, and Kostic a man who made inner tubes in Arkansas and also got $38 per week from the Veterans Administration. Medine tried to join the French Foreign Legion but settled for Louisiana cop, and Young hoped he'd be a mercenary in Mexico, merchant mariner, mercenary in Bosnia, barkeeper, bodyguard, guitarist or novelist while he worked as a Kansas janitor, *bulletin,* worked as a Kansas nurse's aide.

Young and his Mouse broke up. The man who'd married them, Reverend Walls, had told them, "Don' listen to what folks tell you. They goin' to lie," but Young hadn't heeded him, and, one day, when a waitress in Kansas said that Mouse had been effing another man, Young went lifeless, the hills and dales in his voice disappeared, and he said to Mouse monotonously, "You. Opposite direction."

"You. Shut the fuck up," Mouse said.

"I want to get divorced," said Young, and Mouse, closing her eyes, putting her finger on a map, opted to go to Florida to sell popcorn at Barnum & Bailey's. She did, and Young moved in with another girl from the Klub Kamille, a girl who dressed up in cowboy clothes, danced to *Breakfast in America,* by Supertramp,

I'm a winner! I'm a sinner!
You want my autograph?

224

and took off her chaps, et cetera, as off-duty soldiers said, *"Whoo!"*

Some of C stayed happy, some didn't. Spence married the girl he'd met on TOTO, WE'RE NOT IN SAUDI day, and Kostic and Jones got married too, but Grandpa got divorced. Spence and Kostic had baby boys, and Gilliam had a baby girl without a concommitant wife. Russell wanted a baby but Jennifer didn't, and as Fajita, the golden labrador, carried the wedding ring, she married an army helicopter pilot, not Russell. Medine and Carol met just that once, and Walters and Stephanie, who worried that Walters didn't want her, only her $7,000,000, parted, and Walters married his Wal-mart boss. Penn, who, because of the war, had put off his honey-moon on the Mississippi—a showboat, a smorgasbord, a band playing *Ole Man River,* and in the moonlight, *ahh!* the Budweiser brewery south of St. Louis—Penn never went, for Kendrell, his "premature" son, was in fact someone else's, and Penn and Mearrie were off-again, on-again, off. Nor was C saved, for Penn drank beer and McRae said fuck, but, in a church in California, the Samoan, whose name was Aloese, said, *"Ou te lei fasioti!"* "I didn't kill any-one!" *"Ua faaola maiau!"* "I was saved by God!" A true consci-entious objector, the Samoan was now a minister in a church for Samoans.

C led ordinary lives. By 2000, if one can predict, it was mostly civilians, and by 2020, if precedent held, it was older and slower but (in the words of Shakespeare) it still stood a-tiptoe when it spoke of Iraq. By then C had learned that Iraq, where black was black, white white, where a man knew at every crossroad which way to go: go *forward,* where life was dear because death was near, where a man's passions (like *eager,* like *anxious,* like *scared*) were as clear-cut as movies, music and art—that C's greatest moments had been in Iraq, and C recollected them for its sons. It remembered the army's forecast of nine dead, thirty-six wounded, remembered it went to Saudi nevertheless, remembered what the Cavalry had once called the Elephant: *fear,* and remembered the Elephant's bel-lows, *arrrrr!* as C went into the Breach, then galloped to Al Qar-nain, then went to the Battle of Al Qarnain or, as C called it, of

Fright Night, then went to the Battle of the Boogers. As old men do, C remembered with some embellishments (as Shakespeare said, with *advantages*) what feats it did in Iraq, for war is utter confusion and, at the actual battles, most of C hadn't known that a battle was on. It had thought it was shooting abandoned tanks.

In 2020, even in 2040 and 2060, some of C even remembered the Memorial Day parades. Long, long ago in Kansas, it had marched like a crowd of 'cruits up Washington Street, by the Klub Kamille, to a farewell ceremony at Fort Riley. "Halt!" then "Rest!" the first sergeant had said, but C hadn't rested, C was professional soldiers and, as in Iraq, it knew when to follow orders, when not, and it had stood straight while *boom!* the band played one of C's Greatest Hits,

> *I'm proud to be*
> *An American,*
> *At least I know*
> *I'm free!*
>
> *And I won't forget*
> *The men who died*
> *And gave their lives*
> *For me!*
>
> *And I'll gladly stand up—*

as red, white and blue bunting beset it, and as the flags of the fifty states flew over it. Then, C remembered, the colonel had spoken.

The colonel had worn his camouflage clothes. He'd worn his camouflage helmet, and he'd even strapped it to his chin like a quarterback for the Chiefs. He'd known that C was just people, ordinary people, who, in their finest hour, when America called them, had done extraordinary things, and he'd wanted to say to C, "You did what your country asked you to." To say, "You did it with courage, and with compassion toward the Iraqis." To say,

"And things are now *infinitely* better than they once were." War, the colonel knew, was a monster that tramped across the land like the colossus in Goya—war wasn't glorious, war never really ended well, but he'd wanted to say to C, "No war in the twentieth century ended better." No, not even World War I or II.

But that day in Kansas, the colonel hadn't said it. The day was hot as a Saudi summer, the wind from the south was a tank's exhaust, the sweat was a new brown-black on C's camouflage clothes, and the colonel knew that whatever he'd say, C probably knew it. So he'd been succinct: he'd told an anecdote about Iraq, then he'd said, "We are none of us scions of the upper class. We come from Middle America, the barrio, the block, and overseas. But," he'd concluded, the fifty flags flapping over him, the sound like that of machine guns, distantly recollected, the white-black-and-brown-colored boys of C, the Mouse-loving, God-praising, America-cherishing, *Hey-bullets-bullets*-shouting, *We're-gettin'-closer*-shouting, *You-have-been-thunderstruck*-shouting, *My-soul-cries-Halle-lujah*-singing, war-winning soldiers of C standing straight as their guidons—"but I submit," he'd said that day, "that we are the best there is."

Roll Call

T his book is dedicated with affection and admiration to Second Lieutenant Steven Allen of Fargo, North Dakota, *"I got approximately ten"* ☆ Sergeant Tuitui Aloese of Pago Pago, American Samoa, the Samoan ☆ Specialist Samuel T. Anderson of Mansfield, Ohio, Young told him, *"That's interestin',"* *"What's with this Romeo stuff?"* *"No one has ever kissed your hand?"* *"Till it's our time to go,"* *"As long as I'm not in that turret,"* *"There's a faint trace of it,"* Burns's driver, *"I hope no one's seriously hurt,"* he loved in the seventh grade, he stared at the KIM, SHELLEY, MOM, *"The war's only one day old,"* *"The war's crazy"* ☆ Sergeant Tony Applegate of Portsmouth, Ohio, his bone was an osso buco ☆ Sergeant Danny D. Athey of Newark, Ohio, *"Sir. He's fuckin' us"* ☆ Staff Sergeant Daniel Austin, Jr., of Maxton, North Carolina, *"Aw, stop fuckin' aroun',"* *"Y'all want to give 'em the MREs?"* he said to Ross, *"Do it,"* Burns told him, *"Confirm 1850,"* Burns gave him a slow, methodical order ☆ Sergeant First Class Ted Baer of Washington, Illinois, *"We're not firin',"* his right hand gave them the MREs, he drew a square house, the Iraqi told him, *"Saddam fucked us"* ☆ Lieutenant Colonel Sidney F. Baker, Jr., of Odessa, Texas, his unit was Defiant ☆ First Lieutenant Elaine Bayless of Madill, Oklahoma, she sat with ten-dollar bills ☆ Specialist Shane A. Boudreau of Idaho Falls, Idaho, *"Let's shoot 'em,"* he'd done friendly fire in Idaho, *"Let's shoot it,"* *"Oh, what a jerk,"* *"He tried to bullshit us,"* the girl told him, *"Get off my bed"* ☆ Captain Robert A. Burns of Baldwin, Missouri, he erased the Iraqi trenches, *"Another bush,"* he tossed the *Jayhawk News,* *"Allah is telling us something,"* *"Every damn day,"* Mouse told his wife, *"You look patriotic"* ☆ Commander-in-Chief George H. W. Bush of Houston, Texas, *"Why act now? Why not wait?"* ☆ Captain John E. Bushyhead of Oklahoma City, Oklahoma, the Indian captain of D ☆ General Bruce C. Clarke of McLean, Virginia, *"The confusion was—well, I can't describe it"* ☆ Specialist Ronald D. Click of Norwood, Ohio, a loader in C ☆ Staff Sergeant Ronald E. Cline of Shepherd, Michigan, *"I'm receivin' fire"* ☆ Private Phillip R. Cockerham of Jena, Louisiana, *"I'd rather die than lose a leg,"* *"A whole nother company like you,"* *"You never lied"* ☆ Private First Class Melford Collins of Uhland, Texas, who died on D-Day ☆ Captain Joseph M. Conn, Jr., of Monterey, California, *"What darkness"* ☆ Specialist Harold E. Crouch of Columbus, Ohio, *"We need somethin' in the damn chamber"* ☆ Sergeant David Crumby of Long Beach, California, he had steel in his skull ☆ Major Jack Crumplar of Colorado Springs, Colorado, *"We move out at 1900,"* *"I'll name it Axis Thucydides"* ☆ Private First Class Robert L. Daugherty of Hollywood, Florida, he watched the egg-breaking boy ☆ Specialist Manuel Davila of Gillette, Wyoming, he was being shoveled up ☆ Sergeant Lawrence L. Dawson, Jr., of Baltimore, Maryland, the bulldozer driver, the girl asked him, *"How many children did you kill?"* ☆ Sergeant Jay B. De Boer of Racine, Wisconsin, his shirt had Bart Simpson, *"I'm gonna die,"* *"I saw it and you'll be hatin' it,"* *"We're gonna get our shit straight,"* *"Unless it's an Iraqi counterattack,"* the girl told him, *"I need someone to fuck me"* ☆ Staff Sergeant Richard Devereaux of Council Bluffs, Iowa, an Iraqi told him, *"Saudi,"* *"Hey, I'm not into that,"* *"Yeah. He fucked us, too"* ☆ Corporal Patrick A. Disney of Golden, Colorado, *"Daddy goes bye-bye,"* *"I agree,"* *"I hope I don't do a zizz-wheel,"* Young told him, *"I'm never afraid,"* he had caviar, *"Say hi to Irene,"* *"The slaughter is started,"* *"They must be hatin' it,"* he hit the bottle in Germany, he slooowly turned, *"Say hi to Kevin,"* *"You wanna play gunner?"* ☆ Specialist Edward Dopler of Pittsburgh, Pennsylvania, *"I'm gonna fuck her,"* *"Yeah, they're stupid,"* McRae told him, *"Go forward,"* McRae told him, *"Go left"* ☆ Sergeant David Q. Douthit of Tacoma, Washington, he lay dying in the Bradley ☆ Specialist David

W. Dugo of Deltona, Florida, *"No, no, no,"* *"You don't want a rain-coat"* ☆ Master Sergeant James Dykens of Abilene, Kansas, he cracked his skull ☆ Sergeant Dale R. Ferguson of Fosston, Minnesota, *"My camera's packed,"* *"Go get 'em, lobsters,"* he shook the vat, he sent up a flare, he went south with the KIAs ☆ Lieutenant Colonel Gregory Fontenot of Eunice, Louisiana, *"I guess Abdul knows we're here,"* *"We'll pull you out after the war,"* *"Uh, Juliet four"* ☆ Private Kenneth Fowler of Electra, Texas, *"Uno"* ☆ Lieutenant General Frederick Franks of West Lawn, Pennsylvania, the three-star general, *"Can I do something for you?"* ☆ Specialist Michael S. Garrison of Jonestown, California, a driver in C ☆ Specialist Russell C. Gebert of Austin, Texas ☆ Specialist Gregory I. Gilliam of Chattanooga, Tennessee, he put in Beanie-Wienies, *"You want to marry the dancer?"* he moved like in ⚓ and ⚓ , *"Hey you. Hey, you're okay,"* *"I'll fuck that camel,"* *"She's fat and ugly,"* *"I wish we'd move up,"* *"A junior high school team,"* the *thunder* gunner, his mail said, "PEACE RALLY. NOON," *"Mom, I'm in Bangor,"* *"Mom, I can't hear you,"* *"She's cute,"* *"You didn't use your hands?"* *"It's on the wrong foot"* ☆ Specialist Larry Graham of Fairfield, Iowa, *"We got prisoners, babe,"* *"You can listen, babe"* ☆ Sergeant John Guillory of Beaumont, Texas, *"Modus operandi"* ☆ Second Lieutenant Tom A. Guss of West Chester, Pennsylvania, the colonel asked him, *"Did you shave to-day?"* ☆ First Sergeant Robert P. Harn, Jr., of Hot Springs, South Dakota, the first sergeant, *"Look. A hill,"* *"We had this time together,"* *"Ruin the fuckin' neighborhood,"* *"That's the last water we'll get,"* *"Hello, Hugs and Kisses"* ☆ Private First Class Richard E. Harper of Wood-bridge, West Virginia, he said to Jones, *"I see a BMP,"* *"Burns's gonna have an accident,"* he hit a captain in Korea ☆ Sergeant John I. Harris of Appleton, Wisconsin, *"Who is he, Joshua?"* *"Gas! Gas! Gas!"* *"Hey, soldier, shine your boots,"* *"I love you. Goodbye,"* *"On the way,"* he wanted to name it *Cerberus,* he gave an *"Oh, brother"* look, Penny asked him, *"Super Supreme?"* ☆ Sergeant Gary Hartzell of Hagerstown, Maryland, *"Hey, hey, mama"* ☆ Lieutenant Colonel Ralph Hayles of Corpus Christi, Texas, *"It's hard to pull this trigger"* ☆ Private German Hernandez of Aibonito, Puerto Rico, a supply clerk in C ☆ Second Lieutenant Michael Homer of Brown City, Michigan, McRae told him, *"Pizza,"* *"That's Wolfpack,"* the *boom* knocked him down ☆ Staff Sergeant Norman L. James of Suffolk, Virginia ☆ Second Lieutenant Jeffery S. Jones of Pasco, Washington, the lieutenant from West Point, *"I got some anthills,"* *"A lot of body parts here,"* the first sergeant told him, *"He went higher,"* Burns told him, *"Do you not,"* *"We're all gonna die"* ☆ Sergeant Stephen M. Karcher of Mobile, Alabama, Young told him, *"That's interestin',"* *"No, we go to the left"* ☆ Sergeant Patricia Keese of Manhattan, Kansas, she was on cymbals ☆ Specialist Anthony Kidd of Lima, Ohio, his feet were still in a Bradley ☆ Captain John C. Kim of Inchon, Korea, *"Before I'm a soldier, I'm a Christian"* ☆ Private Cleve M. King of Kingston, Jamaica, he boop-boop-a-dooped to Shabba Ranks ☆ Private First Class Gusie F. Kostic of Arbuckle, California, Young played pool with him, *"Hey, Penn,"* *"I don't wanna demoralize her,"* *"It's like the Super Bowl,"* *"You nigger"* ☆ Private First Class David Kramer of Palm Desert, California, he was nothing but soot ☆ Sergeant First Class Esera Lafua of Boloa, American Samoa, *"You tell Saddam,"* Bushyhead told him, *"There may be chemicals there,"* *"Goddammit! Shift fire,"* *"It looks like anthills"* ☆ Colonel Gary L. LaGrange of Marcell, Minnesota, *"Welcome home, heroes"* ☆ Private Kellem T. Lee, Jr., of Riviera Beach, Florida, a medic for Kostic, Saint Bridget ☆ Staff Sergeant Kevin W. Lemon of Kalamazoo, Michigan, *"ID card? Dog tags? Code of Conduct?"* Disney called him *"An I'm-goin'-to-live motherfucker,"* *"The Four M'er,"* his tank was the *Wolverine,* *"Now everyone shit,"* he said to Peterson, *"Hey,"* *"One truck. Range 1150,"* *"More trucks. At 1300 and 1500,"* *"That's not white,"* *"That's Bulldog,"* *"He's fuckin' stupid,"* *"Tank! Direct front!"* *"T-55,"* *"T-55. Range 1930,"* *"We have another T-55,"* *"I can see the gun"* ☆ Sergeant First Class Paul T. Levesque of Lewiston, Maine, *"When you grow up, what'll you do?"* Grandpa, *"Attaboy"* ☆ Private Bryan J. Lewis of Bowdoinham, Maine, Shaffer told him, *"Bang bang bang, then bong,"* Gilliam told him, *"She's fat and ugly,"* Schmidt smeared shit on him, his girlfriend wore spandex, the girls even wooed him, he said to West, *"Yeah"* ☆ Private

Robert Lewis of Cape Girardeau, Missouri, *"Make sure he's conch"* ☆ Sergeant Steven L. Lewis of Chicago, Illinois, *"He's got your eyes and ears?"* *"He'll be a clumsy motherfucker,"* the Mexicans told him, *"Yo tengo hambre,"* *"Heed what I say, XO"* ☆ First Lieutenant Steven M. Light of Chicago, Illinois, *"You eatin' that seagull?"* the XO, *"Tank. Behind that rock,"* he thought of Dante's hell and of Bosch's *Millennium,* *"What is James doing?"* ☆ Private Jhaiphet S. Lim of Savanakhet, Laos, the Laotian ☆ Specialist Charles K. Maddox of Augusta, Georgia, *"Sir, it's the ragheads,"* *"Sand-dune-climbing motherfuckers,"* he had a Georgia license, McRae told him, *"Gas! Gas! Gas!"* he bit one smelly black ball, *"I want to kick his ass,"* he meandered, he sideswiped, he ground the Iraqi in, Moore told him, *"Go left,"* *"Forget that ol' dance,"* *"You had one bad morning"* ☆ Colonel Lon E. Maggart of Raleigh, North Carolina, *"You're right, and if I'm alive tomorrow,"* *"That's right. He's not shooting,"* the colonel radioed him, *"Devil six,"* *"No one likes doing this"* ☆ Sergeant Johnny M. Mares of Denver, Colorado, *"I'm quitting,"* he sang *The Star-Spangled Banner* ☆ Sergeant Guillermo Martinez of Taft, Texas, the Hispanic commander, his tank had a Lone Star flag ☆ Major William McCormick of Boston, Massachusetts, *"Someone got bitten by Taiwan rats"* ☆ Captain William K. McCurry of Fort Worth, Texas, *"We may go north"* ☆ First Lieutenant Bennie J. McRae III of Trotwood, Ohio, the black lieutenant, Young called him, *"Survivor,"* *"Get real, I could die,"* *"They must have worked at Country Kitchen,"* *"What did she do? Slap him?"* *"Get lost, Iraq!"* *"The camel spiders?"* *"Hey, that must be the Iraqis,"* *"Pizza,"* *"I hope the announcement is 'Fuck you all,' "* he thought of his bride in Kansas, Kostic told him, *"No, I won't,"* *"It's time for our payback now,"* Miller told him, *"But that's against their religion,"* *"Why are they shooting that rag?"* *"I confirm 1820,"* *"Fuck permission to fire,"* *"We should go to Baghdad,"* *"Girl, you're to me,"* *"You been to Cairo?"* *"I give you this for that,"* *"It's not like TV"* ☆ Specialist David M. Means of Clewiston, Florida, James's driver, *"It's miserable out,"* *"My grandmama does,"* *"What's happening?"* ☆ Sergeant Scott E. Medine of Baton Rouge, Louisiana, Young asked him, *"Will you be my best man?"*

"It's fuckin' impressive, sir," "Uh-oh. That looks awful close," "Here's your damn $110," he liked music by Mozart, he woke up Burns ☆ Specialist Jeffrey T. Middleton of Oxford, Kansas, the helicopter missile killed him ☆ Private First Class Gary A. Miller of Grant Island, Nebraska, the new loader in C, *"But that's against their religion"* ☆ Private First Class Joseph P. Miller of Portland, Oregon, he had an Oregon license, he sang *The Star-Spangled Banner* ☆ Private First Class Mark A. Miller of Cannelton, Indiana, he picked up an Easter egg ☆ Captain Phil Miller of Lexington, Kentucky, *"Someone got bitten by Taiwan rats"* ☆ Sergeant First Class Mac A. Moore of Jackson, Mississippi, Young borrowed his tape recorder, his tank was the *Phantom Lord, "No, you can't go. There's mines,"* he said to Maddox, *"Go left," "Truck. To your left at 900 meters," "Six might be upset if I shoot,"* he said to Maddox, *"Go left," "Is something wrong?" "What range?"* ☆ Corporal David K. Morris of Weirton, West Virginia, Lemon told him, *"He's fuckin' stupid," "We'll be fuckin' history,"* McRae told him, *"Fuck permission to fire"* ☆ Specialist James Murray of Conroe, Texas, his baby's name was Larissa ☆ Staff Sergeant Donnie L. Myers of Brunswick, Georgia, a tank commander in C ☆ Captain Jim Nepute of Louisville, Kentucky, the D belonged to him and not the Indian ☆ Corporal James E. Newberry of West Plains, Missouri, *"Well, I try," "I don't want to die anywhere," "It takes off my legs," "I wouldn't," "I'm goin' out with a DUI," "Lemme get a whiff of it," "Closest I've gotten to a girl this year," "What is it? Thirty degrees?" "There's probably an Iraqi PFC," "We're gonna get accurate,"* Anderson told him, *"I hope no one's seriously hurt,"* Burns's gunner, Burns told him, *"Don't fiddle-fuck,"* Burns told him, *"Lase 'em and blaze 'em," "When'll it be healed?"* ☆ Private Christian M. Noriega of Miami, Florida, Disney called him *"A better-not-stomp-on-my-peter motherfucker"* ☆ Specialist Douglas E. Northcutt of Iola, Kansas, he'd gotten married, *"How about Satan's Ship?"* he'd batted the mailboxes down ☆ Specialist Wayne Okeson of La Rosa, California, a medic for Kostic, *"We'll be beggin' like them"* ☆ Specialist Marc J. L. Penn of San Gabriel, California,

"Pretty safe" ☆ Private Mark T. Peterson of San Diego, California, Young said, *"He's livin' in the twilight zone,"* he woke up at ten-foot ditches ☆ Specialist Ronald Pierce of Parsons, Kansas, his vehicle hobbled like in *Mother Courage* ☆ Private First Class Kevin Pollak of Tucson, Arizona, he was without long-range goals ☆ Major General Thomas G. Rhame of Winfield, Louisiana, his fingertip hid his 18,800 troops, *"Move up,"* the major general ☆ Lieutenant Colonel G. Patrick Ritter of Macomb, Illinois, *"Ditto, I don't like this,"* *"You shot my Bradley,"* his A, B, C, D were in Indian file ☆ Specialist Pablo M. Rivadeneira of Talara, Peru, *"It's from the gas,"* *"Bullet Bob,"* the Peruvians told him, *"Dame dinero,"* he stomped on the Tokotokos ☆ Captain Robert R. Roggeman of Mishawaka, Indiana, *"You bonehead. You beanbrain,"* *"You can still get killed"* ☆ Sergeant Dwight Ross of Covington, Tennessee, *"Can I engage?"* he booted the carton off, *"T-55! At 1850 meters!"* Burns gave him a slow, methodical order, *"I identify a T-55,"* *"Why won't he let us shoot it?"* ☆ Second Lieutenant David J. Russell of Killeen, Texas, he put in an American flag, *"You still got another one,"* *"No, that's a Bradley"* ☆ Corporal Kenneth Russell of Gallipolis, Ohio, *"You may not be comin' back"* ☆ Captain Wesley G. Saults of Perry, Florida, Personnel, *"All the elements"* ☆ Private First Class Richard A. Sawyer of Hanford, California, *"Paint it black,"* *"I bit some guy's jugular vein"* ☆ Private First Class Steven M. Schmidt of Cincinnati, Ohio, he had an Amazon ass, he avoided rear-enders, he retreated at thirty mph, a girl told him, *"I'll write you in Saudi,"* he smeared shit on Lewis, *"She's dumpin' you, man,"* the girl asked him, *"Why are you eating meat?"* *"What are you? A Californian?"* ☆ General Norman Schwarzkopf of Trenton, New Jersey ☆ Specialist Johnnie L. Seals, Jr., of Dongola, Illinois, he sang *The Star-Spangled Banner,* *"I was involved"* ☆ Staff Sergeant Ron R. Shaffer of Detroit, Michigan, *"Go to War,"* he had $600,000 insurance, *"I can't get,"* he was a recruiting sergeant, he put in his clothes to *The Star-Spangled Banner,* *"Bang bang bang, then bong,"* *"You sell inferior products,"* *"I'll say Gizmo,"* his tank was the *Stranger,* he had more stirring things,

"Dogs of War don't negotiate," "We're like Sergeant Fuckin' York," "We can't see shit," "The hell with Allah," "A high school team," "GONE TO WAR," the Saudis told him, *"We play cards"* ☆ Staff Sergeant David E. Shoulta of Dickson, Tennessee, *"Two tanks. The right tank first," "Mama, mama, can't you see,"* he was a recruiting sergeant, *"Well, he'll get Russell's,"* his *Kellogg's* gleamed, he hoped to make mountain dew ☆ Staff Sergeant Archibald W. Sims of Panama City, Florida, *"It isn't tomorrow, sir,"* he sang *The Star-Spangled Banner, "Truck. About 600 meters," "I got two Bradleys," "They couldn't hear you holler to XO"* ☆ Second Lieutenant Eugene Snyman of Bartlesville, Oklahoma, C told him, *"The yolk's on you,"* he told the engineers, *"Fire," "Hoo hoo," "With unaffrighted eyes"* ☆ Sergeant James V. Spence of Smyer, Texas, *"They're coke whores," "Let's lase and blaze,"* he bit pretty girls' necks ☆ Major Larry Steiner of Minneapolis, Minnesota, *"We're moving out"* ☆ Private Josh Stimpfle of Juneau, Alaska, James's loader, the cannon yanked at his hand, *"What'll happen to us?"* ☆ Sergeant Duane Stubbs of Cleveland, Ohio, *"Can I wear my Cross?"* ☆ Private Robert D. Talley of Newark, New Jersey, the helicopter missile killed him ☆ Staff Sergeant Terry L. Tobolski of Chicago, Illinois, *"A lot of dead enemy here,"* the Iraqi meant *"I'm an Iraqi farmer," "We won't hurt you"* ☆ Captain Juan Toro of Vina del Mar, Chile, the Hispanic captain of B ☆ Warrant Officer Class 2 Kevin Vann of Mildura, Victoria, Australia, *"Oi will pass this moin aroun'"* ☆ Sergeant Jose L. Vellon of Humacao, Puerto Rico, C's supply sergeant ☆ Staff Sergeant Edward Walding of Duncombe, Iowa, the *boom* knocked him down ☆ Second Lieutenant Danny Wallace of Burlingame, Kansas, *"Yes, under your shirt"* ☆ Specialist Samuel E. Walters, Jr., of Hot Springs, Arkansas, he played his *Killing an Arab,* he swerved from an Iraqi, *"Goddammit, XO, answer me"* ☆ Sergeant Shon I. Ward of Norwalk, California, a medic for Kostic ☆ Specialist William C. West of Hunlock Creek, Pennsylvania, Russell's driver, *"I want to get outta here"* ☆ Specialist Nathaniel J. Williams of Elizabethtown, Kentucky, a woman asked him, *"May I?"* ☆ Staff Sergeant Paul

L. Williams of Atlanta, Georgia, *"Gas. One. Two. Three,"* *"My foot. I done fucked it up"* ☆ Specialist John Wilson of Talkeetna, Alaska, he fired a six-inch-wide round ☆ Captain Johnny Womack of Greenville, Alabama, the black captain of A ☆ Corporal Angel L. Yambocancela of Aguada, Puerto Rico, *"Yes, I am goin' crazy," "People here are mad," "It must be gettin' pregnant"* ☆ General John J. Yeosack of Wilkes-Barre, Pennsylvania, the four-star general in Riyadh ☆ Specialist Michael K. Young of Houston, Texas, *"Stress monsters," "The camel spiders," "Latin names," "Someone will kill him," "Eat the cracker, too"* ☆ Major Brian R. Zahn of Bottineau, North Dakota, *"We have movement at 597, 260"* ☆ and everyone else in the U. S. Army.

C was Company C of the 2d Battalion of the 34th Armor, in the 1st Brigade of the 1st Infantry Division (Mechanized) at Fort Riley, Kansas. Its commander was Burns and its first sergeant was Harn. In the 1st Platoon the leader was Russell, the platoon sergeant was Shoulta, and the other two commanders were Myers, who in Kansas was replaced by Martinez, and James, who in Saudi went to the 2d Platoon and was replaced by Shaffer. In the 2d Platoon the leader was McRae, the platoon sergeant was Moore, and the other two commanders were Lemon and Shaffer, who in Saudi went to the 1st Platoon and was replaced by James. In the 3d Platoon the leader was Jones, the platoon sergeant was Austin, and the other two commanders were Ross and Sims.

C was ordered to Saudi as part of VII Corps on November 8, 1990. It flew from Topeka, Kansas, on December 31, 1990, and landed at King Fahd Airport, near Dhahran, on January 1, 1991. On January 12, C left Dhahran, and on January 13 it arrived at Tactical Assembly Area Roosevelt, northeast of Al Qaysumah, Saudi Arabia. The war started on January 16, and on January 18 the battalion became a task force, exchanging its Companies A and D with the 5th Battalion of the 16th Infantry. The 1st Platoon of C was attached to Company D, and the 3d Platoon of D, whose leader was Homer, whose platoon sergeant was Baer, and whose other two commanders were Devereaux and Walding, was attached to C. On January 22, the 2d Platoon of Company A of the 1st Engineers, whose leader was Snyman, was also attached to C. The plows were reassigned from the 1st Platoon to the 3d Platoon of C.

C left Roosevelt on February 13, arrived at Phase Line Cherry, near the Iraqi border, on February 15, and moved to Phase Line Vermont, the Iraqi border itself, east of Markaz Samah al Jadid, Saudi Arabia, on February 18. The plan was, Company D, with the 1st Platoon of C, would raid an Iraqi outpost, 39 Kilo, on February 19, and the ground war would start on February 21, but because of negotiations between the Soviets and Iraqis the raid was canceled and the ground war started on February 24. The plan that day was, the task force would stop at Phase Line Kansas, but because of Iraqis surrendering it continued to Phase Line Colorado. On February 25, the task force went to Phase Line New Jersey, on February 26 it went to Phase Line Smash and passed through the 2d Armored Cavalry Regiment, and on February 27 it fought the Battle of Norfolk Objective or "Battle of Al Qarnain." In this battle were 1800 tanks from the 1st and 3d Armored Divisions, the 1st Infantry Division, and the 1st Armored Division of the United Kingdom Army. On February 27, the task force also went to Kuwait and fought "the Battle of the Boogers." Its secret target was Basra, and it would have gotten there and cut the Iraqi army off if the war had continued another day.

The cease-fire was to start at eight in the morning on February 28, but because of friendly fire it started at 7:23 in VII Corps. C went north to the Iraqi border on March 12, it went to the Iraqi naval base at Umm Qasr on March 22, and it went south again on March 22. On April 6, Burns became the commander of Headquarters Company of the 2d Battalion of the 34th Armor, and

Captain John Greene became the commander of C. C returned to Saudi Arabia on April 17, it returned to Dhahran from April 23 to April 25, and it returned to Topeka, Kansas, and to Fort Riley on May 9.

The official military history of the Iraqi War is *Certain Victory,* by the United States Army, and two excellent unofficial ones are *Crusade,* by Rick Atkinson, and *Triumph Without Victory,* by *U.S. News & World Report.* A history of VII Corps is now being written by Stephen A. Bourque, and a history of the 1st Infantry Division is planned. Some histories of the 1st Brigade are "A Leap of Faith," by Colonel Lon E. Maggart, in *Armor,* January–February, 1992, "Breaching Operations," by Brigadier General Lon E. Maggart and Colonel Gregory Fontenot, in *Military Review,* February, 1994, and *Desert Shield/Storm History,* a photocopied manuscript by the 1st Brigade. Some histories of the 2d Battalion of the 34th Armor are "Anatomy of a Rout," by Lieutenant Colonel Gregory Fontenot, in *Army,* January, 1992, and "Fright Night," by Colonel Gregory Fontenot, in *Military Review,* January, 1993. A videotape interview with Fontenot is on exhibit at the First Infantry Division Museum at Cantigny, Illinois, and transcribed interviews with Crumplar, Fontenot and Steiner are published by the United States Army Center of Military History. The only history of Company C is *Company C,* but a videotape interview with Burns is on exhibit at the First Infantry Division Museum at Cantigny, Illinois, and transcribed interviews with Burns, Harn, James, Means, Penn and Stimpfle (and with Bushyhead and others of Company D) are published by the United States Army Center of Military History. My own 135 hours of tapes, 575 pages of typewritten transcripts, and 950 pages of handwritten notes will eventually go to the John Sack Collection at Boston University.